I have been a pastor for over t
four of whom are now adults.
dozens of Christian books on the subject of the family. However, when it comes to child-rearing, I do not hesitate to say that *Purposeful and Persistent Parenting* by John and Cindy Raquet is the best book I have ever had the privilege and blessing to read on this subject. It is written by a couple who have much proven experience and God-given wisdom. It is soundly and faithfully scriptural. It is gospel-centered and gospel-suffused. It is hands-on, nitty-gritty practical, giving many helpful suggestions and creative ideas without being legalistic, since the writers are careful to distinguish between counsel and Scripture command. Indeed, it addresses many practical and important aspects of parenting rarely addressed in books on this subject. I cannot highly recommend this book enough! I am in double earnest to promote this book and will be urging all the young families in our church to get it and to read it.

–**Jeffery Smith**

Pastor, Emmanuel Baptist Church, Coconut Creek, FL,
board member and lecturer for Reformed Baptist Seminary,
author of *The Rich Man And Lazarus: The Plain Truth About Life After Death* and *Preaching for Conversions*

My wife and I have been blessed by the Lord with the chance to raise and disciple three young children. Though we have read multiple books on parenting, John and Cindy Raquet have produced one of the most helpful books I have encountered. While presenting their advice gleaned through wise reflection on lives lived on purpose, John and Cindy concisely draw lessons out of their failures and their successes. As they do, they do not argue for rigid and absolute formulas for successful parenting. Rather, they invite the reader to inspect their own parenting by providing diagnostic questions drawn from reflection on the Scriptures, and the lessons they have drawn out of their own lives and experience. I highly recommend that any parents who are seeking to parent purposefully pick up a copy of this helpful volume and use it as a way of developing their own habits and patterns of shepherding the children entrusted to your care.

–**Matthew Bennett, PhD**

Assistant Professor of Missions and Theology
Cedarville University

Romans 12:2 commands that we "be not conformed to this world." This includes our parenting philosophy. Christians believe that the Scriptures are sufficient to provide the instructions necessary to raise their children "in the nurture and admonition of the Lord."

Christians also believe that the household of God, which is "fitly framed together," also provides an opportunity to learn from one another in and through our shared experiences as Christian pilgrims. John and Cindy have provided their fellow pilgrim parents with an insightful treasury containing practical parenting advice for first-time and experienced parents alike. As a pastor, husband, and father of three, I particularly appreciated their straightforward approach when treating real issues that my own family has had to face over the years.

Their writing style is refreshingly candid, anchored in biblical wisdom, and free from modern-day pseudo-psychology that seems to clutter many "Christian parenting" books on the market these days.

Moms and Dads, if you desire to cultivate joy, unity, and a renewed biblical purpose regarding your parenting approach, you must read this book. It will it help you. It will help your children, and in fact, it will help the entire Christian community take a significant step in rediscovering purposeful and persistent parenting.

–**Doug Barger**

Pastor, Christ Reformed Baptist Church, New Castle, IN

Purposeful and Persistent Parenting hits a home run for getting things in order from the start of parenting. Every young parent needs to read this book. It is targeted to the first ten years of parenting, where everything matters most. It will get you going in the right direction. John and Cindy Raquet understand with clarity that laying solid foundations early on is critical. It is full of helpful ideas grounded in the Word of God. I can't wait to get it into the hands of my grown children raising their families.

–**Scott T. Brown**

Pastor, Hope Baptist Church, Wake Forest, NC,
president, Church and Family Life

PURPOSEFUL AND PERSISTENT PARENTING

BLESSING OTHERS, BLUE-TAPE BOUNDARIES, AND OTHER PRACTICAL PERSPECTIVES ON RAISING CHILDREN

PURPOSEFUL
AND
PERSISTENT
PARENTING

BLESSING OTHERS, BLUE-TAPE BOUNDARIES, AND OTHER PRACTICAL PERSPECTIVES ON RAISING CHILDREN

JOHN *and* CINDY
RAQUET

FREE GRACE PRESS

Published by
Free Grace Press

3900 Dave Ward Dr., Ste. 1900
Conway, AR 72034
(501) 214-9663
email: support@freegracepress.com

website: www.freegracepress.com

Printed in the United States of America
Published 2021
Second Printing: April 2022

Cover design by Scott Schaller

ISBN: 978-1-952599-19-4

To our parents

You exemplified much of what we talk about in this book

and provided warm, loving, and encouraging homes

in which to grow up.

You truly gave us roots and wings.

To our children

The years God has given us with you

have been some of our greatest joys

and a privilege we will always treasure.

You are precious gifts and uniquely crafted arrows.

We are eager to see how your Creator will use you

to bring glory to Him

as He enables you to make your mark

on this dark world.

Contents

Foreword

I have known and respected John and Cindy Raquet for many years. Specifically, I have admired both their philosophy and practice with regard to child-rearing. They have had a wonderful, godly influence on my daughter. John is one of her pastors, and they befriended and mentored her both as a single and now as a mother of five girls.

After reviewing the manuscript for *Purposeful and Persistent Parenting: Blessing Others, Blue-Tape Boundaries, and Other Practical Perspectives on Raising Children*, I am very happy to see that they have shared with many other parents in this short volume the balanced and wise implementation of a biblical philosophy of child-rearing.

Purposeful and Persistent Parenting is a little gem of a book. I get asked to review many good books, but I have not reviewed a book about which I am more enthusiastic than this one. I am enthusiastic about this book because it takes biblical principles of child-rearing and put the feet of wise application on them. Often, I fear, parents struggling against the tide of our culture react into extremist and foolish applications of perfectly biblical principles. On the other hand, biblical principles of child-rearing do require more than lip-service. They require diligent practice in the everyday world. Parenting challenges like whining, proactive parenting, the practical application of the rod, sitting still, mealtimes, and many other issues are discussed in a biblical, reasonable, and practical way.

Another thing that commends this book is its tone. I much appreciate the kind and generous way in which John and Cindy have written. It allows parents to apply the insights and practices John and Cindy suggest in a way that fits their own situation. It also recognizes that in matters of practical application there is room for discussion and difference of opinion. Nevertheless, I hope that Christian parents will regard the counsel of this book with deep respect and seriously consider the practical wisdom and discernment of which their book is a treasury.

I believe this easy-to-read volume will provide a reason for many parents to thank God for the labors of John and Cindy on behalf of their children and grandchildren.

Pastor Sam Waldron, PhD

Preface

We did not set out to write a book on parenting. With eight children, work and church responsibilities, health challenges, sports schedules, and interactions with relatives, we have plenty of things filling up our schedule and struggle to find time even to communicate with each other as a couple. But over the years, many factors started pressing on us to write this book, even at this current stage of life. It began as a multi-year project, involving many bi-annual "long weekends" away, holed up in a hotel, planning and talking and writing and editing. Several factors contributed to the burden we felt for the work; here are just a few:

- **We learned many things the hard way.** We are absolutely not perfect parents. We've made many mistakes throughout the years and have learned many parenting lessons the hard way. In fact, for the first few years of parenting, we had an approach that was almost the opposite of what is presented in this book. Over time and through the input of many people, we've learned better ways of doing things and have come to truly enjoy our children and the parenting process. While there is not one right way to parent, we do believe that some things we've learned could be helpful to others just starting their parenting journey—those things we wished we had known when we began ours.
- **Hundreds of parenting conversations.** Over the past couple of decades, we have had literally hundreds of parenting-related conversations with other parents we know, usually with them coming to us and asking something along the lines of "What do you guys do about ______?" or "How do you handle it when one of your children ______?" We found that we were addressing some of the same themes over and over again, sometimes even in written form via email, so we decided it

would be more efficient to put some of these thoughts down in one place. Also, we discovered that the questions parents were asking tended to be practical in nature, very much in the "rubber meets the road" realm, and we weren't aware of any resources that addressed some of these highly specific issues.

- **We kept hearing, "You should write a book!"** We tended to laugh off statements like this because we honestly didn't feel like we had anything to say that was worth writing in a book. However, after hearing this repeatedly from a wide variety of people, we at least considered it.
- **We have thoroughly enjoyed raising our children and want other parents to thoroughly enjoy their parenting years as well.** At the time of this writing, all our children are somewhat older than the ten-and-under age range that is the focus of this book. However, we have thoroughly enjoyed the parenting process and interacting with our children as they have moved through the teen years and matured into adults, and we are firmly convinced that the stage was set for these strong relationships in the early years of parenting. We sometimes see other Christian parents struggling with their role in their children's lives and not enjoying parenting. We desire to come alongside them and provide encouragement and what we hope are helpful suggestions based on our own experiences. We are not saying that if you do the things in this book everything will be perfect. Things are not that simple. But we learned many practical ideas along the way that worked well for us, and we think that some of these approaches might be helpful for you too. But keep in mind that there is not a single correct way to parent.
- **We want to communicate our thoughts on parenting to our children before they have children of their own.** One of the factors that has pressed us to get this book finished now is that we wanted to be able to explain some of the reasons behind our parenting to our children and their spouses before their own children—our grandchildren—are in the picture. That way we can freely speak and not have anyone feel like we are specifically "targeting" any of our children's parenting practices, because they are not yet parenting! It's been interesting to see how often our children, when reading through the draft of the

manuscript, said something like, "So that's why you did things that way!" They might have remembered how we did things but didn't always understand the reasoning behind it at the time. We considered writing all this down just for the benefit of our children, but for the reasons given in the previous two points, we decided to make it available to other current or soon-to-be parents. We want to make one thing clear to our children and their spouses and anyone else reading this book: We do not expect that you will do everything we say in this book, and that's okay. We must also be clear that our children are not perfect children and we are not perfect parents—we all struggle with sin, just like everyone else does.

At the outset, we want to be forthright that we write from a Christian perspective, and we believe that the Bible is authoritative because it is what God, the One who has made us, has revealed to us about Himself and all that He made. The Bible does address some aspects of parenting, but not every parenting question is addressed in the Bible. We do reference the Bible but did not limit ourselves to topics that come straight from the Bible when writing this book. For example, the Bible says absolutely nothing about reading books to your children and certainly doesn't give a list of book recommendations. Yet we have a chapter about this. If something is not straight from the Bible, then it is just advice, and you are free to disregard mere advice.

Also, it might be helpful for you to have a sense of what we are like as people, since personality does come into play in how one parents. We tend to be very intentional in how we live life, trying to think things through (perhaps too much, sometimes). We would be described by some as intense and can easily get overcommitted. We love having deep conversations with people on serious topics. We say these things because we don't want you to feel overly burdened by anything we wrote if you are blessed with a more relaxed personality. There are times we would have been blessed to have a few more relaxed, easygoing personalities in our home! We are thankful that God has made His local family, the church, with many different body parts, all with unique functions and gifts (1 Corinthians 12:12–27), according to His good plans for a balanced, functioning body!

How to Use This Book

There is no single "right" way to use this book. We wrote it with the idea that two or more people would be going through the book together. Each chapter has a set of discussion questions designed to help you consider the information in the chapter in light of your own particular situation. We recommend that you talk through these discussion questions with your spouse or, if you're a single parent, with another parent. Even better, get together with a group of like-minded parents and go through the book together. Discussing the material as a group is an effective way to think through the information in a balanced manner. Meeting together every week or two as parents can be a huge encouragement to all involved as you work through things as a group, bounce ideas off each other, and generally support each other in your struggles.

We also would urge you not to rush through the material. We wrote the book with the assumption that parents have lots on their plates and only a limited amount of time to go through a book like this. Each chapter focuses on one topic and can be read and discussed in a reasonable period, perhaps one hour a week. In general, the early chapters emphasize principles, and the later chapters highlight the more practical matters, although we tried to make every chapter address rubber-meets-the-road practical issues as much as possible.

Please don't skip the discussion questions—they are perhaps the most valuable part of the book because they help you think through what you want to incorporate in your own family. Some questions may be more applicable to your situation than others, but we do not recommend skipping the questions altogether.

Finally, do not neglect to pray for your children and for yourselves as you work through this book. Ask God to change you where you need to be changed and to give your child a heart to heed your instruction. But even more importantly, ask Him to grant your child a heart that is soft toward God (Ezekiel 36:26).

Our prayer is that the ideas presented in this book will be a blessing to you and your children, no matter how you choose to work through the material!

Chapter 1

Getting Started

> Everybody knows how to raise children, except the people who have them.
>
> — P. J. O'Rourke

Parenting is an exciting yet daunting task. Voices aimed at parents, many in the form of advertisements, come from all directions, saying, "Do this!" "Do that!" "Buy this!" "Sign up for that!" "Feed them this!" "Avoid that!" and other similarly urgent or essential messages. Even worse, much of this advice is contradictory, so we could never follow it all, even if we wanted to.

If you are reading this book, you likely are looking for good input on how to parent your young children. We wholeheartedly commend you for your interest in parenting well. We have found that good, effective parenting is not generally something that happens naturally—or, more precisely, what we naturally would do as parents is not always a good approach. If we just parent according to how we feel at any given moment, we are almost certainly going to be inconsistent parents who struggle to teach our children the things we think they need to learn.

Additionally, we each come to parenting with our own personal background—some of it positive, and some negative. We tend to parent naturally from our own upbringings, either gravitating toward what we experienced or perhaps wanting to do everything completely opposite from what we faced as children.

Investing intentional time and effort in training your children reaps incredible benefits. Not only do we as parents want our children to grow practically and academically but, more importantly, we desire for them to develop a relationship with God, form good character traits, and have healthy ways of looking at the world that will help them as they mature into adults. God has set things up in such a way that you have the primary role in the training of your children. Certainly, other people will assist in this—teachers, relatives, other parents—but you are the primary trainers of your children. Of all the people in the world, you will likely have the biggest impact on them, for better or worse. Spending time and effort teaching and training your children is of incredible value and can reap significant rewards over time.

This book is focused on the first decade or so of parenting. For those of you at the beginning or in the middle of this period, ten years may seem like a long time (and it is), so we'd like to provide a little perspective to help you value this critical time in your child's life. Let's assume that your child will no longer be living in your home around age eighteen. (Even if they are living in your home, the amount of interaction you have at that age is generally quite limited, with jobs, college, and other outside interests competing for their time.) That would mean that the first decade is about the first half of parenting in terms of calendar time. However, with respect to the amount of direct interaction with your child, the first ten years encompasses much more than half. During those first ten years, most of the time that your child is not attending school is probably spent with you. For the first few years, you must physically attend to many of their daily needs, and you will continue to be involved in much of their "free time," at least until they reach the age of ten. In the "second half" of parenting (ages ten to twenty), children begin to spread their wings and spend much more time in activities where you will have less direct interaction with them. Additionally, it tends to be during these critical first ten years that habit patterns and ways of thinking are established. Laying a good relational foundation during these early years is extremely valuable for navigating the older years of parenting. So, seize this relatively short period of time with your children and seek to parent well for your children's good and God's glory!

With this in mind, we need to address an important balance that must be maintained regarding parenting. On the one hand, what you do as parents will have an undeniably significant impact on your children. On the other hand, parenting is not like an equation, where certain operations will always give the same result. With parenting, there is no guaranteed outcome—you cannot say, "If I do these things, then my children will turn out that way."

We must take care to hold these two truths in tension:

Truth #1: As parents, we have a huge influence on our children.

Truth #2: Ultimately, how our children end up is not completely determined by our parenting.

We are called to be faithful to parent our children with all our effort and ability and to ultimately look to God for the results. If we focus exclusively on truth #1, we might develop a results-focused mindset, sinful pride when our children do well or unnecessary guilt when they don't, or an unhealthy pressure to "do everything right" in our parenting. If we focus exclusively on truth #2, we may neglect the God-given roles we have to train up our children, erroneously thinking, "Kids will be kids" or "It doesn't matter what I do anyway." If we are to parent well, we should attempt to maintain a healthy grasp of both truths at all times.

As you work through the chapters in this book, we want you to consider each like an item in a buffet line, where you have a range of foods before you to pick and choose what you really want to eat. If you felt like you must consume a significant portion of everything, you'd end up with several plates' worth of food and would almost certainly leave that meal feeling utterly uncomfortable. Likewise, you should prayerfully consider what is in each chapter, work through the questions at the end, and then if there are ideas you want to incorporate into your parenting, go for it. If you don't think that a chapter has something for you at the current time, feel free to pass it up and move on to the next.

While guided by biblical principles, much of what is in this book is in the category of "good advice" or "suggestions," and we invite you to prayerfully choose what works for your own unique situation. When Scripture explicitly commands something, we are responsible to God to obey it. Also consider the wisdom of those who are further ahead in their parenting journey, but remember that their input won't have the same weight as the direct commands of Scripture. You are your children's parents, you are responsible to God for teaching and training them, and it is up to you to work out the specifics of what that will look like in the context of your own family.

If you are working through this book with a group of other parents, don't expect them to do things the same way you do. We need to be gracious to one another, especially in the sphere of parenting. Even as we seek to apply biblical principles, there is not a one-size-fits-all approach to parenting for every single detail. So relax, listen with an open mind, and use your judgment as you proceed through the rest of this book.

Discussion Questions

1. What good or bad examples of parenting advice, such as those described in the first paragraph, have you seen?
2. What instruction on parenting or influences on your parenting have you had so far?
3. If you currently have children, what aspects of parenting do you think are going well? In what areas would you like to see things go better? What things are you wondering about or concerned about as you look to the future?
4. If you do not currently have children, what are your biggest areas of concern as you anticipate having a family?
5. What goals are you hoping this book will help you achieve?
6. What is the approach you will take for working through this book? Be specific (e.g., How many chapters will you read at a time? Will you meet with a group and when? When will you pray?). Please see "How to Use This Book" for suggestions.

Chapter 2

Grace-Filled Parenting

> For by grace you have been saved through faith. And this is not your own doing; it is the gift of God, not a result of works, so that no one may boast. For we are his workmanship, created in Christ Jesus for good works, which God prepared beforehand, that we should walk in them.
>
> – Ephesians 2:8–10

Anytime someone writes a book with suggestions for how to think or what to do, a danger of communicating in an imbalanced way arises. Each reader will have unique situations and will bring their own particular strengths, weaknesses, inclinations, and backgrounds. Thus, there is not a universal approach to encouraging parents.

Some people reading this book are naturally strict and authoritarian in the way they go about parenting. These parents especially need to be encouraged to be gracious toward their children. In contrast, some reading this book are innately forgiving and undemanding in their methods of parenting. These parents especially need to be encouraged to teach their children obedience. If you are going to have a balanced approach to parenting, then it is vital for you to be aware of imbalances you may currently have and be open to overcoming them.

As we have talked with people through the years, we've observed that many parents seem to struggle with teaching their children to respectfully obey them (something Scripture commands), so we have some chapters coming up that encourage parents along those lines. However, we wrote this chapter on grace-filled parenting to serve as the necessary foundation from which teaching obedience can be done in a balanced way.

What We Mean by Grace-Filled Parenting

We know that many others have used the term *grace-filled parenting* and that it can have different meanings depending on whom you ask. What we mean by grace-filled parenting is described in the next few sections.

Our Relationship with Our Children Is Not Based on Their Performance

As Christians, our standing before God is not based on our performance but on Jesus's. He lived the perfect life that we could not, and He took the punishment for every sin we've committed. For those of us who are "in Christ"—the term used most commonly in the New Testament to indicate what we call a Christian—our relationship with God is based on His faithfulness and what Christ accomplished and not on what we do. In a similar way, as grace-filled parents our relationship with our children is not based on their performance. We love them whether they obey us or not. We act in their best interest whether they obey us or not. They are just as much our sons or daughters whether they obey us or not. Our relationship with them and attitude toward them is not contingent on how they respond to us.

At least, that is the ideal. As fallen people, we may not succeed in fully living up to those attitudes. But as grace-filled parents, we seek to have these things be true in us. It is helpful for us to remember the parable of the unforgiving servant found in Matthew 18:23–35. In this parable, a servant is forgiven by the king a debt so huge it could never be repaid, only then to not forgive the very small debt that a fellow servant owed him. If we are in Christ, we have been forgiven a huge debt we had no hope of paying, so how can we hold the sins of others (even our children) against them?

We Treat Our Children as Fellow Sinners in Need of God's Grace

When our children sin in various ways, including disobeying us, we come to the situation with the mindset that they are fellow sinners, not that we are perfect and they are the only ones with a sin problem. This kind of attitude changes the way we treat their sin. We will still be faithful parents and appropriately address their sin, but as we do so, we will have hearts of compassion and grace rather than of arrogance and pride—recognizing ourselves as sinners with the same basic problems and struggles. At times, we will need to ask our children for forgiveness when we have sinned against them. This is not a sign of weakness but a modeling of our standing as fellow sinners in need of God's grace and the forgiveness of others.

We Recognize We Struggle with the Same Things

Being grace-filled parents means that we not only recognize we are sinners just like our children but we also understand we struggle with the same root sins as they do and can relate to them. For example, when our children choose to play rather than clean their bedroom like we told them to, they put their own enjoyment ahead of what those in authority over them required of them. We, likewise, often put our own enjoyment or short-term pleasure ahead of what those in authority over us, including God, desire for us to do. (Ironically, we do this even though our enjoyment and pleasure are maximized when we live in accordance with God's commands!)

Grace Doesn't Remove the Requirement to Obey

It is essential to point out that being a grace-filled parent, as we are using the term, does *not* mean we ignore disobedience or treat it as no big deal. God has given us many commands to obey, but these commands are good things, and it is in our best interest to obey them. He gives us these commands not because He hates us but because He has created us, loves us, and knows what is best for us.

Additionally, it is not accurate to say that God just ignores our sin and acts as though we never sinned. Scripture teaches that God's righteous wrath was poured out against each and every sin we commit but that this wrath was fully taken by Jesus, instead of us, when He died on the cross. We say all this not because our relationship with God is a perfect analogy to our relationship with our children. Rather, we want to make the point that even though our relationship with God is based on grace, it doesn't negate the importance of our obeying Him. Likewise, being grace-filled parents does not negate the importance of our children learning to obey us.

Can we occasionally overlook a sin our child committed and "show them grace"? Absolutely! We are not required to track down and punish their every sin, and we couldn't do this even if we wanted to. We should strive for balance in our parenting—a balance between being gracious in our attitude toward our children, encouraging them when they are weak and discouraged, and rebuking them when they are stubborn and hard-hearted. We always want to act in their best interest, which often involves addressing their sin and disobedience in one way or another.

A good summary Scripture to consider is 1 Thessalonians 5:14–15:

> We urge you, brethren, admonish the unruly, encourage the fainthearted, help the weak, be patient with everyone. See that no one repays another with evil for evil, but always seek after that which is good for one another and for all people.

Discussion Questions

1. In your parenting style (or anticipated parenting style, if you don't yet have children), do you naturally gravitate toward being demanding and strict or being forgiving and easy? Do you think this is based on your background or your personality (or both)?
2. If I were to ask you what God thinks of you right now, what would be your response? Is your perception of God's relationship with you based on your current performance?
3. How do you view God's commands? As necessary evils? As burdensome rules? As impossible demands? As loving instructions on how to live? How do you think this attitude affects your view of commands given to your child?

Chapter 3

Children as a Blessing

> Behold, children are a heritage from the Lord, the fruit of the womb a reward.
>
> –Psalm 127:3

I (John) am not a runner. In general, my attitude toward running has been that running is something to be endured, and thus, I have generally not enjoyed it nor done it regularly. At one time, however, I actually did enjoy running. When I was in high school preparing to try out for the varsity basketball team, I realized that being in good aerobic shape would be critical, and running was a means to that end. This fundamentally changed my attitude toward running—rather than something to be endured, it was a principal means to a desired end (making the basketball team), and so I ran often and enjoyed it.

Attitude is crucial, especially when it comes to parenting. Our attitude toward our children will have a big impact on how we parent and how much we enjoy the journey of raising our children to adulthood. Just like with my running, if we see our children primarily as a burden to be endured, our parenting experience will be much different than if we see our children primarily as a blessing from God.

The Bible, in fact, speaks of children as precious gifts, valuable and individually crafted by God. Unfortunately, this is not the predominant attitude of our society. But the western cultural norm considering children as a trial or burden to be endured is not the way they are described in Scripture. In God's Word we see children as a heritage from the Lord and as a reward (Psalm 127:3). It speaks of each child being specifically and individually created (knitted together) in the womb by God (Psalm

139:13–16). At times, the disciples saw children as an annoyance or inconvenience, but Jesus welcomed them into His arms and blessed them (Mark 10:13–16). Generally, the only times the Bible speaks of children negatively is when they haven't been well-trained or brought up in the way they should go (see chapter 10, "Parenting Principles from Proverbs" for more discussion on this topic).

Our modern society increasingly sees sex, marriage, and children as three completely independent things that do not have to go together, contrary to the wisdom of the God-designed sequence of marriage, sex, and then frequently, the gift of children. Along with this perverse, prevailing cultural attitude comes the idea that children are an optional accessory completely up to one's own choice and feelings, which greatly influences whether people have children as well as their attitude toward them if they do. If we are not careful, societal attitudes like these can creep into our own thoughts.

The fact that children are a blessing from God does not mean that parenting is easy or that every aspect of parenting is pure joy and delight. However, just like my example with running, our overall attitude toward our children will dictate how we respond to parenting difficulties and challenges. In this chapter, we would like to provide encouragement to help you maintain a positive attitude toward your children, even when parenting is difficult.

Where No Oxen Are

I (Cindy) appreciate order and cleanliness—things usually hard to maintain in a family with many young children. Several years ago, when I had five young children, I ran across a verse from Proverbs that has been a great encouragement to me throughout the years: "Where no oxen are, the manger is clean, but much [increase] comes by the strength of the ox" (Proverbs 14:4 NASB).

This points out that if we're focusing on the dirty manger (feeding trough) in the ox's barn, our attention is on the wrong thing. Instead, we should be reminded of the productivity that comes with having an ox. The verse helped me to look beyond the messiness of having young children to see the value of the children and what they can (eventually) do. Because this was an area in which I continually needed encouragement, I made Proverbs 14:4 into a "jingle" so that I could sing it to myself by way of reminder.[1] My youngest baby at the time loved to wiggle to the jingle; I think she thought I was singing about her since I sang it so frequently! But it helped me see her and her siblings as the blessings they are. Even now, with older children, we will occasionally encourage each other with the phrase "Where no oxen are" during particularly chaotic times in our household.

When children are very young, it's hard to imagine them making their own bed, let alone becoming productive members of society. However, the truth is that they can grow up to be a mighty force for good, even when they are still children. Just like the ox and the manger, our attitude—what we focus on—is key. Do we see our children as little mess generators or as people in training to be a force for good in the lives of others?

Children and Our Sanctification

Being a parent can be very humbling, in large part because our children are like mirrors, reflecting our own weaknesses and sin back to us. As we train our children, we realize that the very things we are training them to do (or not do) are things we struggle with ourselves. For example, if we lack patience, we might not notice it until we see the same impatience in our children; then our own struggle with patience becomes evident to us.

Being a parent also exposes our selfishness. An adult with no children can live life primarily seeking after their own interests without much difficulty. But once a child is born, parents are forced to look after their children's interests all day long (and sometimes all night long). Parents can't just do what they want to do at any given time. Instead, they must consider their children's needs, which often conflict with their own desires. This "forced selflessness" can be painful, but it is sanctifying as we learn to live less for ourselves and more for others.

Remember, the time when our children need us around the clock is usually short-lived. Indeed, many parents of older children look back on those child-rearing days with longing. Try to keep the perspective that children generally grow quickly and tend to need less active parenting over time. Parenting young children is a short but important time of

1 This song can be found at https://youtu.be/cT4aocJMI8Q or by searching on YouTube.com for "Where No Oxen Are Song."

investing lots of care in one who will one day, Lord willing, be a mighty ox ploughing wherever the Lord leads them.

On the other hand, parenting older children can be an extremely exciting—and humbling—time of life that also goes by quickly. We become aware that our children have abilities and strengths that perhaps neither of their parents had, and they can accomplish things that we never dreamed of accomplishing. They can go and do things we never could. Like arrows sent out from the quiver, they fly and make their mark far from where the archer stood when he loosed them. Exciting, isn't it? It is an incredible privilege to be a part of preparing the next generation to use their gifts and abilities to impact the world.

Verbally Complaining about Children

It is common in many circles to complain about the annoyances and difficulties of having children. While there certainly are occasions where it is appropriate to have open and honest discussions about the challenges of parenting, we would urge parents to be careful about continually complaining about their children. There are several reasons why habitual complaining about children is wrong:

- It is inconsistent with the idea that children are primarily a blessing from God.
- It does not encourage us in our attitude toward our children.
- It can be a discouragement to others who are or will be parents.
- If done in our children's presence, it can demean and discourage them and communicate that we don't love them.

The point here is not to put on a happy face and pretend that everything about parenting is wonderful and fun. We're not even saying that everything you say about children should be positive. However, there is a big difference between an honest statement like "It's been a really difficult parenting week," and comments like "These kids are nothing but trouble" or "Life was great until we had children." One way to evaluate what you are saying is to think to yourself, If God Himself, who created this child and gave them to me, were standing right here before me, would it be appropriate for me to say this? We would suggest that if the answer is no, it shouldn't be said. (This is a good rule of thumb for anything you say, whether it be about children or not.)

Sensitivity to Those Who Don't Have Children or Can't Have Children

While on this topic, please be aware of the needs and emotional challenges of those who do not or cannot have children. We distinctly remember a time early in our marriage when we had become pregnant for the first time but experienced an early miscarriage. It had been several weeks since the miscarriage, and we were still grieving when we went to a work-related party. There Cindy was talking with a woman who mentioned she had thought she was pregnant but was relieved to discover that she wasn't, as though that would have been so obviously a bad thing. The woman didn't mean any harm, but her comment was hard for Cindy to receive, since she was very much wishing she was still pregnant. This incident showed us how hurtful a seemingly innocent comment about children could be.

If you have children, we encourage you to be sensitive to those who do not and who cannot have children. Couples struggling with infertility often are going through an extremely challenging and increasingly isolating experience. There are likely many couples around you who have struggled, are struggling, or will struggle with infertility. Besides infertility, many other experiences are related to children that can result in ongoing raw feelings, such as the loss of a child or simply not being married.

The following are some ways to be sensitive to and, therefore, love those who are struggling in one way or another with issues related to not having children:

- Don't assume that every couple will automatically have children. Avoid phrases like, "When you have children . . ." Having children is not completely under our control.
- Be careful when speaking negatively about your children in the presence of others. Consider what it would be like if you wanted more than anything in this world to have children but couldn't for some reason, and then you heard a friend complain about how their child came in and tracked dirt all over the house. Every part of you would want to scream, "I would give anything to have a child who would track dirt all over the house!"
- When people or couples without children are part of a group, try to avoid focusing all the conversation around children—a

common occurrence when new parents get together with other new parents. Avoid phrases like, "You know how it is when you have kids."

- If you do realize you said something that may have been hurtful to someone without children, ask them about it in private, and seek their forgiveness if necessary. Even if what you said wasn't an issue for them, asking them about it shows love and concern for their situation and can reduce the feeling of isolation that people without children may sometimes feel.
- Be truly thankful for the children God has given you. They are indeed a gift from God.

On a related note, we now move on to considering a vital question.

What Makes a Family?

While children are a welcome addition to a family, they do not make a family. Chapters 1 and 2 of Genesis describe the creation of man and woman, and we see God explicitly instituting marriage: "Therefore a man shall leave his father and his mother and hold fast to his wife, and they shall become one flesh" (Genesis 2:24).

It is interesting to note that this was before the entry of sin into the world (Genesis 3) and that God had declared the situation to be "very good" (Genesis 1:31). What we have here is a married couple who do not have children, but God gave no indication whatsoever that they were incomplete or deficient in any way because they did not have children.

Children, if God gives them, should be a welcome addition to a family, but they do not make a family. It is common in our culture for a married couple to say that they are going to "start a family," meaning they are going to try to have a child. Technically speaking, this is not correct. They started a family the day they were married. It is important for us all to recognize that a couple without children is not deficient or incomplete (in the same way that an unmarried person is also not deficient or incomplete in that situation). It can be a great blessing to be married and have children, but neither being married nor being a parent is necessary for us to have fulfilled lives that are lived to the glory of God as He intended.

Children Are Usually a Limited-Time Stewardship

Finally, if you are married and the Lord blesses you and your spouse with many decades together, recognize that the rearing of children will usually be a short-term, twenty-plus-year segment of those decades together. Most of your marriage may be spent not actively parenting. Keep this in mind as you prioritize maintaining the health of your marriage as the primary long-term human relationship.

> Focus on your marriage. Because that's the nucleus of the home, whatever you do to restore its health and strength will naturally restore what's broken among the other relationships. If you have no children yet, this will make a comfortable nest for them to begin life well. If you have children, the changes you make in your marriage will affect the rest of the household more quickly and dramatically than you think.
>
> – Charles R. Swindoll,
> *Marriage: From Surviving to Thriving*

Discussion Questions

1. On a scale of 1 to 10, how much does messiness and disorder in your house bother you? To what extent has this impacted your thoughts about your children?

2. What areas of your own struggle with sin have become evident to you in the process of rearing children, perhaps things that would not have been as clear if you had not had children? How do you respond when your own sin becomes evident as you parent your child or children?

3. Can you think of examples of negative comments you or others have said about children? Discuss how to best respond when these kinds of comments are made by others.

4. Can you think of people in your life who may be struggling with the inability to have children for one reason or another? In addition to the suggestions given in this chapter, what would be some practical ways you can show love to them?

5. Do you primarily see children as a joy and a blessing or as a burden to be endured? Can you identify things in your life on which you have your heart set (e.g., building a career, being able to visit with friends, having a solid night of sleep, having a clean home, having some time of your own, etc.) but which your children often prevent from happening in some way? To what extent does this color your attitude toward them?

Chapter 4

Be a Parent

> Children are not a distraction from more important work. They are the most important work.
>
> – Charles Spurgeon

As parents, we often turn to many sources of information for help and guidance in parenting, and it's easy to get the impression that the only people who could possibly parent well would be those who have a PhD in child psychology or who have other highly recognized credentials. We almost feel like we need to keep up on the current research to parent "correctly." Parenting can seem quite complicated.

Some of this is due to the many roles we think we're supposed to play in regard to our children. We are expected to be their friend, their advisor, their coach, their entertainment director, their dietician, their tutor, and many other roles. It seems that in the past, life as a parent was much simpler—you were the parent, they were the child, and there was a strong societal understanding of what those roles meant.

If God has given you children, then you can be confident that it is God's will for you to parent them. It is imperative for us as parents to understand that our primary role is to be our child's *parent*. When we feel like we need to be more than that, we lose confidence and can start second-guessing ourselves, to the point that we start looking to the child to be making decisions that we should be making. This is something we learned the hard way early on in our time as parents.

Our Story

Like most parents, we were filled with excitement and anticipation before the birth of our first child. We were looking forward to being parents and wanted to learn all we could ahead of time to be ready for when our child was born. Some well-meaning friends gave us a book on parenting written by a Christian author that we read and thoroughly absorbed. The book was sprinkled with Bible verses speaking of how children are fearfully and wonderfully made (which is all true). This view was then used to assert a primary theme of the book, which we understood to be that your child is well designed, and if you follow their cues well, things will go well for you as a parent. The book also spoke about "new scientific findings" as the basis for many of these cues. While there is a sense that children do give cues as to how they need to be treated, we adopted this viewpoint as an overall philosophy of parenting, as we resonated with all these "new scientific revelations." Surely, our generation had many advantages over previous ones in how they parented. (Groan!)

When our baby was born, we followed this philosophy but had a hard time reading and understanding our baby's cues. Over the next two years, both we and our little girl were miserable. She didn't sleep much, she was the focus of all our attention, our lives were wrapped around her, and we had almost no confidence in what we were doing. She was clearly in charge, but we did not see it.

Thankfully, over time we learned a more biblically consistent viewpoint—that a child is born with a sinful nature and needs parenting to grow and develop the way that they should. We know what is best for the child almost always more than the child does.

Biblical Basis for Parenting with Confidence

Where does the Bible say that children are born sinful and need parental direction? We could write many pages calling out several relevant passages, but in this section, we will attempt to give a summary of what the Bible teaches along these lines.

Parents Can Offer True Hope in the Gospel

Many in our society believe that children are born pure and innocent and are corrupted only by external influences. The Bible teaches the exact opposite—everyone is born with a sinful nature and, if left to themselves, will act in accord with this sinful nature (Psalm 51:5; Ephesians 2:1–3; Jeremiah 17:9). People need resources outside of themselves to overcome this inherent sinful nature. At the most profound level, the only way they can be truly cleansed of their sinful nature is through the saving work of Jesus Christ, when they become followers of Him. When someone becomes a believer in Christ, they are declared righteous and their sin is forgiven. They are also given a new heart, one that is now inclined to follow and obey God rather than inclined toward rebellion. Parents have the role of helping direct the hearts of their children, pointing them the way they should go (the way their heart is not yet inclined to go), and ultimately pointing them to Jesus. Only God, however, can save them and, in doing so, give them new hearts and make them new creations (2 Corinthians 5:17).

When a child is not yet a believer (and therefore does not have a new heart), God uses influences like parents to help them overcome some of their natural sinful inclinations to some extent, for their own good and for the good of those around them. For example, children start to lie on their own; sadly, this isn't something they need to be taught. But parents can instill within their child some level of understanding that lying is wrong. While this parental influence doesn't fix the fundamental problem in the heart of the child that only Christ can fix, it can often mitigate, to some extent, the sinful tendencies of a child's heart. Even an unbelieving child can come to an understanding that it is better not to lie and to live a life not characterized by consistent deceit.

Parents and Children Are Given Distinct Roles

Scripture speaks directly to parents and to children in several places, with an understanding that they have completely different roles in their relationship with each other. In Deuteronomy 6:6–7, parents are explicitly told to teach God's Word to their children, and it is implied that the children should listen to their parents: "And these words that I command you today shall be on your heart. You shall teach them diligently to your children, and shall talk of them when you sit in your house, and when you walk by the way, and when you lie down, and when you rise."

We see in chapter 6 of Paul's letter to the Ephesians that children are told to obey their parents (v. 1), and a few verses later parents are told to bring up their children in the discipline and instruction of the Lord (v. 4). Note that these are distinct and well-defined roles. We see the same thing throughout the book of Proverbs (1:8–9; 6:20–23; 19:18; 23:22).

Children Thrive under Parental Authority

Let's return to the Ephesians 6:1–3 passage. Here it is in its entirety:

> Children, obey your parents in the Lord, for this is right. "Honor your father and mother" (this is the first commandment with a promise), "that it may go well with you and that you may live long in the land."

This passage makes a connection between a child obeying his parents and things going well for the child. In general, it's true that a child who listens to what their parents have to say to them will be more likely to live a long and productive life than a child who ignores his parents and does whatever he wants.

Putting It All Together

We've seen that children are born with a sinful nature, that Scripture gives parents a clearly defined role of training their children, and that children are told to obey their parents so their lives will go well. Putting these together, we can see the Bible doesn't teach that a parent's primary goal is to follow the cues of their children.

Moms and dads, you really do have a God-given role to be the parent to your child, and you can have confidence that you really do know what is best for them. You have lived many more years than the child and have a much better understanding of the world and how it works. If you are a believer, you also have the Holy Spirit working within you, guiding you along the way, as well as God's Word, which reveals who He is and what His intention is for our lives. While you are not perfect by any means, you can trust that God has granted you a specific charge to parent your children.

It's Not a Popularity Contest

What does this practically mean for you in your parenting? If, as you are making decisions regarding your children, you are mostly concerned about what they think, you will be hindered in making good judgments. You are not trying to win a popularity contest with your child. Many decisions we make in the interest of our children will be different than what our children want in the moment. We should not feel bad when our children don't like or even vehemently disagree with our decisions from time to time. You are the one in authority, not your child. If those roles become reversed, the best interest of the child is not served, since he or she does not really have the big picture or the wisdom to make sound decisions in each situation.

It's Okay to Say No

I (Cindy) felt paralyzed in my parenting with my first child because I misapplied some Bible verses. I knew that child-rearing would be a more humbling and service-oriented role than I had previously experienced and that I'd have to battle my own selfishness along the way. But I mistakenly thought it was wrong or selfish of me to deny my toddler's requests if I did not have a good reason to do so. I validated my actions with Proverbs 3:27, "Do not withhold good from those to whom it is due, when it is in your power to do it" and Matthew 7:9–10, "Or which one of you, if his son asks him for bread, will give him a stone? Or if he asks for a fish, will give him a serpent?" among several others with similar themes. However, to assume that what my daughter was asking for was always good or right or helpful for her was a misapplication of these verses. At that point in my parenting I didn't consciously realize the principles described so far in this chapter and lacked confidence to make decisions that went against the wishes of my toddler, causing unhappiness for both of us. "Training them in the way they should go" must involve a realization that all their desires aren't necessarily part of the "way they should go" (We will flesh this out in more detail in chapter 7).

Balance Is Needed

We hope we have encouraged those of you who may lack confidence in your role as a parent. We are not saying that parents should become authoritarian in how they parent or should never consider their children's wishes. Ephesians 6:4 says fathers should not provoke their children to anger, and surely part of this involves respecting our children as individual people created in the image of God. They have unique personalities, gifts, desires, and dreams. It is not our job as parents to crush these things. However, as we interact with our children, we need to remember that we have a unique role as their parent, a role no one else in the world has for them. Your child needs you to be a parent, not a friend or confidant or provider of all whims. None of us are perfect parents, and at times we may make decisions that turn out not to be the best. But the fact that we are imperfect should not dissuade us from attempting to fulfill our God-given role as parents with confidence and to the best of our ability.

Discussion Questions

1. Some parents lack any confidence when parenting, while others are completely comfortable in their parenting roles. Where are you on this spectrum?
2. Have there been times when you have become confused by the advice of parenting "experts"? If so, give an example.
3. What is the most ridiculous parenting advice you have encountered?
4. Can you think of areas where your child may be having too much influence on your parental decision-making?

Chapter 5

Consistent Parenting (Part 1)

> Our children are counting on us to provide two things: consistency and structure. Children need parents who say what they mean, mean what they say, and do what they say they are going to do.
>
> – Barbara Coloroso

A parent's primary concern should be for the hearts of their children, not their external behavior. (By *hearts*, we mean their inner thoughts, inclinations, and attitudes.) We are not seeking to have children who merely conform to an external set of standards (how they *act*) but to have children who have hearts that respond properly to various situations (how they *think*), which then should influence their actions. While we do not have control over our children's hearts, we do have significant influence, and God often uses that influence to draw our children's hearts to Himself.

However, some ways in which we attempt to influence our children can be deeply discouraging to our children to the point of exasperating them and causing them to lose heart: "Fathers, do not exasperate your children, so that they will not lose heart" (Colossians 3:21 NASB.) One way of provoking our children is to parent them in an inconsistent manner. Have you ever been in a hospital where the various caregivers give inconsistent information? One doctor might say she is going to let you go home, then another comes in and says you need to stay overnight for a test in the morning. This can be incredibly frustrating. The same thing can be true for your child if the input they are receiving from you and your spouse is inconsistent in some manner.

It is essential for us to be parents who are consistent in at least four ways:

1. Consistency over time
2. Consistency between what you say and what you do
3. Consistency between the two parents (if there are two parents)
4. Consistency between public and private

Ironically, being consistent in these ways is very much a matter of our own hearts. Most of us naturally tend toward inconsistency in our lives and are frequently unaware of it without careful consideration. It is only by looking to God to show us these things and renew our hearts that we can be truly consistent. We'll circle back on our need for God's work in our lives later, but first, let's look at the first two ways we should strive to be consistent.

Consistency over Time

I (John) struggle with organizing my life. I've read books or taken classes on some kind of organizational method or another and found it quite enjoyable to set up a new program to tackle all the logistical details of my life—ordering my to-do lists, making files and folders, setting up a calendar, and so on. However, it is one thing to set up a method and quite another to follow it consistently. I have struggled to stick to an organizational program consistently over time. To be honest, I've never succeeded in doing this.

The same pattern can be true for parenting. Getting some encouraging parenting input from a book, presentation, or another person is entirely different than putting it into practice. However, it is not so much the initial implementation but consistent parenting over the long term that really makes a difference.

Life can be frustrating for a child whose parents have constantly changing parenting approaches. A child can learn to deal with a parent who is not perfect but is somewhat consistent over time. It is much more challenging to live with a parent who is unpredictable or constantly changing in their parenting methods.

What does inconsistent parenting over time look like? One example is a mom or dad who is primarily driven by their emotional condition at any given time. If they are in a good mood, they may be permissive and let certain behaviors go unaddressed, but if they are in a bad mood, the slightest misbehavior (or even just natural childishness) is immediately pounced on in one way or another.

Another form of inconsistent parenting over time happens when, as described earlier, parents jump on different parenting "methods," only to have the initial energy quickly fade away, and revert to default methods that tend to persist. An example of this would be if you were to read this book (or any other parenting book) voraciously and put a whole bunch of things into practice, but then six months later there has been no lasting change. This, by the way, is why we recommend working through this book relatively slowly so you are more able to develop ideas you'd like to pursue into long-term habits rather than be overwhelmed with everything at once.

Consistency between What You Say and What You Do

The well-known phrase "more is caught than taught" applies when it comes to children learning from their parents. Our children watch carefully what we do, not just listen to what we say. When we tell them one thing but do something completely different, that can confuse and frustrate them. Here are some examples:

- You teach your children not to lie, but then they hear you tell the telemarketer you're not at home or watch you call in sick for work when you're not.
- You instruct them it's wrong to steal, but then they watch as you fail to return the product you accidentally didn't pay for at the store.
- You tell them that they should treat their neighbor as they would want to be treated, but then you aggressively cut off someone so you can get the good parking spot.
- You lecture your children that it's wrong to lash out at other people in anger when they are upset, but they watch as you lose your temper over a bad call at the baseball game.

There are some important caveats here. First, it is sometimes appropriate to give our children greater restrictions than we follow ourselves.

For example, we may live on a busy road and tell our younger children that they may not cross the street though we can. These are generally not cases of morality but of safety and wisdom.

Secondly, we must recognize that sometimes we'll neglect to do the very things we teach our children to do. Suppose that you struggle with anger from time to time. Should you say to yourself, "Since I struggle with anger, I shouldn't teach my children that angry outbursts are wrong so there is not a disparity between what I say and what I do"? Absolutely not. When we respond with a sinful angry outburst, we should openly admit we have sinned, ask for forgiveness (perhaps for simply being a bad example), thank the Lord for His forgiveness, and seek the Lord's help to overcome sinful anger the next time we're tempted. In this way, we demonstrate the heart of the gospel to our children—the concept that our standing before our heavenly Father is not based on our righteousness, such as our ability to "follow the rules," but on Jesus's righteousness, and that there is true forgiveness for those in Christ. Our children will know we are imperfect sinners, and it is crucial for them to see how imperfect sinners deal with their sin.

This example also points out an important principle in parenting: Parents should never "lower the standard" of what is right and wrong so that it becomes a standard we ourselves can accomplish. Rather, we should teach the high standards as presented in Scripture—the absolute moral standards put forth by God, many of which deal with our heart attitudes—and demonstrate the gospel in action when we fail to meet these standards. This is grace, and it includes at the center the idea that, as Christians, our relationship with God as His beloved children is not based on our ability to do what God says we must do but on what Jesus did as the perfect man and expression of God's love. Likewise, our children's status as our beloved children does not change when they fail to live up to the standards we teach. When they—and we—fail to live up to these standards, we point them (and ourselves) once again to Christ. In this way, we are living out the gospel for our children and demonstrating in a very real way the love of God through Christ.

Hopefully you can see that the problem is not so much a lack of consistency between what we say and what we do, because there never will be perfect consistency if we are teaching God's true standards. Rather, the problem is if we apply a standard to our children (what we say) but then hold ourselves to a completely different standard (what we do), without recognition that we have missed the mark.

More to Come

In the next chapter, we will look at two other ways we should be consistent in our parenting. If you're feeling discouraged because of past or anticipated future failures in some of these areas, remember that, ultimately, we can and must look to the Lord to work in our hearts and the hearts of our children. We need God's transforming grace in our lives and in the lives of our children, both to overcome our failures and to transform us into the image of Jesus. More on that in the next chapter!

Discussion Questions

1. On a scale of 1 to 10, how consistent do you tend to be in general (not just in parenting)? What are some areas in which you find it easy to be consistent in living by the standards set in Scripture or taught to your children? What are some areas in which you struggle with consistency?
2. In terms of parenting, have you ever made any significant changes in your approach based on some kind of input from others (e.g., a book, a sermon, a blog, a conversation)? Did these changes "stick," or did they fade after a while? If they faded, what are some reasons they faded?
3. Trying to think from your children's perspectives, are there ways you have been inconsistent in your parenting over time that could easily be frustrating or exasperating to them?
4. Give examples of areas in which you have appropriately held your children to a standard or rule that you yourself did not follow. (Similar to the example given above of not crossing the street.)
5. In what areas of moral teaching has it been relatively easy to be consistent between what you say to your child and what you do? What are some areas where you struggle with this consistency? (If you are not a parent, give examples of what you've seen with other parents.)
6. What is your response when you fail to live up to the moral standards you teach your children? How much of this do your children see?

7. What changes can you make to more openly live out the gospel in your life?

Chapter 6

Consistent Parenting (Part 2)

> Children do need the guidance of their parents, and we guide them more by the example we set than by any other way. We need to be firm and sane and fair and consistent.
>
> – Billy Graham

This chapter continues the theme begun in the last chapter—consistency in parenting. Previously, we covered the need to be consistent over time, the need to be consistent between what we say and what we do, and what to do when we're not consistent.

In this chapter, we will cover two vital areas in which consistency is very much needed—consistency between parents and consistency between public and private. A significant lack in consistency in these areas will undercut just about anything you attempt to do in your parenting. We have talked with many moms and dads who have struggled in significant ways in parenting their children, and in some cases the topics covered in this chapter were at the root of many of their problems.

Consistency between Parents

Since a mother and a father are two distinct people who are together parenting a child, an obvious potential for inconsistency exists between what one parent says and does and how the other parent responds to the same situation. This can cause understandable confusion and exasperation in the child. Inconsistency between parents can take on two different forms.

The first form of inconsistency between parents is *unintentional inconsistency*. This is when parents are trying to be consistent but they simply make different judgment calls from time to time. For example, suppose a child asks if they can play outside, and the mother says yes. But when the child starts to go outside, the father notices that a required chore has not been done, so he tells the child they cannot go outside until they finish their chore. Are the parents being inconsistent? Yes. Is it intentional? No. They are following the same philosophy and trying to be consistent in their parenting, but in this case one of them had information the other didn't, so their parenting decisions were different.

Unintentional inconsistency is bound to occur occasionally, so what can be done to make it less frustrating for the child (and the parents)? Here are some principles we found to be helpful:

- **Always back each other up.** When an unintentional inconsistency is recognized, both parents should do everything they can to become united and do this quickly. In the example of a child asking to go outside, it probably would make the most sense for the mother to say that she didn't realize that the child hadn't finished their chore, and that she, like Dad, would like the child to finish the chore before going outside.
- **Do not allow your child to "fish" for a favorable answer.** Sometimes, if a child gets an answer they don't like from one parent, they will go to the other parent and ask the same question in hopes of getting a better answer. This must be prohibited and discouraged in every way possible. If you get a sense that your child does this, get in the habit of asking your child if they've asked the other parent before you answer. If they have asked the other parent before coming to you, then ideally, both parents should jointly declare that the child shouldn't do that, and perhaps make a decision together that makes the situation more negative from a child's point of view to dissuade them from "fishing" in the future.
- **Teach your child what to do if they get conflicting input from parents.** What is the best thing for the child to do when the authorities (parents) in the child's life give conflicting commands? It would be the same thing we should do when our authorities give conflicting inputs—appeal to them respectfully, let them know they are giving conflicting responses, and ask what you

should do. It is fine for a child to identify when parents have given conflicting inputs as long as it is done with an attitude of submission—not to play the parents off against each other but to request resolution of the conflict by the parents.

This might be a good thing to practice as a family. Give your child a scenario. For example, Dad asks the child to go pick up sticks off the lawn so he can mow. As the child is heading out to do that, Mom stops the child and reminds them they need to make their bed. What should the child do? Help them figure out how to present the situation respectfully to Mom so she knows there is an unintended conflict for the parents to resolve.

Unintentional inconsistency will happen, but if parents work to minimize the effects as described above, then occasional inconsistency will generally not be a big problem. A much more harmful form of inconsistency between parents is *inconsistent parenting philosophies*. When parents have inconsistent parenting philosophies, they have a fundamentally different approach to parenting in any given situation, which will result in the parents often disagreeing on what should be done. If inconsistent parenting philosophies persist and are significant, it can cause major frustration all around: between the parents and between the child and one or both parents.

It is critical for your child's sake and your marriage's sake to "get on the same page" in terms of your parenting philosophy. This will likely mean that one or the other parent (or both) needs to make some adjustments to his or her parenting philosophy. In our opinion, it is more important for parents to be consistent between each other than to be "right" in their parenting methods. As an example, consider many of the topics in this book, especially the later chapters, which are in the category of helpful suggestions but not biblical truth. If one parent thinks the suggestion should be implemented, and the other thinks it shouldn't, then it's more important that the parents agree to be consistent than to adopt any particular idea.

The classic example of differing parenting philosophies is having one parent who is strict and demanding and another parent who is laid back or more lenient. If this situation is not addressed, it will be problematic to put into practice anything described in this book unless both parents can come to agreement on parenting philosophy, both in theory (what they think) *and* in practice (what they do).

It is likely that any two parents will have different personalities. There is no problem with having one parent who is more detail-oriented and one who is more laid-back and perhaps "play-oriented." However, our natural personalities do not need to completely determine how we act. We may need to parent in a way that is unlike our personalities or our natural inclinations. For example, if you are naturally laid-back, you will probably need to parent with more intensity and strictness than is natural for you. And if you are naturally driven by order, you may need to parent in a more flexible way.

By our observation, parents who see little positive change when they try to implement changes in their parenting often have, as a root cause, an inconsistency between them in terms of overall parenting philosophy. Parents, you must work hard to align your approaches and realize that this may mean learning to bring up and care for your children in a way that does not come naturally to you. It may also mean spending significant time and effort communicating with each other about parenting issues. For the sake of your children, we plead with you not to cling to your own personal preferences only but to honor God and love your children by parenting in a consistent manner with your spouse.

Consistency between Public and Private

The final area in which consistency is needed is in how your family operates in private versus how you operate in public. Here are some questions to consider:

1. Does the way you interact together change significantly if a visitor is present in your home?
2. Are there negative actions accepted and common within your home that are not ever seen when out in public (e.g., regular outbursts of anger or unkindness at home but always calm and respectful in public)?
3. Do you have significant "family secrets"—an understanding (stated or implied) that certain negative things should never be spoken of in public?
4. Is there an implied understanding that your family needs to put on a good face in public that is different than the reality when at home?

5. If someone who knows you from mostly public interactions were to come live with you for a month, but you didn't change anything about the way you operate as a family, would they be disturbed or surprised by what they see?
6. Is it somewhat common to have major conflict, disagreement, and arguing instantly change into cooperative cheerfulness once the car doors open and you step out in public?

If your answers to these questions reveal a significant inconsistency between your public and private lives, then you may have some serious family issues that need to be addressed. However, let's recognize that there are some caveats. We are not saying that nothing should be private and that everything should be in the open. Some things, such as disciplining a child, are more appropriately done in private and generally will not be done in public. Also, some amount of conflict is present in every home, and some of that should be dealt with in a private manner. Often there will be a suitable slight shift in observed family culture when a visitor is present so that attention is focused on welcoming and visiting with the guest.

The real question is how big the gulf is between public and private. From the child's point of view, do they really see two completely different families—the one in private and the one in public? We believe that a disparity between public and private can be extremely damaging to a child, for several reasons:

- It implies that appearances are more important than the heart reality. In a sense, it trains the children to be good at creating a disconnect between how things appear on the outside and what is truly going on in their hearts.
- If there are significant "family secrets," then they learn not to ever open up too much to people outside the family, for fear that the secrets will get out.
- It makes dealing with heart issues in our children difficult because of the pattern of ignoring heart issues and focusing on external appearances. For example, if unkind or disrespectful conduct and communication is allowed in the home but not in public, then the child may begin to think there is nothing inherently wrong with those attitudes and behaviors—just don't do them in public. Not addressing these issues at home allows

them to "rehearse" wrong heart habits and inconsiderate actions in the home environment rather than having their home life prepare them to be considerate of others around them.

- They develop the mindset that there are two standards of behavior: a high standard when other people are present and a low standard when other people aren't around. This is an unbiblical and dangerous mindset.
- If children are taught that they really only need to be civil with other family members when in public, they may begin to think their parents and siblings aren't worthy of consideration or respect. The home is a training ground for their future homes, and we want to teach our children the "one anothers"[1] in Scripture, starting with their own families.

Every family has some differences between public and private, but if you perceive major and consistent public versus private discrepancies in yours, then we would encourage you to attempt to deal with these issues within your heart. Seek help from a pastor or a trusted friend. Openly admit to your children when wrong has occurred, and seek their forgiveness. Show your children, by your actions, that what happens in private at home or in the heart is just as important as what happens in public.

Sadly, we must briefly address the extreme case of public versus private inconsistency—abuse. A detailed coverage of physical or sexual abuse is outside the scope of this book; however, if you are in a situation in which there is imminent danger to you or your children, you need to seek outside help immediately. If this is your situation, improving your parenting is not the issue at hand—protecting yourself or your children should be your focus.

Need for God's Grace

Looking back over these last two chapters, we recognized the need for parental consistency over time, consistency between what we say and what we do, consistency between both parents, and consistency between

---

1 The Bible contains dozens of passages about how we are to treat "one another." Some examples are: "through love serve one another" (Galatians 5:13), "forgiving each other" (Ephesians 4:32), and "encourage one another and build one another up" (1 Thessalonians 5:11). We encourage you to search for the words "one another" and see the breadth of Bible teaching on this subject.

public and private. However, most of us look at ourselves and realize that we don't measure up and need to grow in one or more of these areas. Here again we come face-to-face with the need for God's grace in our lives. Thankfully, our standing before God is based on Christ and not on our "performance" as parents. Still, our ability to be consistent in these areas (or not) will impact our children. We need God's grace to cover up our inadequacies as parents, and we must look to Him to give us hearts truly consistent in these different ways.

Discussion Questions

1. If you have children, have you ever caught them "fishing" for a better answer between parents? If you can, give an example. What was your response?
2. When you grew up, were your own parents on the same page in terms of parenting philosophy? What impact did that have on you as a child?
3. Go through the questions in the "Consistency between Public and Private" section with your spouse (or, if a single parent, consider them on your own). Assign a number between 1 and 10 to each of them, where 1 indicates that what the question is asking is almost never true and 10 indicates that what the question is asking is almost always true. If you're in a group, summarize your findings from this question to the rest of the group to the extent that you are comfortable.
4. If you have identified some significant inconsistencies between public and private, choose a person outside your family you can talk to about this, and schedule a time to discuss it with them and get their help. For the sake of your children, do not just sweep this under the rug and pretend it's not there!

Chapter 7

Center of the Universe

> When they discover the center of the universe, a lot of people will be disappointed to discover they are not it.
>
> – Bernard Bailey

Every child begins life seeing the world only from their own perspective. For example, when a newborn baby's stomach is empty, she knows she is hungry and wants to be fed, and that is all that matters. She has little perception of what is going on around her. Even if Mother is rushing to finish her own meal before feeding her child, the newborn baby cannot possibly understand the reason for her mother's delay. To her, she is hungry, but Mom is not there.

As children get older, they understand more of the world around them, but due to their natural selfishness, they still tend to think that everything revolves around them. Children with a "center of the universe" mindset will be characterized by a demand for things to go the way they want (a desire for control) and a lack of submission to those in authority over them (e.g., parents, teachers). They have a mindset that the world around them exists for the purpose of pleasing them, and often become manipulative to get their way.

Children, left to themselves, will suffer greatly if they are allowed to persist with a "center of the universe" attitude. A child who is unable to live contentedly under those in authority will almost certainly struggle in many areas of life, especially if he doesn't learn to do so before adulthood. A child who thinks she should be the center of everyone's attention will become an attention seeker and will struggle to notice or pursue what is in the best interest of others. A child who thinks the world exists to serve him will have an entitlement mindset and may become devastated when the realities of life show him that the world doesn't exist to serve him.

We do our children a great disservice if we allow them to persist with a center-of-the-universe attitude, or even worse, if we encourage it. Ironically, we commonly do things that tend to encourage a self-centered attitude in our children. In this chapter, we seek to help you identify a few of these unintentional "pitfalls" that we ourselves have done (to our later regret) and have seen others do as well. It is easy for well-intended, intentional parents to fall into these pitfalls, especially with firstborn children.

Pitfall 1: Too Much Attention

One common pitfall is simply to give our children too much attention. This may sound funny to you—is it really possible to pay too much attention to your child? Every child needs nurture and will benefit from intentional, loving interaction with his or her parents. However, if our child is constantly the focus of our attention when we are with them, they can develop a mindset that life really is all about them.

We distinctly remember an evening many years ago when we, as relatively new parents, were visiting some friends of ours. Our child was a toddler, and we spent most of the evening sitting with our friends in the living room watching our child toddle around in front of everyone. We cringe a bit when we look back on that evening for several reasons. First, while our friends may have found some of our toddler's antics funny, they likely did not share the passion for watching them that we did. (Thankfully, they were gracious to us.) Secondly, from our toddler's point of view, she spent a couple of hours as the sole focus of attention of four adults whose only desire (so it seemed) was to watch her. This one event by itself would not make a large impact on her life. However, it was somewhat consistent with how we were parenting at the time, so it was one of a long string of interactions in which our child was the primary focus of her parents (and any other adult in the room). She clearly was getting the picture that everyone else existed to pay attention to her!

It is valuable for children to spend time with their parents when their parents are focused on other things (like working on a project, cooking, etc.). We do not need to feel guilty going about our necessary work with our children nearby while they are not the center of our attention. It is beneficial for children to observe what "normal" parents need to do so they can develop an awareness and appreciation for what is needed to care for a family. Clearly, balance is necessary in this area. It is neither good to be a parent who never gives individual attention to their child nor one who gives nearly constant individual attention to their child.

This issue tends to be greater with firstborn children because, by definition, they start their lives as the only child and normally have much of the parents' attention. A child who is the second or later child in a family will have much less of an illusion that they are the center of attention!

Pitfall 2: A Conversation "Trump Card"

It has been said that a conversation is like a game of tennis—the control of the conversation is passed back and forth between two (or more) people like a tennis ball. But sometimes children are given a "trump card" in this conversational back and forth between two adults. This happens when a parent makes a habit of immediately stopping conversation with another person to respond to any and every request or comment of the child.

For example, consider the following interchange between a mother, her child, and her friend Janet:

> Mother: Janet, where did you stay the first night of your trip?
>
> Janet: We stayed in a hotel because they had a nice pool. We like to swim when we take—
>
> Child (interrupting): Mommy, can we go swimming?
>
> Mother (turning to child): We are planning on going swimming tomorrow.
>
> Janet: As I was saying, when we travel, we—
>
> Child (interrupting again): But can't we go swimming tonight?
>
> Mother: Tonight won't work because Mommy has to go to a meeting.
>
> Janet: we like to have a chance to—
>
> Child: What's a meeting?
>
> Mother: A meeting is when people get together to talk about something.

Janet: have a chance to unwind after—

Child: What are you going to talk about at your meeting?

Mother: We are talking with teachers at the school.

While this example may seem contrived, you might be surprised how often a parent will allow a child to interrupt them at will. In fact, it can become a habitual pattern of interaction, and the parent may not even consciously recognize that it's happening. Not only is this somewhat rude to whomever the parent is talking, it also reinforces the child's perception that they are the most important person present and that everyone stops to address them when they speak.

In the above example, what message are we giving to the child about the importance or respect that should be given to the person talking to the mother? It is crucial to teach our child how to listen to a conversation and try to find a time to interject a necessary question at the least disruptive time. We have found it helpful to give our children a signal they can use of coming and laying a hand on our arm so we know they want our attention. When we see this signal, we will try to acknowledge them at the soonest possible break in the conversation. We don't want to frustrate a child with a legitimate need who feels unable to get our attention, but we also want them to develop the skill of waiting and listening.

Pitfall 3: Strengthening the Want Muscle

We have a family joke that every child seems to be born with a "want muscle"—that is, they naturally want things. Many of these wants are necessary and helpful (like wanting food when they are hungry, which is a good thing!). But that want muscle seems to get stronger and stronger as they get into their toddler years. If a child crumples to the floor because they did not get something they desire, they have a powerful want muscle.

In a sense, we strengthen a child's want muscle when we regularly give them whatever they want. However, it is healthy for a child to sometimes want something but not receive it. It takes some wisdom on a parent's part to discern when it is good to grant the requests of our child and when to say no (or "not now"). However, we should do it regularly enough that our child realizes it's okay for a want or request to go unfulfilled. As a parent, it is acceptable to say no sometimes, even if there is not necessarily a good reason to do so. We can do this and still be a parent who is characterized as saying yes to reasonable requests.

How can you discern if your child's want muscle has become too strong? A good way to tell is to observe what happens when your child is denied something they want. If they regularly have an extremely negative reaction to a denial, then there may be a problem.

Once again, balance is necessary. We do not need to be characterized by always saying no to any request from our children. But we should work to ensure our children are completely okay with a no from their parents from time to time.

This is another area where our parenting can have a big impact on how our children deal with life in the future. They will certainly not be granted everything their hearts desire as they grow older, and when they do get their desires (like a spouse) it won't always happen in the time and place of their choosing. So much of what we do when parenting smaller children influences how they respond to the challenges of life later.

As I mentioned in a previous chapter, when my children were young, I (Cindy) felt like I was supposed to grant any reasonable requests from the children based on some improperly applied passages of Scripture:

> Do not withhold good from those to whom it is due, when it is in your power to do it. Do not say to your neighbor, "Go, and come again, tomorrow I will give it"—when you have it with you.
>
> – Proverbs 3:27–28

> You have heard that it was said, "An eye for an eye and a tooth for a tooth." But I say to you, do not resist the one who is evil. But if anyone slaps you on the right cheek, turn to him the other also. And if anyone would sue you and take your tunic, let him have your cloak as well. And if anyone forces you to go one mile, go with him two miles. *Give to the one who begs from you, and do not refuse the one who would borrow from you.*
>
> – Matthew 5:38–42 (emphasis added)

> Or which one of you, if his son asks him for bread, will give him a stone? Or if he asks for a fish, will give him a serpent? If you then, who are evil, know how to give good gifts to your

> children, how much more will your Father who is in heaven give good things to those who ask him!
>
> – Matthew 7:9-11

Having read these, I concluded that I was always to respond as positively and generously as possible to all my children's requests. I was concerned about battling my own selfishness and knew that serving my family and my young children in particular would require sacrifice, so I tended to see requests from small children to be opportunities for me to be selfless and sacrificial. I had not stopped to consider whether always responding as positively as possible might actually be harmful for my children. Later in my parenting, after a few pretty challenging years with a toddler ruling my home, other passages from Scripture caused me to reflect on the possible negative impact I might have on my children's character if I treated all their requests as wisdom-filled, good things for them to have or do. Here are a few of the verses I considered:

> Do not answer a fool according to his folly, or you will also be like him. Answer a fool as his folly deserves, that he not be wise in his own eyes.
>
> – Proverbs 26:4–5 (NASB)

> Do you see a man who is wise in his own eyes? There is more hope for a fool than for him.
>
> – Proverbs 26:12

> Woe to those who are wise in their own eyes, and shrewd in their own sight!
>
> – Isaiah 5:21

Clearly, every request a child makes is not foolishness. However, if we allow our children to develop a mindset that every question they have will be immediately answered or that every reasonable request will be granted, we can inadvertently set them up to be "wise in their own eyes"—that is, to think that they are in control and always know what is best. There is a delicate balance here. On the one hand, we do not want to attack or demean our child and regard them as though they know nothing. On the other hand, we don't want to treat them as though they are wise rulers who know what is better than the people around them. This wise in their own eyes attitude is frustrating to deal with coming from a two-year-old, and it doesn't improve with age emanating from an older child!

We are now firmly convinced that if a child struggles to be content (becoming mopey or grumpy) with a kind but firm negative response to a request, there is some heart-training work to be done in that child so they can learn contentment. Our heavenly Father, in His wisdom, does not always answer our requests affirmatively, and He does so for our good and His glory. He knows what is best, and earthly parents often do too. It is a great blessing to our children to begin to learn the art of contentment and gratefulness toward those who help and serve them and provide for their needs. They will be far better served in their later lives to have developed these heart attitudes.

Pitfall 4: Too Many Choices

As another variation on the same theme, one area where many parents (including us) fail to realize they are reinforcing a "center of the universe" mentality is in giving too many choices to our children. For example, suppose it is snack time for your three young children, and in the refrigerator you have apple, grape, and orange juice. You may not really care which juice they drink, so you're tempted to let them make that choice for themselves. However, it may not be the wisest thing to allow each child to choose which kind of juice they have whenever they have juice. Why is that? Besides not encouraging our children to think we run a short-order kitchen, it comes down to a matter of who has authority. In a parent-child relationship, the child is not the one who is (or should be) in charge in a general sense—that's the appropriate role of the parent. A young child who is always given choices can start to think they are really the one calling the shots (and they are if they get to consistently exert their will by making many of the decisions). Our goal is to encourage contentment with good things, like a cup of juice.

Sometimes we might not directly give our young children choices, but they may request to make the choice. In the juice example, perhaps we grab the apple juice but the child says, "No, I want orange juice." It is easy for this to become the kind of thing where the child is trying to wrest control away from their parent, and the parent may not even realize what is happening. We can inadvertently create little rulers who are calling most of the shots within their sphere of influence.

An easy way to determine if this is a problem with your child is to simply not allow your child to make the choice, and observe what happens. In the above example, when you start pouring apple juice and the child says, "I want orange juice," you simply say, "No, I'd like you to have apple juice," and then see what happens. If your child is okay with that, there is no problem, and you could probably allow them to choose which juice, at least some of the time. However, if the child whines, throws a fit, or keeps requesting orange juice, then you have a battle of wills going on, and you need to give the child many opportunities to learn contentment with the treat of having *any* kind of juice, not just the one they want at that moment. It's not hard to picture a sulky teenager, or even young adult, very bent out of shape when there is no milk in the fridge or the cookies are all gone and shopping day isn't until tomorrow. The roots of that attitude start young.

Most parents are concerned about teaching their children to make good choices, and this is an important goal of parenting, particularly as children get older. However, for very young children, it is much more important that they are willing to abide by the choices of the authorities in their lives cheerfully (in our example, to be content with whatever juice is placed before them) than it is to make "wise" choices, because they often don't yet have the understanding needed for making wise choices. In our example, is there really a wise choice between apple, grape, and orange juice? No. From the child's point of view, it's more about personal preferences than a wisdom issue. There will be plenty of opportunities to teach them about decision-making as you begin to include them in your thought processes when making decisions yourself, but this is generally more appropriate later in their childhood.

Rejoice with Those Who Rejoice

The apostle Paul instructs us to "rejoice with those who rejoice" (Romans 12:15). This is something we need to teach our children because it does not usually come naturally. When a child is accustomed to being the center of attention, it can be very upsetting for them to be in a situation where someone else is in the spotlight (like a birthday celebration). This kind of situation provides a good opportunity for us to encourage our children to start to see things from another person's perspective, by being happy when others are blessed. Change in this area does not come quickly, but if we consistently encourage our children to think about things from other people's perspectives and rejoice with those who rejoice, eventually that concept can start to sink in. (By the way, the second half of Romans 12:15 says to "weep with those who weep." The same principles apply here, as we teach our children to have sympathy for those who are suffering.)

Concluding Thoughts

If you are a parent, you may read this chapter and think to yourself, "Oh no, I'm doing all these things!" If, after honest evaluation, you realize that you have fallen into any of these pitfalls, don't panic. It's never too late to turn things around and change how you do things. If your child is older, you might want to talk with them and tell them that you have learned some things and want to better help them to become grown up. You can explain how you may be changing things and tell them how you expect them to respond. For younger children, you can just start changing the way you operate. If it's a big change, there may be a time of adjustment, but you might be surprised at how quickly your child can adjust to the new reality.

Also, it is wise to recognize your own personality tendencies when considering the suggestions in this chapter. For example, if you are the kind of person who reflexively says no to anything your child requests, then you may actually need encouragement to say yes more often. It can be helpful to have an honest discussion about these things with someone who knows you well (like your spouse) to ascertain how much you should strive to change and in what areas.

So take a deep breath. Addressing this kind of selfishness and self-orientation in our children is a daunting task and clearly one of the more nuanced and challenging aspects of heart training for our children. We won't be able to completely prevent the sinful self-orientation in our children. However, by recognizing and identifying things we are doing that feed their selfish tendencies and making suitable changes, we can help our children become less self-oriented.

Discussion Questions

1. On a scale of 1 to 10, how much do each of the four pitfalls apply to your current children? (1 = it's not really an issue, and 10 = it's a huge issue)

2. If you have more than one child, have you seen differences between your children in terms of how much they feel like they are the center of the universe? Has your parenting changed between children, and if so, in what ways?

3. Each of the pitfalls described requires an element of balance. For example, avoiding giving too many choices does not mean that you should never give a child any choices at all. Describe the balance required for each of the four pitfall areas.

4. Do you find yourself naturally unbalanced in any of these areas? (In other words, if you don't consciously think about it, do you lack balance?) What changes can you make to become more balanced?

Chapter 8

Setting Boundaries: How We Learned to Love Blue Tape

> A man's worst difficulties begin when he is able to do as he likes.
>
> – Thomas Huxley

Parenting can be a humbling experience, especially when we realize that, despite good intentions, we have headed down an unhelpful path in one way or another.

One area where we started out in the wrong direction was in setting boundaries. Initially, this was not much of an issue since infants don't have much mobility. But before long, our first child started rolling over, and we were thrilled with her accomplishments. When her crawling began, we realized that we had to think about how to keep her out of certain areas. Thus began our childproofing adventure. We bought all kinds of devices and barriers designed to keep a child out of harm's way, including various gates and cabinet and door latches. After a whole day of installing the cabinet latches and putting up the gates, we were able to create an environment in which our child could freely explore but wouldn't get into the cabinets or dangerous areas of the house. Problem solved, right?

Well, it was somewhat solved—for a while. Then an older, more experienced father stayed with us and made some gentle comments about how they worked on houseproofing the child rather than childproofing the house. Looking back, we wished he had been less gentle and, instead, hit us over the head with a two-by-four to get our attention. But no, we thought we had this all figured out.

The problem with the strong childproofing approach is that it only works for so long. Eventually, the child will learn how to get around whatever barriers we put up, even if it takes a couple years. I think our hope was that when our children got older, they would be more mature and would just know that they shouldn't get into those areas. However, this was all premised on the fact that they would have magically developed sufficient self-control to constrain themselves when the physical barriers were no longer sufficient. A common example of this is where a child has learned to crawl out of the crib or toddler bed, and with no internalized boundaries, the parents are then burdened with continually monitoring the child to keep them safe.

After a couple years of living in a childproofed home, we ended up moving to a new house in a new city. In the process of moving in, we wanted to keep the children from crawling or walking into the kitchen, which would pose many dangers for children their age. Because this particular house had a vinyl floor in the kitchen and carpeting just about everywhere else, on a whim, we decided that, at least for the short run, we would see if we could simply get our young children to stay off the vinyl floor. To our surprise, it worked amazingly well! It took a little training, but soon they learned that they were not to cross the well-defined dining-room-to-kitchen boundary. As a result, we never put up the gate we had been planning to install there.

This started us wondering if we could do the same kind of thing for other places in the house. Would it be possible to simply train the children to respect physical boundaries on their own, rather than attempt to physically constrain them? We discovered that yes, it was possible, but it required giving our children a clear understanding of established boundaries.

Eventually, we migrated to using blue painter's tape on the ground to demark boundaries for crawling children and toddlers. (We initially used regular masking tape but found that to be extremely hard to remove after a while, especially on carpet.) We could put blue tape at the top or the bottom of the stairs, and they knew that the stairs were off-limits. We put tape on the floor around a fireplace, and they stayed away from the fireplace. We could also put it around fragile things in a room, and they would stay away from them. This led to an amazing amount of peace within our home, since we could place young children in various areas and know that they would be safe. Over time, we gained just as much, if not more, confidence in these boundaries as the physical boundaries.

At this point you might be thinking, *How do you get them not to cross the tape?* Stay tuned—that will come later in the chapter. It is possible—normal children can be trained this way.

As time went on and the children gained maturity and responsibility to handle access to areas like the kitchen floor, we could remove various strips of tape to broaden their horizons. It was quite fun to watch our children when we removed the tape at the bottom of the stairs so they could go between floors at will. Each child, in turn, spent most of that first day of "stair freedom" simply going up and down the stairs.

We would even bring the tape with us when we went to the grandparents' houses or stayed at various other places away from home, like hotel rooms. After a minute or two of tape placement, the youngest children knew where they were allowed to be, and everyone was happy. From the child's point of view, this was just an everyday part of life—a limitation they had learned to live within.

It was quite funny to watch what would happen when a guest had been holding one of our young children and unknowingly set them down on the floor of our kitchen—one of the "forbidden zones." Usually the child would stand paralyzed at the spot where they were placed, looking to us as their parents to rescue them and take them to a safe place (which we always did with a chuckle).

We also found that once the children got the idea of staying within boundaries, we could extend that concept to other areas that didn't involve blue tape. For example, we could put a large beach blanket down on the ground at a picnic and tell the children that they needed to stay on the blanket, usually putting some toys there for them to play with. They obeyed, and it was much easier than dragging around a large fence to deploy wherever we went!

When the youngest of our eight children was old enough to enter the kitchen—the last remaining forbidden zone—we were reluctant to remove the last piece of blue tape, knowing it was the end of an era for our family. Eventually, we had to remove it, however, so we had a "tape removal" ceremony. It seems like a funny thing, but we were choked up about it because removing the last of the blue tape meant we were leaving the "little kid" phase of parenting, which, for us, was a sad thought.

Using blue tape to train your children to stay within boundaries falls in the category of "advice" rather than biblical truth, and you can be a faithful parent and never use a single piece of blue tape. However, we found it to be extremely helpful to us, and whether or not you use blue tape, we would strongly encourage you to teach your children how to exert self-control to stay within boundaries. Do this from their early ages, and you may be surprised at how it can pay off long-term dividends for having a degree of order in your household as well as in their development of the skill and virtue of self-control.

Practical Considerations

The most common question we get about the use of blue tape is "How do you train your children not to cross the line?" We found that the earlier we did it, the easier it tended to be. For a very young child who had just learned to crawl, we would spend some time pointing at the line and gesturing that they shouldn't cross it, and saying, "No." We would then watch the child for a while, and if they started going across the line, would give them a firm verbal "No!" while pointing to the line. If they persisted, we would give them a flick of our finger across the top of the hand that had crossed the line. This would cause a small amount of short-term pain that would make our intentions clear. Usually, after some intentional training along these lines, they would "get it" and would become more or less compliant. Sometimes it would take continual refresher training. It was also vital to deal consistently with infractions. If the children interpreted the tape line as a mere suggestion, then it would not have worked very well.

You should use your judgment—there may still be truly unsafe things where use of physical barriers would be wise, such as putting a gate at the top of stairs and locking medicine cabinets. The point of this is not to avoid all physical constraints at all costs but to work on training your children to practice physical self-control, rather than to apply only external constraints.

When to Set Boundaries

We believe there are two basic considerations about setting boundaries for children:

1. It is harder to add a boundary than to remove a boundary.
2. It is harder to add a boundary for older children than for younger children.

Taken together, these considerations imply that things will go better if we set boundaries early and then relax them when appropriate. In contrast, most parents naturally wait until there is an issue and then start "clamping down" by setting more and more boundaries as time goes on.

Let's consider the example of allowing children to go into the kitchen. If a child is taught from the start that the kitchen is off-limits, then this restriction seems normal, and it is unlikely to require a battle of wills to make this happen. However, if a child has been able to enter the kitchen at will and at some point later in life (perhaps as a three-year-old) they are suddenly told that they are no longer allowed to enter the kitchen, this will take some adjustment on everyone's part. This late enforcement of a boundary is much more likely to lead to frustration and a battle of wills that could have been avoided had the boundary been set at an earlier age.

Many parents are delighted when their child learns to crawl and can open a kitchen drawer and play with the plastic storage containers. They are excited to see the growth in coordination and think of this as being really adorable. Here is where it is good to consider the long-term implications of this freedom. At some point, it is no longer cute for a child to be emptying kitchen drawers onto the floor repeatedly while you're making dinner. How much better would it be not to allow this freedom from the beginning? Carefully consider what freedoms you allow your crawling child to have and what that might look like when they are an active toddler.

So far we have been talking about setting physical boundaries, but the same principles apply for all types of boundaries we might set for our children, including things like computer usage, curfews, and whom they can play with.

Of course, none of us are perfect parents, and there will likely be times when we find ourselves establishing a new boundary later than we might have hoped. In these cases, it's still better to go ahead and do it, even if it takes more effort on our part than it would have earlier.

Won't Setting Boundaries Limit Them?

Some parents are concerned that setting boundaries will in some way limit their children, preventing them from exploring on their own and from learning to make their own decisions. It is true that a boundary is, by its very nature, a limitation. Everyone, however, must live within boundaries that others have set for them, whether they are a young toddler or an adult. (Take, for example, speed limits.) Parents set up boundaries not just for training but also for their children's protection. Training our young children not to go near the street is good for them!

Learning the skill of functioning within boundaries is an essential part of everyday life. While it's true that a parent can set too many boundaries or set boundaries that are not age-appropriate, the negative impact of doing these things is probably less than the impact of not setting enough boundaries.

As in many things, this is an area where we need wisdom. Remember that *you* are the parent and the child is the child, and *you* are given the role to protect and nurture your child. Setting boundaries is an important tool to this end.

Discussion Questions

1. What boundaries do you remember from when you grew up? Were the boundaries fuzzy or clear? Were there any boundaries you knew must not be violated at all?
2. How did the nature of your boundaries change as you got older?
3. If you have young children, what boundaries do you currently establish by physical constraints (door locks, gates, etc.)? Are there any you could instead establish as a taught boundary using other, non-physical means (such as blue tape)? What would be the benefit to your child by switching some to non-physical means?
4. Thinking ahead, is there any type of boundary you should establish now, before it is needed, so as to avoid adding it later when it will be more difficult to enact?

Chapter 9

Chores

> Whatever your hand finds to do, do it with all your might.
>
> – Ecclesiastes 9:10 (NASB)

> Whatever you do, work heartily, as for the Lord and not for men, knowing that from the Lord you will receive the inheritance as your reward. You are serving the Lord Christ.
>
> – Colossians 3:23–24

What parent wouldn't want to have their child:

- regularly engaged in routine activities that greatly increase the skills that will help them succeed in life?
- develop a legitimate feeling of satisfaction in being able to use their abilities and skills to bless and serve those who live closest to them?
- know they are an important part of the family, sharing in the necessary work that keeps the family functioning?
- have a part in working to reverse the effects of the fall by helping to bring order, sanity, and peace to our homes and their future homes?
- find joy in showing Daddy or Grandma what a nice job they did folding and stacking the clean washcloths as part of their twice-weekly chore?

We have truly grown to think of chores in this way and cannot overemphasize the value of them in the lives of children.

However, in our society, chores get a bad rap. Most people don't like to do them. They see them as a necessary evil. Add children to your home, and the number and types of necessary chores grow. When you are surrounded by little ones under five, it can seem like trying to include them in the necessary work of cooking and cleaning and tidying would just make the process take longer and make tensions rise. We would like to strongly challenge some assumptions you may have about chores and encourage you to get your children involved in them regularly and at a young age.

Never Too Young to Get the Feel of the Ball (or the Dust Rag!)

We have an uncle who, when seeing one of our youngsters with a ball in their hands, would comment, "They're never too young to get the feel of the ball." The implication was that for a future sports enthusiast, getting your hands on the particular ball of that sport, even at a very early age, had some gain. We aren't sure about that, but we do think there is great gain in getting those adorable toddler hands in on housework as soon as possible—while they still want to be included and before they've developed the wrong opinion that they are just there to be served and not to serve others.

Young children love to imitate their parents. Who hasn't seen a toddler "cooking" with play pots and pans, "building" with mini tools, "changing diapers" on their doll, "going to work" with a makeshift briefcase, or staring at an open book like they are reading, even if the book is upside down, all because that is what they see others doing?

We encourage you to tap into this inherent desire to be "just like mom and dad" by giving them areas of their world to take dominion over and learn to work. It will be a matter of small beginnings but should grow into accepted habit. The benefits are great, not just to you, the parents, but to the children as well.

How do you get a toddler started with chores? It's fairly simple. When they are rested and in a reasonable mood and while you are doing some of your necessary work, take a few minutes to show them their "new job." It could be:

- Folding a bin of washcloths into smaller squares (quarters) and then putting them in the drawer or shelf where they belong.

They won't look as neat and tidy as if you did them, but it's a start, and they might surprise you.

- Unloading the silverware from the dishwasher or dish drainer into the silverware drawer, after you have removed the sharp knives. (This may involve a stool and handwashing, but those can be part of the taught steps.)
- Picking up toys or blocks and putting them into a specific toy bin.
- Gathering the paper or cloth napkins off the table after a meal and putting them where they belong (garbage or laundry).

Use your imagination. What task can you break down into a doable piece for them? Make sure that you assign chores appropriate for their age and skill level.

Once they have been trained and have made a decent effort at accomplishing the task, it's time to tell them legitimately how thankful you are for their help and to start letting Dad, siblings, grandparents, or neighbors know that you have quite a helper working with you. Make a few phone calls or do whatever it takes for your child to know how excited you are that they are working hard to help the family.

After a child knows the routine, you can ask them to do "their washcloth job" or their "silverware chore," and usually it becomes a habit, even a joyful one at times. Not that you will never get pushback or a sinful response from your child when asking them to do their chores, but you may be amazed at how easily this becomes accepted routine—and even enjoyable.

And having older siblings who do meaningful chores is a real benefit to young children. The younger ones see them having responsible jobs around the house and often aspire to one day have such a privilege (really!). One of our five-year-olds was so excited to get dish gloves for her birthday because she was now old enough to load the dishwasher. She even eagerly mentioned that when she was older we could clean the bathrooms for our whole street! Her older siblings groaned, but it was a precious example of how she viewed the value of work and how it was a gift that could be shared for the benefit of others. She had caught that by watching her siblings work.

The Research

We were not at all surprised to hear of a 2014 University of Minnesota report entitled "Involving Children in Household Chores: Is it Worth the Effort?" describing a study by professor of family education Marty Rossmann in which Rossmann determined that the best predictor of young adults' success in their mid-twenties (measured by a variety of factors including success in college, getting started on their careers, relationship status, and not using drugs) was that when they were three or four years old they participated in household tasks where other family members were depending on them.[1] We encourage you to read the study. You may be surprised and very encouraged by the results. What they found resonates with what John had noticed in the challenge of hiring new employees: people who are highly responsible stand out from the crowd. What an awesome opportunity you have to parent your children, even at a young age, to be highly valued in their vocation and known by their responsibility!

Yes, you will have to deal with the sinful tendencies of your children to be lazy and irresponsible, just like you deal with those tendencies in yourself. These are character issues you should be addressing anyway. And, yes, the work you entrust to your young children will not be done as well as you might have done, but it is completely worth it to take the time to train them. Allow them to make a few mistakes along the way too. We have had some dishes broken, even some dishes that meant a lot to our family because of their history, but entrusting our children to share in the real work of the household was more valuable. We hope that some of those broken dishes taught our children about the consequences of their judgment and how quickly or slowly one should do their work to do it well.

The Progression

Once you have toddlers doing small tasks, they can grow into doing more substantial chores (e.g., loading the dishwasher, hand washing dishes, sorting laundry, folding laundry, sweeping, shaking off a tablecloth with crumbs, wiping a table, putting away canned goods, tidying

---

1 College of Education and Human Development, "Involving Children in Household Tasks: Is It Worth the Effort?" University of Minnesota, February 5, 2014, http://ww1.prweb.com/prfiles/2014/02/22/11608927/children-with-chores-at-home-University-of-Minnesota.pdf.

a shoe closet or mudroom). It would be a good idea to review the necessary work needed in your family every year or so to consider which tasks would be best to shift around so others can learn that skill or so things are done more efficiently.

We have had a variety of plans for how we have divided up chores over the years and have observed some creative ones our friends have developed—feel free to come up with your own and use your creative talents. If you would like some outside help, we were recently pointed to a resource called *Managers of Their Chores* by Steve and Teri Maxwell. This helpful book goes into much more detail about chores and helps you think through your plan of chores and how to follow up on their completion, which is also important. We've recently given it a try and find it solves many chore problems, especially accountability and acknowledgment of completion of a chore.[2]

Follow-Up and Accountability

A friend of mine from Canada used to say, "Children won't do what you expect but will do what you inspect!" If it is known that you will never really notice if they do their chores or not, don't be surprised if they don't get done. We highly recommend some regular follow-up and inspection, though this is probably the hardest part for parents. The point isn't to run a militaristic review with white gloves—though occasionally you could do this with a twinkle in your eye and in good fun if you think your family would enjoy it—but, rather, just letting them know you do care if the work gets done and if there are any factors keeping them from completing their chores. After all, you don't want to exasperate your child, and there may be factors making the completion of a chore challenging that you might not discover if you don't follow up.

Serving or Robbing?

I (Cindy) ran across an old friend I hadn't seen in quite a while, and in the course of our conversation, as we were comparing notes on the details of our lives, she commented that she had tended to do all the housework for her family because she was able and saw it as a way to serve and bless them. But she realized that instead of blessing and serving her two children, now teenagers, she had instead robbed them of the opportunity

2 Steve and Teri Maxwell, *Managers of Their Chores: A Practical Guide to Children's Chores* (Leavenworth, KS: Communication Concepts, 2006).

to learn to work and bless their family with their labors. At this point it was too late to start this foundation naturally in her family. Consider this, especially if you have only one or two children and actually enjoy housework yourself. It is still worthwhile to take the time—and risk the broken plates—to teach your children to work while young.

I'm in Management

Many times over the years people have expressed amazement that we have so many children and might comment that we don't look too crazy or hassled. Sometimes they ask, "How do you do it all?" I think they are implying something like how do John or I possibly do all the work to support a family of ten, as though the workload was on any one person. My usual response is "I actually don't do much of the work—I'm in management." Many years ago, John looked at our family schedule and decided that I no longer had time to make the family lunch each day or do all the laundry, and he began to divide these responsibilities out to the eight-year-old and the ten-year-old. I think it was harder on me than it was on those children, who really rose to the occasion, and seemed to take pride in making a good lunch for the family or doing a good job of the laundry.

Humorously, an acquaintance was once asked, when someone discovered she had ten children, how she fed all of them. With dry wit she exclaimed, "I've taught them to feed themselves." You could fill in that blank with any useful life skill, and smile at the future, knowing your children are equipped for facing any number of adult challenges with the skills they learned in your home.

Family Projects

There are many benefits to having your children from a young age just absorb the expectation that they own some of the responsibilities for the work of a household. Some you may not have considered are the areas of hospitality and mercy ministries.

When your children are folded into sharing the workload, they see themselves as part of the team when you are gearing up to host a family in your home for a meal or an overnight stay or making a meal to take to a family in need. Perhaps there is a family in your church or neighborhood who just had foster children join them or who have a family member going through cancer. In time, you can have your "small army" equipped to come to the aid of families such as these. Many hands make light work. It's amazing what a family can do when working together!

We vividly remember being blessed in this way by a family with several teenagers from our church. I was greatly pregnant with our second child and had come down with the flu while bringing John home from knee surgery from a city several hours away. We had a toddler, John was on crutches, and I was sick in bed. The kitchen was a mess, and dirty clothing was all over the house. We couldn't do much for ourselves. Word got out to this family, and they swooped in. In just a few hours, a pot of soup was cooking on our stove, our house was clean, laundry was going, and the baby was well entertained and ready for bed. It was a huge encouragement to us. You can be preparing your family *now* for being this kind of encouragement.

Similarly, when you are planning to add folks to your table for dinner, it is an easier prospect when you can, eventually, ask Joe to make a salad, Sally to set the table, and Little Suzie to go tidy up the living room. If you get your children in on helping with these tasks at a young age, you will likely be more willing to invite folks in and be hospitable, which is a great benefit to your children in many ways.

Want to see your little one light up with the joy of a job well done as they enjoy the inherent reward of using their labor to bless and serve others? Grab your toddler, a bin of clean laundry, and start preparing them for future job success now.

Discussion Questions

1. What was your experience of doing chores when you grew up?
2. If you have children, what chores do you have them doing now?
3. What would you say to a mom who would say, "I'm serving my family by doing all the chores"?
4. Brainstorm chores that your children could be doing but are not. Be creative.
5. Do you have a chore tracking system that has worked for you? Explain.

Chapter 10

Parenting Principles from Proverbs

> Train up a child in the way he should go; even when he is old he will not depart from it.
>
> – Proverbs 22:6

Proverbs is one of the "wisdom" books of the Bible, and it has quite a bit to say that is relevant to parenting. In this chapter, we will not attempt to go through everything the book of Proverbs has to say about parenting. Instead, our focus will be on a few key themes from Proverbs we have found especially helpful when put into practice. There is very little in this chapter that has not already been said by many others, yet we think it is good to go over these themes because they ripple through many of the other topics covered in other chapters of this book.

Train Up a Child

One of the most well-known parenting verses in the Bible is Proverbs 22:6: "Train up a child in the way he should go; even when he is old he will not depart from it." This proverb clearly emphasizes the real need to train up a child in the way he *should* go. Children, by themselves, will not naturally "go" in directions that are good for them in the long run. They are, like every person who has ever existed, made in the image of God, but also like every other person (except Christ), they have a sinful nature from birth. A parent's primary calling is to train their child in the way he or she should go, which is contrary to the way they would naturally want to go without parental input.

The specifics of how we train a child in the way they should go will vary somewhat from child to child. Personality differences and the strengths and weaknesses of each child will affect how we train them. A shy child will need more instruction about being friendly toward others (rather than impolitely ignoring them), while an outgoing child will need more training on the importance of holding back and giving other people the chance to talk in a conversation (rather than rudely dominating a discussion). A child who is academically or physically talented will need more training on how everything they have is a gift from God and to not look down on those around them, but a child who struggles in these areas will need to be shown how they are a unique individual created in the image of God with a unique purpose in the world. Parents are often the only people in the world who can recognize and address weaknesses in their children, and this is the loving thing to do.

Though many people treat Proverbs 22:6 as a promise, it is not. It's vital to understand the intent of the sayings found in the book of Proverbs—they are not promises or guarantees but, rather, wisdom that is generally true. This proverb is pointing out the strong connection between the training of our children and how they act when they are adults, which should motivate us to take our child-training seriously, knowing that it will have a lifelong impact on our children. That being said, we recognize that how our children turn out as adults is not completely under our control.

Training Example: Lying

Let's again consider the example of lying. Children do not need to be taught to lie—just about every child will develop the ability to lie to their parents as well as others. At first, they are not particularly good at it, but they tend to get better and better at lying until we have difficulty identifying dishonesty in our children. Should we throw our hands up and just live with the fact that our children will become accomplished liars by the time they leave our house? Absolutely not. Not only is it a clear teaching of Scripture that lying is wrong but we can also consider our child's future as an adult and see that dishonesty would cause significant problems in their life: "A man of crooked heart does not discover good, and one with a dishonest tongue falls into calamity" (Proverbs 17:20). Besides the negative practical consequences of lying, God also states that lying is something that is an *abomination* to Him: "Lying lips are an abomination to the LORD, but those who act faithfully are his delight" (Proverbs 12:22).

So, developing a habit of truth-telling is a way our children should go, and it is our job as parents to train them up to be honest. What does this practically mean? First, when we see dishonesty in our child, we should directly and strongly address this and discipline them for lying. At its root, lying is a sin and is against God's commands. We should also proactively teach the child the value of a good name and the value of having others believe you and trust your words. We want to show them how honest living really is an attractive way to go. (Of course, we must be honest ourselves, since they are watching us like a hawk.) The goal is that they develop an inward revulsion against lying and value honesty as they get older and grow into adulthood.

Please believe us that even young children can be skilled liars, and the older a child grows, the more proficient they may become. This can be disheartening when you realize you have been taken in by the "innocent" face, words, and demeanor of your child. Apart from them having a regenerated heart to want to obey God and their parents, however, this should not be surprising. We have often been asked, "How can you tell your child is lying?" It is difficult. If you have any doubt, pray that their sins will find them out. It is much better for your child's heart and future that they be caught in a lie—in any sin, really—than to persist in lying. God can reveal the truth to you, and He can convict your child of their sin. Second, whenever you have doubt, ask questions. Usually, children are not prepared for serious cross-examination from a skilled prosecutor. Experience has taught us to trust a bit less and ask probing questions more. As with all discipline, it is never convenient to catch a child in a lie and deal with it, but this is a vital part of parenting. Pray and ask whenever you have an unsettling hunch.

Answering a Fool According to His Folly

One of the most helpful and practical parenting "tips" for us came directly out of Proverbs 26:4–5 (NASB): "Do not answer a fool according to his folly, or you will also be like him. Answer a fool as his folly deserves, that he not be wise in his own eyes." In a previous chapter, we discussed how this verse might encourage parents not to grant every request made by their children. There are some other applications of this verse that come into play as well.

Sometimes we think that whenever someone asks a question, we are obligated to answer directly and at face value. This proverb would encourage us to evaluate the characteristics of the person asking the question, and if they are being foolish, we should not fall prey to their line of questioning but, instead, answer them as they deserve. This may involve refusing to answer or telling him that what he is saying makes no sense. A non-parenting illustration would be how some salespeople ask a series of questions that really only have one reasonable answer, as they try to back you into a corner where you almost have to say yes to what they are selling:

"Do you love your family?"

"Yes, of course."

"Do you think it's important to spend quality time with your family?"

"Yes, of course."

"Is your family a high priority in your life?"

"Yes, of course."

"Would you be willing to invest time and resources in your family?"

"Yes, of course."

This continues and eventually ends with "Is there any reason not to buy this timeshare condominium in order to live according to your priorities?" His questions really aren't genuine. The salesman isn't interested in how much you value or prioritize your family time; he just wants to sell condominiums and is using this line of questioning as a way to manipulate people into buying something they probably weren't prioritizing, budget-wise, before this conversation.

What does this have to do with parenting? Children can sometimes act foolishly in the way that they interact with their parents, often in a desire to manipulate them. For example, some children will exert an inappropriate level of control over their parents by asking a long series of *Why?* questions:

Child: "Why is the grass green?"

Parent: "Because it has chlorophyll in it."

Child: "Why does it have chlorophyll in it?"

Parent: "Because chlorophyll is needed to convert light into energy."

Child: "Why does light need to be converted into energy?"

Parent: "So plants can grow."

Child: "Why do plants need to grow?"

Parent: "Because God made them to start small and become big."

Child: "Why did God make them to start small and become big?"

Anyone who's been around children knows that line of questioning can continue indefinitely.

It's possible that the child is truly interested in all these answers, but as the line of questioning goes on, it becomes clearer and clearer that the child is actually just manipulating their parent, knowing that they feel compelled to answer these kinds of questions. Sometimes they are asking them not so much because they want to know the answer but because they are enjoying captivating the attention of their parent. In reality, the child here is being foolish by asking questions that aren't genuine questions, and a parent should feel free to call them on this and simply not answer.

Of course, we would strongly encourage you to engage in conversations with your children about the world around them. Part of training them up is education, and you are in a prime location (around them the most) to be able to connect the dots and fill in the blanks as they learn about the world around them. What we want to caution you about, however, is being diverted from other legitimate God-given responsibilities by a bored child who has become skillful at asking "why" as a way to manipulate their parents to pay attention to them.

The second part of this proverb is also important: "that he not be wise in his own eyes." To be "wise in his own eyes" would mean that the child thinks he is wise when he really is not. It is the opposite of being a humble learner who is aware they have need of input from others or of patience in waiting for the right time to ask a question. There are times when our child asks us something and our right response is to not answer directly but to respond in some other way, such as saying, "That's not something you need to know," or "We would be happy to talk about that subject at a more appropriate time." We have noticed that these types of nonessential questions from bored or manipulative children tend to come when Mom or Dad is busy navigating in crazy traffic, talking with another adult, or concentrating on some mental work at home.

For those of you with only very young children, this section may sound like we are just very uptight and enjoy undisturbed mental space free from children's questions. This is not the case. Answering questions from children is important and can be an enjoyable and essential part of parenting. In fact, we often linger at the dinner table discussing many topics with our children. But we have noticed a trend in preschool and elementary-aged children that can become a significant means of their controlling their parents and all the adults in a room. We want to encourage you to recognize this and to feel free not to answer questions when they represent foolishness on the part of your child—when they come at an inappropriate time or when they are more about the child controlling the situation than having a legitimate question. We would strongly encourage you to develop natural, conversational interaction with your children of all ages, which is an ideal time to teach them many things. A great time for this is around the table for meals and when going about the normal tasks of daily life. We also want a child to have the appropriately humble perspective that they are just one of many people in the room (or wherever they happen to be) and that they may have things to learn from the conversation. They should also realize that every moment in life is not meant for their personal entertainment.

Expressing Opinion

One valuable proverb for parenting is Proverbs 18:2: "A fool takes no pleasure in understanding, but only in expressing his opinion." As they learn more and more about the outside world, it is natural for a child to "try out" various theories about why things are the way they are. But we have noticed that this can grow to the level of "foolishness" when a six- to ten-year-old, or even older, child starts making a regular habit of explaining the way things are to any adult who is willing to listen, and does so with an attitude of wanting to enlighten the adult, thinking themselves wise, with no interest in learning anything themselves. Unrestrained, this leads to the child becoming more "wise in their own eyes," as mentioned above, and fosters the kind of pride the Bible speaks so clearly against.

It is crucial to recognize when this is happening but not to overreact or squash all "verbal processing" that your child may be doing. Normally, this kind of attitude is not outright rebellion and should not be treated as disobedience. Rather, it is an attitude we want to gently discourage in our children. We have found that this can be difficult, taking concerted effort over time to see improvement, but that addressing the issue directly seems to have the greatest benefit. In other words, talk to your child and ask them questions like, "Do you think that you know more about _____ than Mrs. Miller?" "What should our attitude be toward those who are older and have more life experience than us?" We normally talk to them in private about issues like this to enable more direct and blunt communication and to avoid publicly embarrassing the child.

It is not a good idea to ignore this proud attitude and just hope it goes away. Remember, our goal is ultimately to address our child's heart. While it's true that a child will sometimes grow out of telling adults "how it is" because they realize this is socially unacceptable, if we fail to address the heart attitude behind this we have missed an opportunity to train the heart. An older child can still very much harbor this internally prideful attitude without wearing it on their sleeve like a younger child does.

There are many more proverbs about pride and humility, foolishness, listening rather than talking, and gaining wisdom. You can systematically teach them to your child over time to help address these attitudes. The beauty of teaching these proverbs to our children is that they are hearing these lessons from God's Word directly, and it is coming from an even higher authority than just their parents. God's Word is living and active, powerful and effective. Don't be afraid to hide it in their hearts for the Holy Spirit to use as He wills. Here is a small set of examples from the book of Proverbs:

- "When pride comes, then comes disgrace, but with the humble is wisdom" (11:2).
- "The way of a fool is right in his own eyes, but a wise man listens to advice" (12:15).
- "The ear that listens to life-giving reproof will dwell among the wise" (15:31).
- "Whoever ignores instruction despises himself, but he who listens to reproof gains intelligence" (15:32).
- "Pride goes before destruction, and a haughty spirit before a fall" (16:18).
- "Listen to advice and accept instruction, that you may gain wisdom in the future" (19:20).

- "Cease to hear instruction, my son, and you will stray from the words of knowledge" (19:27).
- "One's pride will bring him low, but he who is lowly in spirit will obtain honor" (29:23).

One easy way to expose our school-aged children to the wealth of wisdom in Proverbs is to read a chapter aloud each day for several months in a row. There are thirty-one books in Proverbs, so you can read the chapter that corresponds to the day of the month. Have your children who can read take turns reading the verses with you. Even if you don't have the entire book memorized, you will familiarize your children with the proverbs, and perhaps it will make it easier to direct your children to specific ones at relevant times. Another thing we've done is to pick out one relevant proverb, read it, and discuss it. Many of the proverbs take some thought and insight to discern the point that is being made, and it's helpful to have a discussion of the proverb to ensure the children understand its meaning.

The Need for Discipline

The book of Proverbs often points out the need for children to be disciplined. For example, Proverbs 29:17 says, "Discipline your son, and he will give you rest; he will give delight to your heart." The Hebrew word translated "discipline" is actually fairly broad in its meaning and can mean both *correction* (to discipline, to chasten, to punish) and *instruction* (to instruct, to teach). We sometimes use the word *discipline* with this broader meaning, such as if we see a sports team playing well together, we say that "they are disciplined" or "they play with discipline." What we really mean by this is that the coach has worked hard to get them to play well, understanding that this almost certainly involved aspects of both correction and instruction.

This proverb is instructing us to actively discipline our children—to teach and instruct them and, when necessary, to correct or punish them. This is a weighty matter, as seen in another similar proverb: "Discipline your son, for there is hope; do not set your heart on putting him to death" (19:18). This verse implies that failing to discipline our children is like giving them a death sentence! It simply is *not* an option for us to take a pass on disciplining our child. A child left to his own way without parental discipline will surely suffer.

There is a stark example of a parent failing to discipline his children found in 1 Samuel 2. Israel's high priest Eli had two sons, Hophni and Phinehas. Apparently, Eli did not discipline or restrain them as they spent years grossly and publicly violating and ignoring God's clear commands. Toward the end of Eli's life, he calls them in and gives them a mild verbal rebuke, but they completely disregard it because, by that point, their hearts were completely hardened. It seems clear that, at least to some extent, Eli's lack of disciplining his sons did result in their deaths and the removal of Eli and his family from the priesthood.

So, parents, take heart and have courage. It is your God-given role to discipline your child, to include both the positive aspects (instruction, teaching) and negative aspects (rebuke, punishment). Because it is a role that God gives you, He will provide help and strength as you faithfully seek to obey Him. This is a task of great magnitude, and of the billions of people in the world, you are the ones God has appointed to do this for your own children. No one else can, so you must. Our desire in writing this book is that your children would give delight to your heart and be a blessing to those around you as a result of God's grace working through your discipline, in the fullest sense of the word.

Discussion Questions

1. How confident are you overall as a parent? Do you generally have a sense of "the way your child should go" in any given situation, or is this something with which you struggle?
2. If you are feeling uncertain about how to parent your child in a particular situation, how does this uncertainty affect your ability to parent?
3. How can you improve your confidence along these lines?
4. Can you think of examples of either you or another parent falling into the trap of interacting with their child by "answering a fool according to their folly," as described in the chapter?
5. While you were growing up, what was your family like on a scale of 1 to 10, where 1 means that children are to be only seen and not heard and never express their opinion, and 10 means that children

are always given the floor if they have something to say. How does this background affect your current parenting?

6. What is your emotional response when you see proverbs about disciplining your child?

Chapter 11

A Parenting Theme: Others-Orientation

> Let each of you look not only to his own interests, but also to the interests of others.
>
> – Philippians 2:4

Unlike teaching a child to walk or to use the potty, some parenting topics are relevant throughout the life of a child. These would more appropriately be called *parenting themes*—matters we come to again and again, day by day, month by month, and year by year.

One such theme is to be others-oriented, which is well stated in Philippians 2:4 above. It is another form of the golden rule: "You shall love your neighbor as yourself" (Matthew 22:39). Like other character traits we've discussed, this does not come naturally to a child, because all children are born with sinful, selfish hearts. We do not need to teach children to be selfish—they are born that way. Part of our job as parents is to instill within them a response contrary to this natural selfishness—a response that considers the interests of others, even above one's own interests. This is a long-term project—a parenting theme.

A few years ago, it occurred to us that there is a close connection between what we call *maturity* and others-orientation. We would go so far as to say that maturity and others-orientation are really one and the same thing. A person who is mature is a person who has a consistent ability to see things from others' perspectives and to put the needs of others ahead of their own. Maturity is not defined by age as much as by the level of others-orientation. There are fifty-year-olds who live self-oriented, immature lives, and there are sixteen-year-olds who have developed a high level of others-orientation that we consider to be mature. We believe that developing an others-orientation in children is a worthy, long-term goal of parenting. Parents should consciously strive to develop this trait in their children to the best of their ability.

But practically speaking, how do we do that? There is no simple, single answer to this question, but we have found it helpful to teach our children to ask themselves two questions as a habit:

1. How is what I'm doing impacting others?
2. How can I be a blessing to others in this situation?

Computers run programs called *background tasks*. These background tasks are continually operating "in the background," meaning they are running behind the scenes, not necessarily visible to the person using the computer, and usually in addition to the main program currently operating. Like background tasks on a computer, we want these two questions to be constantly in the back of our children's minds as they go through life—a consistent theme that affects how they think and what they do.

How Is What I'm Doing Impacting Others?

There are lots of things we tell our young children *not* to do:

- Don't throw trash on the ground.
- Don't handle the vegetables in the supermarket.
- Don't pull things off the store shelves.
- Don't run in the building.
- Don't scream.
- Don't make lots of commotion in church.
- Don't throw your food on the floor.
- Don't leave your toys on the floor or stairs.

The list goes on and on. However, when we stop and ask ourselves *why* we don't want our children to do these things (or when our children ask us why), the answer often comes down to the fact that these things have a negative impact on others. When we throw trash on the ground, we are being inconsiderate of—that is, *not considering*—others who will come after us and be faced with the mess we left. When we handle vegetables in the grocery store, we are not considering the person who will later be buying the vegetables. When we leave toys out on the floor or stairs, we are not considering the people who will need to walk across that room or use the stairs and will have to contend with obstacles. Showing consideration for others as a reason for right behavior should be a common theme.

One of the easiest ways to have our children start thinking in this others-oriented way is to simply bring in the "why" along with our commands to not do something. Rather than just saying, "Don't run in the building," you can say, "Don't run in the building because it will make people who have trouble walking nervous." Providing the reason why in these cases teaches the child to consider how what they do impacts others. Even more powerfully, providing the "why" enables a child to respond correctly in a new situation they've never seen before. By way of example, imagine a situation where a child has spilled some water on a seat in an airport. Even if they've never been in that situation, a child who is accustomed to considering others will realize that it would be good to wipe up the water to prevent someone from sitting in it.

Bringing up how our actions impact others is something we can do for the very youngest of children. It usually involves things we should not do. However, the second question is more applicable to older children and involves things we *should* do.

How Can I Be a Blessing to Others?

In whatever situation children are in, they should be thinking about how they can proactively be a blessing to others. Believe it or not, this is a learned skill. It requires stepping outside of one's own frame of reference and seeing things from another's perspective, which once again is not natural. We propose some examples below.

Nursing Home Visits

There have been times in our life when trips to visit our parents also included visits to other elderly relatives in a nursing home near them. As you can imagine, leaving the excitement of playing at their grandparents' house to spend a few hours visiting in a nursing home is not naturally at the top of a young child's list of fun things to do. From the child's viewpoint, instead of playing, such visits involve mostly sitting and talking, and even the talking may not be very interesting (depending on the health of the person we're visiting). Additionally, lots of strangers, who may have various physical challenges not normally seen outside a nursing home, may want to interact with them. The reality that a typical nursing home visit holds little intrinsic interest to an unprepared child actually makes it a fantastic opportunity to work on this concept of thinking how we can be a blessing to others.

When visiting a nursing home, we found that it was very helpful for us to talk with our children ahead of time (usually in the car on the way there) about how much they can be a blessing to others during a visit like this. We would discuss how people in a nursing home don't get to see lots of children, and that they can be a great blessing by just being friendly. We would try to have our children think what it must be like to live in one room, day in and day out, and how exciting it would be to have visitors come. Sometimes, we would simply ask our children to tell us how they could be a blessing to the person we were going to see in the nursing home.

This kind of interaction really helped our children to shift their focus from their own interests to the interests of others. Now, rather than only thinking about how much they didn't want to be there, they had a mission—to be a blessing to others—and had some idea of how to truly do that. We still had our share of behavior challenges during these visits, but the quality of the visits greatly improved to the extent that our children bought into this idea. One of the great things about this was that, in the end, if our children did have an others-oriented mindset, they would enjoy the visits much more! And when we left, we were able to encourage them with how they really were a blessing to someone else.

Talking to a New Person

It is also important to have an others-oriented mindset when interacting with people who are new to a group. A classic example is when a new family visits our church and has children the same age as ours. It is always easier and more comfortable for our children to play with their existing friends than to interact with guests. However, we want them to be thinking less about what is easy and comfortable for themselves and more about how they can be a blessing to others. We want them to recognize that it is awkward to be a new visitor and that being friendly to them is a way to be a blessing to them.

Instilling this kind of visitor-welcoming mindset in our children is something that normally takes training and encouragement, since the vast majority of children (even the outgoing ones) will find this personally challenging. How, practically speaking, can you encourage your children to welcome visitors? They need to have two things:

1. The ability to perceive what being a blessing to others looks like
2. A desire to be a blessing to others

The first part, perceiving what being a blessing to others looks like, is something we can talk about with them. Explain how it feels to be a visitor and how by just going up and saying hello, we can be a blessing. The second part, wanting to be a blessing to others, is something that needs to be a consistent parenting theme over many years so that it just becomes the way the child thinks and interacts with the world, at least to some extent.

Other Situations

Here are several more example situations in which a "pep talk" with your children before beginning these activities could help them learn how to bless and serve others while participating.

Going to visit or play at a friend's house:

Mom: "Children, what are ways we can seek to bless the Smiths today while we visit?"

Children: "Say thank you for lunch." "Say thank you for letting us come visit." "Remember to ask them what they would like to do next, and not just do what we want." "Not whine!" "Remember that these are their toys." "Ask Mrs. Smith before going in the backyard."

Mom: "What about when you are done playing with toys and it's time to go? How would you want your visiting friends to leave the toy area in our house when they leave?"

Children: "Oh, yeah, we should pick up everything and put it back where it belongs before we leave!"

Attending a church service:

Dad: "What are some things to remember to do to bless those sitting around us and behind us during the service?"

Children: "Not distract others by fidgeting or touching." "Not turn around and smile at people, because it distracts them from worshiping God."

Going to a wedding:

Mom: "Why are we going to this church building today?" "How can we help everyone who is there celebrate this ceremony for Uncle Joe and Miss Sally?"

Children: "Not distract others with our bodies." "Not ask how long it is going to be." "Smile at people and answer them when they talk to us." "Make people feel welcome to the church building." "Ask the ladies hosting the reception how we can help." "Not run and play during the in-between times since it is not playtime." "Help clean up and put things away afterward."

Having people over to your house:

Dad: "We have the privilege of having a new couple in the neighborhood over for dinner tonight. How can you all help Mommy get ready today, and how can you help the Joneses feel comfortable and enjoy their evening here?"

Children: "Put away the toys." "Shake the crumbs off the tablecloth." "Sweep the Cheerios up in the kitchen corners." "Make sure there is toilet paper and a dry towel in the bathroom." "Sit quietly and listen at the dinner table until we are excused." "Take their plates to the kitchen when they are done eating." "Ask them if they would like more of some food we can pass."

Going to the store:

Mom: "I have to stop at the grocery store for a few things and then the drugstore. How can you all be a help to me while we get these errands done for our family? And how can we be a blessing to the other shoppers and workers at the store?"

Children: "Not fuss and argue while we are shopping." "Keep our hands to ourselves and not touch the stuff in the stores so it stays nice and we don't make the store people worried about us." "Be quiet so Mommy can think and concentrate so we can get shopping done sooner." "Hold on to the cart so Mom isn't worried about losing us!"

Coming home from an outing

Mom: "We are almost home, and I'm going to be working on getting lunch ready. How can you bless the other members of your family as we head into the house?"

Children: "Put our shoes in their cubbies so others don't trip over them in the mudroom." "Hang up our coats so everyone doesn't have to step over them." "Not leave things in the van so it's nice for whoever rides in it next." "Put away the library books we just got."

Obviously, most children won't come up with these on their own, and the answers they might give are learned over time with some training. These are typical answers we might have received from our van full of kiddos before these kinds of outings, after years of this pep-talk practice. To get these answers early on, the key is to ask leading questions to get them thinking about how to be a blessing in new situations and how their actions will affect those around them, or perhaps more abstractly, how their actions will affect those who will use a space or resource after they have left it.

Sibling Discord

We are called to be a blessing to others, and this certainly includes siblings. However, many parents of multiple children struggle with some form of sibling discord. In our family we attempted to address this in multiple ways:

- We asked our child, "Are you treating your brother/sister the way you would want to be treated?"
- We talked with them often about what a blessing their brothers and sisters are.
- We proactively and repeatedly told them that as siblings they are going to be lifelong best friends and that God has given them their brothers and sisters as a gift.
- When a new baby was coming, we talked about what an incredible blessing it was—God's gift to everyone in the family! As much as it was possible, we did not ignore the real needs of our other children when we brought a baby home from the hospital. We tried to treat our other children with the appropriate concern and kindness they required. Yes, they may

have needed to learn to wait until the baby's needs were met, but with training they were able to understand that.

- When there was something specific they were bickering about, we told them they needed to come up with a plan of how to deal with it they could both agree on and let us know their agreed-on plan. This helped them learn the very practical skill of interpersonal problem-solving.

We also believe that when many of the parenting principles described throughout this book are put into place, parents will have the ability to address sibling discord as the heart issue it really is. The reality is that sibling discord is just one of many heart issues we must address in children.

The Remaining Problem

Teaching and training our children to think about how they are impacting others and how they can be a blessing to others is a worthy goal, and we can expect to have some level of success in doing so if we are consistent over time. But we need to have the humility to recognize we cannot completely remove the selfishness naturally occurring in the heart of each child and replace it with a pure others-orientation, especially one that is motivated by a love of God. God is the only one who can cause this kind of deep heart change.

We have generally observed significant growth in this area when God has softened our children's hearts and brought them to believe in Him. Prior to conversion,[1] they exhibited a level of others-orientation, but it was limited in scope and generally appeared to be more out of duty than out of an inward delight in pleasing God. However, having an others-orientation is one area where God's work in their lives was generally quite evident. After conversion, they would have a much stronger inherent desire to think of the needs of others, and this would be driven by and connected to their relationship with God. It seemed as though we as parents, prior to our children's conversion, helped to carve out some small streams that they could follow along from time to time, but God, in the process of conversion, turned those streams into deep rivers of living water that consistently flowed with resources provided by Him.

1 By "conversion," we mean a child turning away from their natural bent toward sin (repentance) and believing in what Jesus Christ has done for the forgiveness of their sins—this is covered in more detail at the end of the next chapter.

Discussion Questions

1. Was others-orientation, or thinking of others, something that was a part of your family when you were a child? If so, was it something explicitly talked about or just something your parents modeled? Can you think of positive or negative examples of others-orientation from your childhood?

2. What is the difference between asking how what we do impacts others and asking ourselves what others think of us? What happens if we are mostly concerned about what others think about us?

3. Think of some specific areas where giving instruction to your child but adding some explanation of why could help grow an awareness of others in your child.

4. At times, giving the reason why behind our instructions can be helpful, but we don't want to give a sense that we need to explain our rationale for everything we do as parents (thus, not encouraging our children to be "wise in their own eyes"). How, practically, can we avoid the trap of feeling like we need to justify ourselves to our children?

5. Children will learn not just from what you say but from what you do. In what ways do you need to grow in others-orientation in your own lives so that you're not holding your children to a standard you don't adhere to yourself?

Chapter 12

Spiritual Training of Children

> Bring [your children] up in the discipline and instruction of the Lord.
>
> – Ephesians 6:4

As Christian parents, we all have a sense that we should be involved in the spiritual training of our children, but many of us feel like we are inadequate for this task. We don't know where to start, we don't know enough ourselves, we're spiritually struggling in our own relationship with the Lord, or we are afraid we'll make significant doctrinal mistakes. It just feels easier to leave spiritual instruction to the "professionals" such as pastors and Sunday school teachers.

We want to encourage you to take heart. There are lots of simple ways you can train your children in spiritual things, and you don't need a doctorate in theology to do these things well. We firmly believe that normal parents living regular lives can spiritually train their children through many routine activities of life. Our desire is that this chapter encourages you and helps you see an assortment of simple ways in which you can bring your children up in the discipline and instruction of the Lord. You don't need to do all the things described below, but figure out what will work well for you and your family at your current stage of life, and give some things a try (if you're not already doing them).

Bring Up God

An important passage that deals directly with spiritual training of children is found in the book of Deuteronomy:

> Hear, O Israel: The Lord our God, the Lord is one. You shall love the Lord your God with all your heart and with all your soul and with all your might. And these words that I command you today shall be on your heart. You shall teach them diligently to your children, and shall talk of them when you sit in your house, and when you walk by the way, and when you lie down, and when you rise.
>
> – Deuteronomy 6:4–7

This passage, in verse 7, encourages us to "bring up God"—that is, talk about His commands—during our everyday activities. We don't think the intent here is to have a specific list of times at which we must do it but, rather, that we should just bring up God as we go about our regular lives. What can this look like? Here are some examples:

- Comment on how creative God is when you see an unusual plant or animal.
- Comment on God's amazing power when you see the power of nature (like a thunderstorm).
- If you find and attempt to return a lost item to its owner, comment that you are doing it because God has said we should treat others the way that we would want to be treated.
- Talk with your children about what you are learning spiritually.
- When you are in a difficult situation (like stuck in traffic when late for an appointment), talk about how Christians can trust God's plan, even if we don't always understand it.
- Say, "This is the day that the Lord has made; let us rejoice and be glad in it," (Psalm 118:24) when you get up in the morning.
- Say out loud what you are thankful to God for in any particular circumstance.

These are just illustrations to get the juices flowing—the idea is to talk about God and His desires for us as we encounter regular situations every day.

It's good to notice that before God tells us to talk about these things with our children, He says that His words should be on our hearts (Deuteronomy 6:6). This is the precursor to being able to talk about God's thoughts with our children—they must first be something that are on *our* hearts. If needed, ask God to help you grow in this area. Ask

Him to open your eyes to His working in the world around you and to help you tell of His greatness to your children.

Family Devotions

Another aspect of spiritually training children is to have some form of family devotions. There are lots of ways to do this, and we would encourage you not to feel constrained by any one approach. Figure out what works well for you and your family. Some families read through devotional books. We tend to read the Bible together, which is simple but enjoyable.

When the children were younger, we called that time "Bible Story," and it involved reading through a book of the Bible, one section at a time. I (John) would read several verses and then ask each of the children, usually going from youngest to oldest, an age-appropriate question. As a result, the questions went from really simple to more advanced. Sometimes we had a brief discussion about a topic that came up, but that didn't always happen. I sometimes found it helpful to read a commentary of some sort on the passage we were about to read, but that's not completely necessary. You can also ask questions like, "What does this passage tell us about God?" "Is there a command to obey?" "Is there anything you don't understand?"

By the way, at times you may come across a passage as a family and you don't know offhand the answer to a question that comes up. It's perfectly okay to tell your children that you're not sure and will think about it, pray about it, research it, and get back to them. This is not a bad thing—it models for them how to deal with difficult questions they will encounter.

Praying with Our Children

As we pray, our children see how we interact with God and naturally absorb truths about who He is, how we relate to Him, what Jesus has done, how we are thankful, and the like. Also, it is a time that specific needs of the family or people you know can be brought before God in prayer.

Don't make this more complicated than necessary. The point is not to have amazing, impressive prayers but to come before God regularly, recognizing Him as our Creator and Savior, and admitting our dependence on Him. This can be done as part of devotions, but it can also be part of a bedtime routine or some other regular time of the day.

Church Engagement Is Caught, Not Taught

The Bible is filled with instruction about how we should interact with other believers, and this is most often accomplished in the context of a local church. Being involved in a church is not an optional activity for believers—it is an essential part of how God sustains and strengthens His people, as we see in the book of Hebrews: "And let us consider how to stir up one another to love and good works, not neglecting to meet together, as is the habit of some, but encouraging one another, and all the more as you see the Day drawing near" (Hebrews 10:24–25).

How you engage in church life will have a big impact on how your children will engage in church life. If you see the church as a place in which you invest time and resources and where you develop meaningful, spiritually encouraging relationships with other believers, your children will be more likely to follow that model when they grow up. Demonstrate active, healthy church interaction to your children—they need to see it, and you need it as well to benefit from all the ways God works through His church to sustain and grow His people. If, instead, you treat church simply as a place you go once a week and are more like a spectator or consumer than an integrated participant in the life of the church, then your children will likely pick up that consumer mindset as a model for church involvement, to their detriment.

Catechisms

A catechism is simply a set of questions and answers used for teaching a summary of core biblical truths. Think of them as a topical Bible summary that is easy to mentally reference. When questions come up in life, the answers will be right there on the tip of your tongue—or mind. Catechisms are an excellent, systematic way to teach children (and adults) many of the basic truths or principles of our faith. They are easy to go through and take some of the burden off you, the parent, to come up with what you need to teach your children.

There are many faithful catechisms to choose from that have stood the test of time and doctrinal examination. Two that we appreciate are the Children's "Prove It" Catechism and the New City Catechism.[1] Both are

1 http://www.vor.org/rbdisk/html/proveit/index.htm; http://newcitycatechism.com

available online and can be purchased in book or pamphlet form. The New City Catechism even has phone app versions with other helpful tools and YouTube videos to go with them. Many other historical catechisms are available online or as book versions.

Children are quick at memorizing things, so it can be a good idea to help them commit the catechism answers to memory. This will give them a framework for thinking about God and their relationship to Him that can help carry them throughout their lives.

Bible Memory

Helping our children memorize Scripture is another way we can spiritually train them. We wanted to mention it here for completeness, but we will devote an entire chapter to the topic of Bible memory. Chapter 29 has more information and practical ideas for parents to help their children memorize Scripture.

Singing Together

Paul wrote to the church in Colossae about singing to each other: "Let the word of Christ dwell in you richly, teaching and admonishing one another in all wisdom, singing psalms and hymns and spiritual songs, with thankfulness in your hearts to God (Colossians 3:16). He speaks here of singing as one way to teach and admonish one another in all wisdom. This is true within a church, but it can also be true within a family. Singing is a good way to recall many truths about God and about living as a Christian this side of heaven. There is something about a song that is different than words by themselves. There have been many Mondays when the songs from church the previous day are running through our heads or being sung by our children as they go about their chores, which is a good thing.

Songs do not need to be long or complex. When our children were little, we usually sang a song before we put them to bed—usually something that taught a simple spiritual truth. Two of our early favorites were "God Is So Good" and "My God Is So Great." We still sing these once in a while, but as our children have become older, we have moved to more in-depth songs or hymns.

When you are singing as a family, the point is to have fun and sing together, not to sound like a professionally trained choir. So, sing out, and make a joyful noise unto the Lord (Psalm 98:4), even if it's more like noise than beauty!

Recordings

There are many good resources available that children can listen to that can also provide spiritual instruction. We would encourage you to be discriminating and choose things with solid, biblical truth. If you're going to have them listen to something, make sure that it's good.

Among the numerous resources available, here are three that we have found helpful:

- **Judy Rogers Music (judyrogers.com).** These are creative, catchy songs about spiritual truths that are understandable by children. Our children report thinking about the theological truths in the songs as they listened to them through the years.
- **A Visit with Mrs. G (biblestoriesalive.org).** These are Bible stories told in a very engaging and informative way. They do a good job of helping children (or any listener) place themselves in the situation as it would have been when the stories given in Scripture were happening. They are engaging enough that our children listened to them again and again and gained a broad and deep understanding of many of the narrative stories of Scripture.
- **"What's in the Bible?" video series (whatsinthebible.com).** At the time of this writing, there are thirteen engaging, fun, but content-filled videos that cover many important biblical topics you may not normally get with children's materials. For example, there is a good description, at a child's level, of the "cycle of apostasy" described in the book of Judges, complete with a song!

While these are some that we have appreciated, there are certainly other resources you may find helpful. Ask around, but be picky. Don't assume that everything labeled as Christian or talking about spiritual concepts is worthwhile or even true. We remember, with concern, buying some "Christian" early readers when our youngest child was learning to read, only to realize that in simplifying the flood account with Noah, they actually implied that Noah noticed it raining and ran into the ark! This is not the biblical account. So be discerning.

Be Creative

We have listed many ways you can spiritually train your children, but feel free to be creative and find approaches that work well for your family. Spiritual training does not need to be a chore—in fact, it can be one of the most enjoyable things you do together as a family, even part of some of your favorite family memories, depending on what you do and how you do it. Try different methods until you settle into those that work for you, and feel free to make adjustments as your children get older.

It's crucial to recognize that doing the things listed in this chapter does not guarantee your child becomes a Christian; but they can teach your child important spiritual truths that can be of great value to them in their lives. This type of teaching can be used by God to build a God-centered worldview into your children and give them the resources to understand how to think of and respond to the world around them. Exposure to these sources of biblical truth can also show your child their need of the gospel.

Is My Child a Christian?

The Bible describes what we call "true Christians" as those who believe in Jesus (John 11:25), are "in Christ" (Romans 8:1), have been "born again" (John 3:3), or have been "saved" (Acts 2:47). The Bible teaches that we are not saved by the things we do (including all those in this chapter) but by grace through faith in Jesus (Ephesians 2:8–9). It also speaks of a fundamental transformation that occurs within a person when they are saved—they are given a new heart and are a new creature (Ezekiel 11:19; 2 Corinthians 5:17). In fact, the Scriptures teach that there has not been true conversion if there is no evidence of change within a person (James 2:17, 26).

Christian parents earnestly desire for their children to become Christians, but we should be careful not to follow this desire to the point that we declare our children to be Christians apart from God's actual working in their life. Young children are impressionable and will believe most of what an adult tells them. We can tell a group of young children about the wonders of heaven and the horrors of hell and that if they believe in Jesus they get to go to heaven, and then ask how many of them want to follow Jesus. (Most will.) So, then we pray a prayer with them and declare them to be Christians. Everything's good, right? The problem is that this is not at all consistent with the biblical description of conversion, which always involves a lasting change of heart. It is not something we can force or coerce in our children.

We believe that rather than pressure our children into a confession of faith or expect them to be acting like believers when they're not, we should constantly point them toward Christ and pray for their salvation but ultimately depend on God to save and perform the necessary "heart transplant." The practical question does come up, however, "Is my child a Christian?" We think it is important not to "inoculate" our children against the gospel by telling them that they are a believer when they really are not. If they falsely think themselves a believer, they may be less prone to listen to the many calls in Scripture (and hopefully from others) to repent and believe in Jesus, and to recognize their dire need of Him.

While it may not always be possible for us to discern perfectly whether our child has been converted (1 Samuel 16:7), we have found several guiding principles helpful in thinking this through. Fundamentally, to discern conversion in a child, we are looking for a change of heart: "And I will give you a new heart, and a new spirit I will put within you. And I will remove the heart of stone from your flesh and give you a heart of flesh" (Ezekiel 36:26).

More specifically, what can we observe when God changes the heart of our child from a heart of stone to one of flesh (when He regenerates them)? Here are some thoughts, observations, and Scripture references:

God's Commands

Before conversion, a child may comply with God's commands out of duty or good training, but after conversion they have an inner desire to follow God's commands that is *not* based only on external encouragements. We observe this when we notice our child seeking to understand what God desires and to obey on their own—prompted by the Holy Spirit—without the need for direct encouragement by parents or anyone else. We will also observe them obeying in ways contrary to their natural disposition, especially in areas that are a challenge to them.

What Scripture says:

> But this is the covenant that I will make with the house of Israel after those days, declares the LORD: I will put my law within them, and I will write it on their hearts. And I will be their God, and they shall be my people. (Jeremiah 31:33)

> And by this we know that we have come to know him, if we keep his commandments. (1 John 2:3)

Repentance

Before conversion, a child may readily ask for forgiveness when prompted simply out of good training or because they have learned that this is the easiest path to get through the situation. After conversion, they have genuine grief over their own sin and a heartfelt desire to seek restoration with God and others. We see this when we observe our child being convicted of their sin on their own, without any prompting on our part. They will also have a sincere hatred of their own sin.

What Scripture says:

> For see what earnestness this godly grief has produced in you, but also what eagerness to clear yourselves, what indignation, what fear, what longing, what zeal, what punishment! At every point you have proved yourselves innocent in the matter. (2 Corinthians 7:11)

Belief

Before conversion, a child can know all the right answers regarding who Christ is and what He has done and might be able to explain the gospel accurately, especially if the child grew up in a Christian home where these things were well taught. After their conversion, we can observe a true love for God that comes when one truly believes in Christ and recognizes that their only hope is in Him and His work. Evidence for this includes things like:

- A heart inclined toward God and what He says rather than inclined toward their own desires
- A true hunger for God's Word, as evidenced by their turning to Scripture on their own for encouragement
- A desire to pray on their own, apart from external encouragements to do so

What Scripture says:

> No one born of God makes a practice of sinning, for God's seed abides in him, and he cannot keep on sinning because he has been born of God. (1 John 3:9)

Also, the whole of Psalm 119, which depicts a love of God's Word.

How Much Is Enough?

No child or adult believer will perfectly exhibit repentance, belief, and a desire to follow God's law always and in all circumstances. We are not looking for perfection here or for some checklist of behaviors perfectly followed. However, a true believer *will* exhibit many of these consistently over time. An unbeliever may show glimmers of interest in these things occasionally (for example, an unbelieving child may be really interested in reading the Bible), but it will generally not be sustained. We are looking for a deep-seated, permanent change of heart, which will mean that we will see some level of consistency over time in each of these areas.

What if you're just not sure? That's okay! Your role is to bring up your children in the discipline and instruction of the Lord and look to God to perform the true work of conversion within them (Ephesians 6:4; 2:4–5). From a practical level, whether your child is a true believer or not, it is always right and good to point them to Christ for repentance and forgiveness. Be faithful to train your children in spiritual matters, fervently pray for God to work in their lives, and recognize that the results are ultimately His to accomplish.

Discussion Questions

1. What kind of spiritual training, if any, did your parents use with you when you were growing up? What things did you appreciate, and what were not all that helpful?

2. Describe the nature of your involvement with your church. Are you more of a spectator or a participant? How are you investing in the church and its people with your time and giftings?

3. Which of the topics covered in this chapter do you feel like you're currently doing? Of those, are there any adjustments you'd like to make?

4. Are there things you are not doing but would like to try, either listed in this chapter or other ideas you may have?

5. Come up with a specific plan with any changes you would like to make in the spiritual training of your children. What short-term steps do you plan on taking?

Chapter 13

Obedience (Part 1)

> Children, obey your parents in the Lord, for this is right.
>
> – Ephesians 6:1

God has commanded that children should obey their parents and has stated that this is right. As any parent of a toddler well knows, obeying parents is not an automatic response that children come preprogrammed with. Parents are commanded in the Bible to train their children in the way they should go, to discipline them, and to teach them diligently. This brings us to the big challenge in Christian parenting: How do you teach children to obey?

Whether or not they realize it, all parents have created a standard of obedience for their children. For some, that standard is clear, consistent, and well understood by both the parent and the child. For others, that standard is unclear, inconsistent, and not well understood. There is a big difference between these two extremes, and there is great benefit when both the parent and the child have a well-defined, shared understanding of what obedience truly looks like. This is a foundational issue in parenting, and making positive changes in this area can result in transforming the relationship between parent and child for the better.

Is Obedience Objective or Subjective?

It is imperative to consider the fundamental question of whether obedience is an objective standard or merely subjective. An *objective standard of obedience* is based on a well-defined standard, not on how the parent feels or reacts. A child has either obeyed or disobeyed in accordance with this external standard. A *subjective standard of obedience* is based on the parent's thoughts or feelings at the time.

When parents enforce an objective standard of obedience, what constitutes obedience or disobedience is well understood by both the parent and the child and is consistent over time. In contrast, when parents discipline or correct their children based primarily on their own feelings of frustration or annoyance, this subjective standard is inconsistent and leads to exasperation or aggravation for both parent and child.

For example, consider a situation where a parent is busy getting the house ready for guests and tells a child to pick up their room. The child doesn't respond to the parent's request. The parent sees this and recognizes that disobedience has occurred, so it must be dealt with as disobedience right away. Even though the parent is busy getting ready, they stop what they are doing and deal with the disobedience immediately with some form of discipline or correction. This is not because the parent has become angry but because there has been an infraction to an objective standard of obedience, and they have made a commitment to hold the child to this standard, regardless of whether they are emotionally worked up about it or not. This parent knows that letting the child persist in not responding to their command to pick up their room is teaching the child that obedience isn't required.

In contrast, consider another parent in the same situation—guests are coming, they ask the child to pick up their room, and, as before, the child doesn't respond to the parent's request. In this case, however, the parent decides to keep going with their own preparations rather than address their child's disobedience because they have a lot to do and there's still time to get the room cleaned up later. The parent may think to themselves, "It's not that big of a deal that my child isn't cleaning their room right now, as long as they get it done sometime before the guests come." However, as the time for the guests to arrive approaches, the parent is feeling more and more pressure to get everything done, and upon walking by the still uncleaned room, they emotionally lose it and start yelling at the child, "I told you to clean up this room—get over here right this minute and start cleaning, or you'll be in more trouble than you can imagine!" At that point, the child realizes that they really do need to clean the room, so they go do it. This is an example of enforcing subjective obedience—the child realizes that there are no real ramifications to disobedience until the parent is emotionally worked up.

This contrast between objective and subjective obedience may seem to be more philosophical than practical in nature, but in reality, there is a night-and-day difference between the two approaches. If you discipline only when your child's behavior has become annoying to you, then you almost certainly will experience great frustration as a parent, and your child will likely be aggravated as well.

Changing to an objective standard of obedience can be a challenge, but the rewards for both parent and child are great. We know this from personal experience. With our first child, we initially did not have a clear standard of obedience, and not only were we frustrated but our child was too. We would ask her to do things, but these were essentially suggestions because there were no ramifications if she didn't obey. We would get frustrated that she wasn't doing what we wanted or needed her to do, and it wasn't clear to her why she should do what we were suggesting when she didn't feel like doing it. Once we consistently enforced the standards described later in this chapter, our relationship with our young daughter was much more mutually enjoyable, and there was a level of peace and harmony in our household that we had never experienced.

To have an objective standard of obedience, there must be mutual understanding between the parent and the child of what obedience looks like. What are the characteristics of true obedience?

Characteristics of Obedience

Children can be quite creative in finding ways to disobey authorities in their lives while appearing to be obeying. Obedience is a multi-faceted issue, and we (and many others) have found it helpful to define three characteristics that must all be true for a response to be considered true obedience in our house:

- **It must be done right away.** The child does not have the option to hold off obeying until they finish something they are doing or until they simply feel like it. When asked to do something, they must do it right away, without delay.
- **It must be done completely.** Sometimes children will start to obey, but then not complete whatever it is that they've been asked to do (e.g., they begin picking up their room, but when the parent leaves, they stop). They must do what their parents have asked them to do until it is finished.

- **It must be done with a good attitude.** The child should obey without a grumbling, negative attitude. We don't demand that the child be artificially happy about doing what we've asked them to do, but they should obey with a "good spirit"—as opposed to "obeying" in a grumbly manner, murmuring to themselves as they head off to accomplish your requested task with a "poor, pitiful me" attitude. Going back to the "clean up the room" example, a child may do it right away and do it completely without stopping, but if they angrily put their toys away, this is actually a form of rebellion and disobedience. This is the most challenging of the three characteristics of obedience for children to fulfill and for parents to discern, but in some ways, it's perhaps the most critical (more on that later).

True obedience means all three of these responses are present. There's a sense that objective obedience is binary—someone either obeys or doesn't. Partial obedience is really disobedience. Sometimes children are not disobeying but simply don't understand the instructions. It is appropriate to teach them to respectfully ask a question if they don't understand or are not able to obey for some reason.

We should point out that there's nothing particularly special about this exact formulation of what obedience looks like. You may come up with some variations on the same themes. What is important is that both you and your child understand what constitutes true obedience in your household and that you address both external and internal (heart) compliance.

Value of a Verbal Response

We also included a fourth item, which isn't so much a true "characteristic of obedience" but a helpful habit to teach children: there should normally be a verbal response. This means that when the parent asks the child to do or not do something, the child responds verbally. (The exact form of the verbal response is not important—we taught our children to say "Yes, Mom" or "Yes, Dad," but many other types of responses would be appropriate as well). This may seem to be a somewhat forced response, but it is incredibly helpful for several reasons:

- **It makes it clear that the instruction was heard and understood.** It is challenging to discipline a child for disobedience if it's not evident whether they heard and understood what the parent told them to do. For example, you might ask, "Were they too focused on what they were doing to hear me, and therefore I am not just in disciplining them for not obeying?" Having a verbal response makes it certain that the message has been heard and establishes that there is now a need to obey.

- **It gives better visibility into what is going on in the heart of the child.** The tone of voice can help parents to discern whether the child has a good attitude. If their "Yes, Mom" or "Yes, Dad" is done in a whiny, complaining sort of way (e.g., with the voice really dropping when they say it), then we can see that they are really not doing it with a good attitude.
- **It helps the child to obey.** We found that when our child verbally responds to us as parents, it helps them in their heart to "move" in the direction of obeying. We can't really explain why this is the case, but it's something that we observed. It's as though the act of saying "Yes, Mom" or "Yes, Dad" is an act of submission that starts them moving in the direction of obedience, and this initial momentum helps them to fully obey.

While we tried to teach our children to give a verbal response without prompting on our part, the reality was that sometimes they did need a prompt ("say, 'Yes, Daddy'"). Giving them this prompt was often all that was needed to get the ball rolling toward obedience, especially if they were in a distracted situation.

It's a Heart Issue

The last thing we want to do is teach children to obey only externally, without addressing the need for heart obedience as well. Teaching only external obedience creates little "Pharisees," who were known for the appearance of external obedience but not true obedience from the heart (Matthew 23:25–28).

It really *is* possible for parents to train their children to have a heart desire to obey them out of love and respect. And this kind of training is a good thing! It is not just for the purpose of making our lives as parents more pleasant—though it certainly can. More importantly, it helps children be obedient to God's calling on their lives as children right now (Ephesians 6:1), and it helps prepare their hearts to respond to God-given authorities with respect and attention as they grow older.

While we can train our children to obey us from the heart, we cannot make our unsaved children obey God from the heart—that is, to obey out of love and respect for God. Only God can work this change in their hearts. While we can't, through training, give them hearts that love God, we should continually point them to Jesus as the only One who can give them a new heart that truly wants to obey Him. It is at the level of these heart struggles where we most see our need for Christ. We can verbally sympathize with our children in this struggle. We can tell them we, too, struggle to obey God right away, completely, and cheerfully and must ask God for forgiveness when we disobey and for help to obey. In a sense, it is a good thing for our children to see that it is frequently hard to obey, and to recognize, over time, that they are battling their own sin and are in need of the Savior.

Benefits of Enforcing an Objective Standard of Obedience

We'll close the chapter by listing some of the benefits of having an objective standard of obedience and holding our children to it:

- **It reduces our incidents of getting angry with our child.** When disobedience is clear and we address it right away, we tend to deal with the issue *before* we get angry. A police officer who is giving out a speeding ticket does so not because they are angry with the speeder but because the speeder broke the law and it's the police officer's job to enforce the law. That should be our attitude as parents—we enforce obedience because it's our job to do so, not because we're angry with our child.
- **It avoids exasperating our children.** Since the standard for obedience is well understood and not arbitrary, we do not exasperate our children like we might if obedience is subjective, based on our current emotional state. We'll discuss this more in the next chapter.
- **It reduces the impact on the parent/child relationship when there is disobedience.** If obedience is primarily based on the mental state of the parent, then disobedience feels more like a personal offense. But if obedience is based on an objective standard that is external to both the parent and the child, then disobedience is merely a violation of that standard, not a personal offense.

- **It enables regular discussion about the gospel.** As already mentioned above, when there is a clear, objective standard of obedience (including the heart) that has been violated, we can point the child to their need for Christ to give them a new heart that wants to follow and obey God.

Discussion Questions

The following questions are addressed to those who are currently parenting. If you do not have children, answer the questions not in terms of how you parent but in regard to how you were parented in the family in which you grew up.

1. How would you describe the type of obedience that characterizes your parenting—do you have a subjective standard of obedience or an objective standard of obedience?
2. Of the three characteristics of obedience, which do you find the most difficult to enforce? Are there other aspects of obedience you can think of that are not covered by those three?
3. Do you expect a verbal response from your children? Why or why not?
4. What topic within this chapter seems the most foreign or unusual to you? Is this something you would like to change or not? Why?
5. What percentage of the time are you angry or annoyed when you're dealing with disobedience in your children? What ideas covered in this chapter do you think would be the most helpful to reduce those feelings in responding to your children's disobedience?

Chapter 14

Obedience (Part 2)

"But you don't know my child!"

– Many parents

In the previous chapter, we talked about a fundamental principle of parenting—that we should have an objective standard of obedience both we and our children understand and that we should hold them to that standard. In this chapter, we will be discussing some related issues that come about with this way of thinking.

What You *Really* Expect

Children will generally live up to the standard of what you really expect of them when you're training them to obey. If you ask your daughter to do something and she doesn't obey, but you count to three before actually taking any corrective action, then she learns that what you *really* expect is for her to obey once you get to three and not when you first say something. Or if you give a command in a normal tone of voice but then repeat it in a firm or elevated tone of voice if your son doesn't obey, he learns that what you *really* expect is obedience when you elevate your voice. If you sometimes hold your children to an objective standard of obedience but sometimes don't, then they learn that what you *really* expect is that sometimes they need to obey, but not always. (And they will get very good at discerning when it is that they really don't need to obey, such as when you are not paying attention.) If, instead, you teach your children to obey you the first time you tell them to do something in a normal tone of voice, and you always hold them to that standard, they will learn that this kind of obedience is what you *really* expect.

So, should you count? Should you repeat your command in a firm or elevated tone of voice? Should you sometimes let disobedience be unaddressed when it's not convenient to address it? Realize that your children will generally respond to whatever it is that you really expect along these lines, so how this goes in your family is up to you. If you continue to count to three, as we hear constantly in grocery stores by aggravated, bedraggled parents, then know that your children will generally only obey you when you count to three, and then only if you have consistently had some consequence at that point.

We think there is great blessing for all (parents, children, and everyone else around) to teach and truly expect our children to obey at the first command given in a normal tone of voice. This is a well-defined standard that can be easily understood by both parent and child. It is also practically helpful in that it enables parents to deal with disobedience *before* they get emotionally worked up, because obedience or disobedience is discerned right at the start, not after a lingering "battle of wills" between a parent and a child. Finally, we found that enforcing obedience at the first command in a normal tone of voice led to a much higher level of contentment and enjoyment in both us and our children as well as less interpersonal stress.

Sounds great, right? This is an achievable goal, but it requires consistent enforcement. Parents must address disobedience after the first command in a normal tone of voice. For some parents, this may be a significant change from the normal mode of operation and will take some getting used to. If you are accustomed to only disciplining when you've counted or raised your voice, then it can seem odd to discipline your child if they don't respond after your initial command in a normal tone of voice. We strongly recommend, if this is going to be a new mode of operating in your family, that you sit your children down and acknowledge that you have not been expecting obedience as you should but that you are asking God to help you and this is going to be much better for them (as they will have a more cheerful mommy, for example). It would also be wise to practice and role-play what obedience will look like from now on.

Say What You Mean and Mean What You Say

To help our children obey right away, it is important for us to be clear in our instructions to them. When we ask them to do something (or not to do something), we must really mean it.

For example, if Mom and Dad are trying to have a conversation together in the car and the children are being overly noisy (as often happens when everyone is in a car), it is common for a parent to throw a "shhhh" in the general direction of the children, often without even consciously thinking about it. Sometimes this is done so quietly that the children can't even hear it. Simply tossing a "shhhh" back to the children is vague and certainly not crisp from a "discerning obedience" point of view. If we are going to hold our children to a well-defined standard of obedience, we need to make sure we are clear in our instructions to them so there is no ambiguity as to what is truly a command to be obeyed versus other communication. If we really do want our children to be quiet, then we need to tell them that clearly and plainly and, more importantly, be prepared to follow up if they don't obey. In general, the more explicit our instructions are, the better. For example, Dad can say, "Children, Mom and I need to be able to hear each other as we talk about what we need to take care of when we get to Grandma's house, and we need you to be much quieter. Please read a book or do something quiet for the last fifteen minutes of this trip."

Avoiding Exasperation

In Colossians 3:21, fathers are explicitly told not to exasperate their children. The word translated "exasperate" in the NASB and "provoke" in the ESV means to "stir to anger." By implication, mothers should not do this either—clearly Paul's intent was not that it is just fine for mothers to exasperate their children. There are many ways we can exasperate our children, but some are especially relevant to this chapter.

First, as implied earlier, we can exasperate our children by being inconsistent in how we enforce obedience. If parents have been inconsistent, it is then challenging for a child to be able to predict how their parent will respond when they act a certain way.

Second, we need to understand that our primary goal for teaching our child to obey at our first command is for the child's good, not our own. Just because our children are required to obey us does not mean that we then can treat them primarily as our own personal servants. It would be exasperating to a child to feel like they are being ordered around only for your entertainment or convenience, rather than as a helpful member of the family.

Third, it is important to take into account the ages, abilities, and even current mindset of our children when we give them various commands. We should not command a child to do something they are not capable of doing, thereby setting them up for failure. Likewise, we should strive to make it easy for our children to obey. There may be times when a young child is overtired or particularly cranky, and in this case, we might try to avoid giving them direct commands, knowing that they will find it very hard to obey. Or, we might give them an alert that a command will be coming up soon so they have time to prepare their hearts (e.g., "Children, we are going to be leaving our friends' house soon, and in five minutes I'm going to ask you to pick up the toys").

We must distinguish between childishness and disobedience. If a child unwisely tries to carry too many dishes to the sink and they fall to the floor and break, we may feel upset and disappointed, but this is an example of childishness, not outright disobedience. When our children are childish, we should be patient with them and point out how they had not been wise, but we shouldn't consider this an example of disobedience. Disobedience is when a child intentionally fails to obey a parent's clearly understood command or instruction, whereas childishness is when a child does something unwise or foolish. We may still enforce some kind of consequence in the case of childishness, such as having a teenager help pay for a broken window if they were unwisely playing baseball too close to the house, but this is in a different category than enforcing obedience.

Be careful as well about making excuses for our children's behavior in public—things like "She's tired" or "He's shy"—usually to cover for our child's disobedience to known expectations. It's not wrong to be tired or to have a shy personality, but using tiredness or shyness as a justification for not obeying parents or being rude to others is not appropriate or helpful. Making excuses for our children's behavior can give them a message that there are any number of excuses for disobedience in public settings that aren't true at home. While we want to be grace-filled and understanding toward our children, we want to help them learn to obey God the rest of their lives, even when it's difficult or they don't feel like it. Two- and three-year-olds are much more savvy about these kinds of things than we tend to think, and our children are only too willing to enjoy milking the excuses for all they are worth.

Finally, use your head—parenting is not a formula, and there may be times when you make exceptions to what is normal. It is good to be consistent and predictable for your children, but that does not mean that you need to be mechanically rigid in how you define and enforce obedience. Occasionally, situations pop up where you may end up making exceptions to your general rules—just be careful that this doesn't become the norm.

Common Objections

We have talked about this kind of obedience with many parents, and some have a high degree of skepticism and take a very different parenting approach. Let's address their common objections head-on.

"But This Is Impossible"

Some parents think there is no way that children can be taught to obey in this manner, however, many parents have been able to teach their children to generally obey cheerfully at the first command. We don't think this is because the children in these families are somehow born categorically different than other children. In fact, we know this is not the case, because when we started parenting, we were not following these principles, and everyone was miserable. When we overhauled our parenting approach, a significant change occurred in our relationship with our children, and we were all much more content and enjoyed each other more. The difference was mostly in how we parented, not that our children somehow changed. Yes, we still had some friction and disobedience, but it had lessened considerably. Teaching our children to obey cheerfully at the first command is not a miracle cure that removes all sin and every parenting challenge, but it tends to reduce the constant friction in the parent/child relationship as everyone understands what is expected and what the consequences are.

It is not necessarily easy to make these kinds of changes, but realize that the primary challenge is not so much for the children to adjust as it is for you as parents to make and consistently enforce the changes. As we've stated, children tend to know what their parents *really* expect from them, and if their parents change what they expect (and enforce), the children will generally adjust quite quickly to the new reality (especially if the parents are consistent). It is a significant challenge for you as a parent to change your default approach to parenting, but the benefits of doing so are worth it for your children and for you.

"But You Don't Know My Child"

Clearly, every child is different, and some children will more quickly learn to obey the first time, from the heart, than others. Parents are sometimes quick to attach labels to their children that are really not helpful—we say our children are "always pushing the boundaries" or "constantly pushing my buttons" or that they are stubborn or strong-willed. The reality is that most children are strong-willed boundary pushers, and those who are exceptionally strong-willed, stubborn, and good at pushing boundaries are especially in need of training in this area of obedience. It is the strong-willed child who will most benefit from having a consistently enforced, clear standard of obedience. If their natural bent is to rebel against any outside authority telling them what they should do, then this very much needs to be regularly addressed at the heart level and not ignored, because carrying that kind of attitude into adulthood is only a recipe for trouble (not to mention how this kind of attitude is something that is completely against the attitude that Christians are to have toward their Savior).

You're right. We don't know your child like you do. However, we would say that training in this area is even more essential for children who struggle more with this. Don't be the kind of parent who shies away from the difficult parts of parenting and focuses on the easy parts. Loving our children means that we train our children, especially in the areas where they most struggle.

"But This Sounds Selfish or Wrong"

As we stated earlier, the point of teaching heart obedience is not to have well-trained house slaves that can carry out our every whim. This is not about us—it's about our children. The reason we want to teach our children to obey us from the heart at the first command is that it is best for them to learn to do so. They will need to learn to submit to the authorities in their lives, and ultimately our desire is that they learn to submit to the ultimate authority in their life—God Himself. We can't "save" our child by teaching them to obey, but by working on this area, they are able to see their lack of obedience to God and their need for Christ more explicitly.

"But This Sounds Harsh and Overly Demanding"

At first glance, it might seem that holding a strict standard of obedience would create an oppressive environment in which to grow up, and that the relationships between parents and children would be hollow because it would be all about enforcing obedience. But what we have observed is that exactly the opposite tends to be the case. When there is a clear, enforced standard of obedience in the family, there is also a measure of peace and harmony and a lack of anger and frustration. When obedience is not taught or enforced, significant relational friction occurs because parents are often annoyed or angry at their children's behavior and children are often frustrated or exasperated by their parents' inconsistency. Once parents have been able to establish and enforce a clear standard of obedience, less time is spent dealing with disobedience (because it happens much less often), and more time can be spent on positively building family relationships. If a child never gets to the point of cheerfully submitting to their parents as a habit, then it's much harder for other aspects of the parent/child relationship to thrive.

Remember from chapter 2 the need to be grace-filled parents, even as we encourage our children in obedience. Can we be overly harsh as parents? Yes. And we know we may be becoming harsh when we lack compassion for our children as they struggle with their sin, perhaps not recognizing that we are fellow sinners. Just as God is compassionate with us, we need to be compassionate with our children.

It's Worth It

We are the weak link here, parents. Addressing disobedience when we see it is what's needed. This will require getting off the couch, turning off the stove, setting down the laundry, and otherwise putting aside what we want to do at any given moment to address the more important issue of our child's disobedience. We'd prefer to ignore it, but that isn't going to help.

As we mentioned at the beginning of the last chapter, this area of how we understand and enforce obedience is a foundational part of parenting, and how we do this will have a huge impact on the training of our children. Making the difficult changes in these areas is well worth every bit of effort it takes.

Discussion Questions

1. Based on how you currently operate, what do you *really* expect in terms of your children's obedience? Has this changed over time? How consistent is it from your child's viewpoint?

2. What are examples of times where you have said things to your children that you didn't really mean? (Consider things like empty threats, vague commands, etc.)

3. What are your biggest objections to teaching your children to obey from the heart at the first command?

4. Give an example of childishness you've observed in your children or others' children. What things should you consider when trying to decide whether something is childishness or disobedience?

5. What would you say is your default mode of parenting in terms of enforcing obedience; that is, what happens when you don't consciously think about it?

Chapter 15

Proactive Parenting

> Train your child in the way in which you know you should have gone yourself.
>
> – Charles Spurgeon

Imagine a brand-new student pilot named Joe who has never before flown an aircraft and knows nothing about how to fly. When he shows up for his very first class, the instructor pilot says, "All right, Joe. Let's start by having you get in the cockpit with me. You go ahead and try to fly the airplane, and I will tell you if you do anything wrong." Clearly, this would not be a good approach to teaching someone how to fly an airplane. In fact, it would likely be a recipe for disaster. A student pilot must be taught many things before he or she steps foot inside an airplane—things like how the controls work, what the gauges mean, rules for safe flying, and how to transfer control to the flight instructor. Teaching someone to fly by only telling them when they do something wrong simply does not work. Why, then, do many of us parent as though the primary input our child needs is correction when they do something wrong?

We strongly believe that most of our input to our children should be along the lines of proactive instruction rather than reactive correction. However, proactive instruction requires a high level of intentionality on the part of the parent, which is why we often are weak in this area. Our lives tend to fill up with many activities and thoughts, and we don't get around to thinking proactively about how to train our children. Yet proactive training is extremely valuable and effective, especially at times when conflict isn't already occurring.

What do we mean by proactive training in times of non-conflict? It's a matter of thinking ahead about situations our children will encounter and anticipating what sorts of challenges they may face. Then, in a calm moment, we talk to the child about this and perhaps practice it with them so that, when the time comes, they are appropriately prepared to handle the situation we have anticipated. While most parents do this well for things like "what to do if a stranger talks to you" or other safety issues, many other situations are also excellent opportunities for proactive training, for instance, training our child to sit quietly at a doctor's office, a concert, church, or some other public event. (This is specifically covered in chapter 24). Other examples of this type of proactive training follow in the sections below.

Practicing Obedience and Self-Control

Teaching children to obey is a significant parenting challenge that requires both proactive training and correction when children do not obey. Recall from chapter 13 that obedience required three things to be true:

1. It must be done right away.
2. It must be done completely.
3. It must be done with a good attitude.

Just as in the pilot training example, there is great benefit to teaching these three things proactively at a time when the child is not currently disobeying. We began a family activity called "training time" that consisted of several different components. When we were initially trying to teach the concept, we would do some role-playing, where one parent pretended to be the child, and the other parent acted as a parent. We would then demonstrate what true obedience looked like, incorporating all three of the above standards and modeling the helpful verbal response.

I (Cindy) might ask John, the pretend child, to pick up the red block and bring it to me. He would initially begin to comply right away and, with a smile and happy body language, would say, "Yes, Mommy!" and bring me the red block. Then, after a few similar examples of what obedience looked like, we would then have John comply in all but one area. For example, if I asked John to sit on the couch, he might do it right away, while saying, "Yes, Mommy," but have a very grumpy voice and body language. We would then ask the children, especially the younger crowd between ages three and five, whether Daddy had obeyed, and if not, what was missing. Next, we would enact a similar example, but this time John would comply cheerfully but perhaps get distracted on the way to the couch. This was always done in a lighthearted way, even with a humorous and exaggerated manner, so that the children were usually giggling and even asked to have training time because it was fun.

Once we had completed several examples of this kind of obedience and recognizable examples of disobedience in each area (either by a parent or perhaps demonstrated by an older sibling) we would then practice. It is important to pick a time when the children are well rested and fed so that this part goes as well as possible without setting up the child for unnecessary conflict. We would ask the younger children (the ones who most needed practice with obeying) to do a variety of simple tasks (e.g., go hug your mother, put the pillow on the couch, pick up the blocks). We would expect these things to be done following the three requirements mentioned above, plus the verbal response. If they weren't completely accurate in following these things but did not seem willfully disobedient, we would point out what was lacking and have them do it again.

Sometimes we would add in some crazy things or a long sequence of tasks if the child was old enough to remember them: clap ten times, walk into the kitchen, and sit down. When they got skilled at this type of thing, we might even add in some immediate response practice. For example, while they are on their way into the kitchen in compliance with a previous command, we might loudly say, "Stop! Run back here!" having explained that there may be times when we need them to respond to something urgently, for safety reasons, and that they should do that quickly, before even saying, "Yes, Mommy!" Believe it or not, the children very much enjoyed this kind of practice.

One reason we think the practice sessions are so powerful is that they enable a child to get into a habit of responding the right way. Having this habit is a large part of the battle when you must ask them to do something while they are distracted in the middle of some other activity. Also, because it is done in a fun way and not in a time of conflict, they tend to buy into it much more readily than when they are in the heat of a battle of wills with you already. And when you are regularly practicing what obedience looks like, and you know the child is aware and is able to obey, then disobedience is easier to distinguish. You will then have more confidence recognizing when a battle of wills has begun, and the child will not get away with feigned obedience (by pretending not to understand or hear you correctly).

Advanced training in this area, which is also fun, is to give them a quick series of commands while they are in the middle of something in another area of the house, and see how well they do. For example, let's say two children are playing a board game, and you want to test them in a more real-life situation. If you have recently been practicing obedience and you know they will understand this is a test because you said you would be testing them, you can call from another room and ask them to run to the kitchen and do jumping jacks. Since you have been practicing recently, they might just comply, trying to outrace each other and giggling, saying, "Yes, Daddy!" as they run by.

Talking about Expectations before an Event

Anytime you are about to bring your children into a new social situation, it is helpful to talk about what kinds of things they should think about to be a blessing to others in this new context. Remember in chapter 11 when we talked about being others-oriented? We mentioned asking them how they might be considerate of others in the grocery store. Ahead of time, you could ask several leading questions, like:

- Why will it be important to stay near the shopping cart?
- Should you touch things on the shelves?
- What should you be doing with your voice?
- How can we show honor and consideration to other shoppers while in the store?
- Mommy will have a lot to think about and read. How can you be helpful and considerate to her while we are in the store?
- How can you help keep the baby entertained while we are shopping, in a way that does not distract others?

Rather than seeing this as a big lecture or list of rules, we would encourage you to frame this as a positive, empowering thing for the child. They have a special mission and opportunity to be vitally involved in an important family project—shopping—instead of viewing it as something to be endured. Then, when the shopping is done and you are headed home, you have lots of specific things for which, hopefully, you can praise them.

Even taking this approach, there may be times they do not obey well and behave badly in the store. However, attempting to prepare them ahead of time can significantly reduce the amount of disobedience and correction that is required.

Role-Playing Social Situations

Many children do not naturally exhibit polite responses to social situations—things like shaking someone's hand, looking them in the eye, greeting adults with their name, or responding to questions from well-meaning adult friends. Children generally need help being prepared for these social encounters. Looking back, we wish we had worked harder in this area in our family. However, at times we have had some measure of success by remembering to practice these things at home. For example, one of us might pretend to be "Mr. Brown" or "Mrs. Smith" and ask the children a series of questions:

Parent: Hi, Jack!
Jack: Hi, Mr. Brown.

Parent: Hi, Mike, how was your week?
Mike: Hello, Mr. Brown. It was very nice. I caught a fish!

Parent: My, Joshua, you have grown. How old are you now?
Joshua: I'm now eight, Mrs. Smith.

Parent: Elizabeth, would you like some ice cream?
Elizabeth: No, thank you, Mrs. Smith. I'm allergic to milk.

This chapter gave just a few examples of proactive training as a springboard for you to consider what would be most helpful in your unique family situation.

Discussion Questions

1. What would you estimate is the percentage of your child-training that is proactive in times of non-conflict versus reacting to disobedience or negative behavior?
2. What benefits are there when you train your child in a time of non-conflict versus attempting to train them in the middle of a conflict?

3. In what areas have you, as a parent, been proactive in training your child or children?

4. Can you think of other areas where being more proactive would be beneficial? Of these, which one or two do you think would be the most important to work on soon?

Chapter 16

Relating to Extended Family, Other Children, and Other Parents

> Happiness is having a large, loving, caring, close-knit family in another city.
>
> – George Burns

Parenting styles become evident when we get together with other families, and this can be particularly awkward when it comes to family gatherings. If you are an intentional parent who has worked hard at teaching your children to obey you from the heart at the first command, but others in your family have a different parenting style, you can be put into spots where you have to make difficult choices. Thankfully, this has not been a big issue within our extended family, but we have talked to many friends who have struggled with these kinds of situations.

For example, suppose the extended family (consisting of three to four family units) are at Grandpa and Grandma's house. You have worked hard at teaching your children to consider how what they do impacts others and how they can be a blessing to others, and your children have also learned to obey you at your first command. However, suppose there is another family unit where these are not at all the case, and the children from this family are loud and disruptive to the point of physically jumping all over the furniture. You have taught your children that they need to respect other people's property and to be considerate with their voices, but they are starting to join in with the other children (as children tend to do). What do you do? There is no single right answer, but let us suggest a few principles that can help guide you:

- **Your primary responsibility is to parent your own children, not other people's children.** You are not responsible for everyone else's children—just your own. In situations like this, it's good to recognize that everything is not in your control and that you may not be able to completely "fix" everything.
- **Context is important when enforcing expectations on our own children.** If your children are lured into things that they wouldn't otherwise do, like jump on the sofa, the context of the situation should be taken into account. If it would have been almost impossible for them to "go against the flow," then it would be wise to consider this when deciding how to interact with them, especially for very young children. For older children, this is a good opportunity to follow up after the event with a discussion on peer pressure.
- **Removing a child from the situation may be an option.** Sometimes, the most effective thing to do is to simply remove your child from the temptation to misbehave. For example, you might tell them they need to come sit with you, or you take them somewhere else to participate in a different activity. This way, you don't need to make a big deal that what the other children are doing is disrespectful—you are just finding a subtle way to remove your children from the activity.
- **Explaining the "why" to your own children may have a positive effect on the rest.** Another way to indirectly address the issue is to talk with *your* children about why what they are doing is not a good idea (e.g., "Jumping on the couches breaks them so others can't enjoy them anymore"). The other children will overhear what you're saying to your own children and may respond to it. While it's usually good to make it clear you're primarily addressing your own children, perhaps by calling just them over to talk with you, speak loudly enough that the other children can hear too.
- **It is always good to have a gracious attitude toward others.** No matter what, we should be gracious toward others—both other parents and their children. Rather than looking down on parents who are really struggling with unruly children, foster an attitude of genuine compassion. Most of us can appreciate the

> struggle to train our own children and might keenly remember a time when we were not as attentive to the impact our children's behavior was having on others. Our job is to help our children in this tough situation and to train up our children, not to judge or criticize other parents. Also, remember that we are not walking in the steps of those other families and may not be aware of all the situations going on in those households that may be contributing to their children acting out.

In situations like this, your children will undoubtedly notice that they are doing "what's right" and the other kids aren't. This leads us to another important area of parenting—teaching graciousness to your children.

Teaching Graciousness to Children

Pride is an insidious sin that can easily creep in without notice. If our own children are learning to obey us and to be respectful of others, there is almost certainly a potential for pride or even arrogance to build up when they see other children who don't "measure up" to the standards they have been taught.

By way of example, consider a situation in a grocery store. You have taught your children to be respectful of others by not running around and jostling things on the shelves and to hold on to the cart so that Mom or Dad knows where they are. While you're in the store one day, there is a harried mom with a few children in tow trying to shop, but her children are somewhat out of control and doing all the things yours were taught not to do.

What should you do? Your children cannot help but notice the difference, and if you never address the situation, the natural, sinful response of your children will be to have pride grow within their hearts. Without you saying anything at all, they'll start thinking to themselves, "We're good children, compared to those bad children over there." How do you fight against this attitude?

Rather than ignoring these kinds of situations, we found it helpful at times to talk about what we saw and point out that those children may not have been taught yet about how important it is to obey their mommy and be respectful of others. What we were trying to do was help our children see the other children through the eyes of compassion rather than judgment. For slightly older children, we might also discuss how we don't know what the situation is for that particular parent. We point out that they may have various challenges in their lives we don't know about that limit their time or ability to teach their children about these things. We may want to teach our children that some children have come from traumatic situations and may be in foster care in temporary homes, and help them understand how stressful and disruptive that could be on a child.

On a related note, we also need to teach children discretion in a wide variety of contexts, including the grocery store situation described above. Suppose your child sitting in your shopping cart points at the misbehaving children and says out loud, "Look, those children are not obeying their mommy!" While true, that statement is showing a lack of discretion. In that case, not only would we address reasons the other children might not be obeying but we would address what our own child did: "When you pointed at those children and said they weren't obeying their mommy, how do you think that would make them feel? How do you think it would make their mommy feel? Why is it not a good idea to point at other people?" Part of learning discretion is learning when and where not to say something in any given situation. The need to teach discretion increases as our children get older, even into their teen years, but there are times, like the one described above, when even young children can learn to be discreet in what they say.

The Distraction of Visitors

We are big fans of inviting people into our home, either for a meal or for a longer stay, such as when distant grandparents come for a visit. Hosting guests presents a challenge to our parenting, however, because we often focus on them more than on our own children, as is appropriate. Additionally, when visitors are present, the standard home routines are often changed, sometimes we all get less sleep than usual, and we will probably find it hard to be as consistent a parent as we normally might be. All these things put together can make hosting visitors challenging from a parenting perspective.

That being said, hospitality is of great value, even to our children. Not only is it something commanded by Scripture (Hebrews 13:2; Romans 12:13; 1 Peter 4:9), hospitality is valuable to our children as they participate in giving to others (time, perhaps their room, etc.). Much can be learned from others who live in our home and share meals around our table since they have had different experiences and backgrounds—it broadens our world. Hospitality also provides some level of protection from having inconsistencies between our public life and our private life. When people are in our home, particularly for an extended period, it's hard to maintain a false façade. Our children have commented that practicing hospitality by having a variety of people stay in our home and gather around our table has had a huge positive impact on their adult lives. It was an unexpected blessing and benefit of following this Scriptural command.

So, if we want to be hospitable to others, how do we deal with the parenting challenges of hospitality situations? Here are a few suggestions:

- **It's probably acceptable to let things slip a little bit on occasion.** If you are being consistent overall, relatively brief periods of less consistency are not going to undo the work you've done, particularly if the context has changed from normal life. It's worth it for the breadth and value providing hospitality affords to your children.
- **Avoid establishing a "discipline free" zone.** While you may not be as consistent on following up with your children when visitors are around, it's important not to create a situation in which your child knows they can do anything and won't be held accountable. This means that even when guests are present, there will likely be times when you dismiss yourself from your visitors and go deal in private with a child who has disobeyed.
- **Have a humble attitude about your own parenting.** No parents are perfect parents, and no children are perfect children. Your goal is not to impress anyone by your parenting, and there should be no sense in which any personal embarrassment you may experience by your child's behavior in a visitor situation be "taken out" on your child. Remember, how you respond to your child's misbehavior should be based on enforcing an objective standard, not based on your feelings (including the feeling of embarrassment).
- **Avoid making excuses for your children.** It is very tempting when a child is misbehaving in the presence of visitors to try to make excuses for them by saying things like "He's overtired" or "She's been out of sorts with all these extra people around." As we mentioned in chapter 14, while these things may be

true, making excuses for our children, particularly in their presence, essentially teaches them to make excuses for their own misbehavior. One good response we've heard parents say is simply, "We're working on that."

True hospitality requires humility because we open up our imperfect homes to outsiders who will see the imperfections, and this includes our children, who are never really finished projects! Whether you're interacting with others in a multiple family situation or hosting people in your own home, we hope that the principles described in this chapter can help guide you through some of the tricky situations that invariably arise when we interact with others.

Discussion Questions

1. Describe some family gatherings that were challenging from a parental point of view, either from when you grew up or involving your own children. What was particularly difficult about the situation? What was done by the parents involved? Looking back, what might have been done better?
2. What is your normal response when other people's children are misbehaving in a public situation? If your normal response is fairly judgmental or critical, what would be a godlier attitude to have in these situations? What can you do to foster that attitude within your own heart?
3. Have your children ever noticed other children who were misbehaving? What was their response? What was your response? If their response was critical or lacking grace, what could you do differently next time to develop a humble attitude within your children?
4. Can you think of examples where your children showed a lack of discretion by saying something that would have been better left unsaid? Describe your response when that happened. How can you teach your child to have more discretion next time?
5. In what other ways, besides comparing themselves to other children's behavior, might your children be tempted to have prideful

attitudes? What can you do or say to address these other areas of growing pride?

6. For you, what is the most challenging aspect of (1) having visitors for a meal, and (2) having people stay overnight? How are your children involved in either of these activities, for better or for worse? What are proactive ways you can have your children participate more directly and helpfully in these activities?

Chapter 17

The Rod: Biblical Principles

Fathers, do not provoke your children to anger, but bring them up in the discipline and instruction of the Lord.

– Ephesians 6:4

Perhaps the most controversial aspects of parenting center around what the Bible calls the use of "the rod," sometimes referred to as *spanking* or *corporal punishment*.[1] We fear that the existence of this chapter in this book will result in some people completely dismissing everything else we have written. Some other parents may have a vague sense that use of the rod is good and appropriate, but they lack confidence that they are doing it correctly or may find their efforts ineffective.

Whatever your current disposition is toward the use of the rod in disciplining children, we challenge you to consider what is said in this chapter and the next with an open mind. Recognize that many of the ways in which the rod is applied in the modern context (and perhaps in your own background) are not at all what we are talking about in this chapter. For example, striking a child in anger or out of frustration is *not* a proper use of the rod, and doing so for those reasons is *never* appropriate. In this chapter, we are talking about something completely different than this faulty conception.

So, just to be clear at the outset, we do not condone:

- Using the rod in anger or frustration (striking a child because you're angry or frustrated or letting anger or frustration affect how you treat a child)

---

1 For consistency, we will refer to the general concept of spanking or corporal punishment as "use of the rod" or just "the rod."

- Doing anything that causes physical damage to a child
- Anyone who is not a child's parent administering corporal punishment (what we are calling "the rod")
- Interacting with a child in any way, shape, or form that is sexual in nature

We would also highly recommend that you look back and reread chapter 2, "Grace-Filled Parenting," to remind yourself of the mindset that we should have for all parenting, including the use of the rod.

Our goal in writing these chapters is to help parents learn how to use physical discipline confidently and appropriately as one important tool for training their children. Even if you are positive about the general concept, you very well may lack confidence and wonder if you're "doing it right."

In this chapter, we'll glean several principles related to the rod found from passages in the book of Proverbs. This is not an exhaustive exposition but is intended to hit the highlights.

One important passage from the book of Proverbs that deals with the use of the rod is Proverbs 13:24: "Whoever spares the rod hates his son, but he who loves him is diligent to discipline him." This verse describes a parent who fails to discipline when they should be as hating their child, while conversely pointing out that true love for our children will make us diligent to discipline them when appropriate. Disciplining our children is an act of love for them and a desire for their good—not an act of revenge or retribution or a venting of frustration or anger. If we love our children and want their best, we will discipline them. If we really don't care about their well-being, we will just let them go their own way and not bother disciplining them when necessary. The reason we have been given several proverbs about the rod is because a parent is likely to need encouragement to use this tool.

But use of the rod is not the one and only way we train our children. Note that in this book on child-training there are thirty-one chapters and only two of them deal with the rod. There are many things we should be doing to train up our children in the way they should go, and much of that training does not involve using the rod. However, use of the rod is an important tool for parents, and if we neglect to use it, our parenting will not be as effective as it would be otherwise.

Also, as covered extensively in chapters 13 and 14 on obedience, we should discipline our child based on an objective standard of obedience out of love for them, *in contrast to* disciplining them when we are finally at an emotional breaking point. Proverbs 13:24 speaks of our use of the rod as an act of love toward our children, not a way to vent our frustration. Using the rod out of frustration or anger is *never* a proper use of the rod.

Another related verse is Proverbs 29:15: "The rod and reproof give wisdom, but a child left to himself brings shame to his mother." This verse points out that a child "left to himself"—without any parental discipline—will lack wisdom and act in shameful ways. Note that this verse speaks of both the *rod* (corporal punishment) and *reproof* (verbal correction). We will almost always include both.

When we use the rod, we should also talk with our child and explain at an age-appropriate level how they disobeyed and what they should do differently next time. We may also choose to:

- Provide other instruction
- Talk about how they need to ask Jesus to change their heart so they can obey
- Reassure them of our love for them
- Pray with them
- Express that we don't enjoy using the rod but are doing it to be faithful parents and for their good (say things like "I'm sad to do this" or "I wish that I didn't need to do this")

There is no need to bring up all these additional topics every time as a checklist kind of activity—use your judgment, and bring them up when you think it is most appropriate, given the age and maturity of your child and the current situation.

Proverbs 22:15 speaks of one of our goals in the use of the rod: "Folly is bound up in the heart of a child, but the rod of discipline drives it far from him." Children are not born inherently wise. They, like every other human being ever born, have a heart that will eventually desire to rebel against the authorities in their lives and, ultimately, rebel against God. This is the natural condition into which each of us is born—we are self-proclaimed enemies of God. We understand from other parts of Scripture (such as Romans 5:10) that the ultimate fix to this problem is to be reconciled to God through the death of Jesus, and this is something that only God can accomplish in anyone's life, including the lives of our children. But we still have the responsibility to teach and instruct our children, and an important part of that is teaching them how to live under authority. It is folly for any young child to think that they know what is best, more than any authority in their life, especially their parents, who have the God-given authority to train them in the way they should go and to discipline them. The rod can be used to help our children learn to obey and prevent them from thinking that they can live as the sole authority in their lives.

One final passage from Proverbs 23:13 speaks of a common fear that parents have regarding using the rod: "Do not withhold discipline from a child; if you strike him with a rod, he will not die." This passage is making the point that there is benefit to the child by appropriate use of the rod. Rather than harming our child, we are steering them away from a path that could lead them in harmful directions, possibly even death. Many parents fear that using the rod will cause more harm than good to our children, but this simply is not the case. The rod can and should be used in such a way that it will be for the child's good and not to his or her harm. In these cases where a parent is struggling with doubt about the appropriateness or effectiveness of this form of discipline, it is often better for the child that the rod be used than that it be withheld.

Somewhat humorously, there was a time when we were speaking with a group of parents about parenting, and we brought in our oldest children for the younger parents to ask questions of, thinking it would be encouraging for parents of younger ones to hear what older children thought of how they've been parented. Our children said they thought we should have used the rod more than we did. We think this is because they knew their own hearts and understood that there were many times when we weren't completely sure of the details and opted not to use the rod. They knew they had pulled the wool over our eyes and that it would have been better for them to have their sin exposed and addressed in those instances. We were surprised by this.

So, in summary, we have learned the following principles from Proverbs:

1. If we love our children, we will discipline them.

2. Failing to discipline our children when we should is actually a form of hating them.
3. Use of "the rod" (spanking) is a valid, biblically-prescribed form of discipline.
4. It is not proper to use the rod to vent our own frustration or anger.
5. Normally, verbal correction goes along with use of the rod.
6. Use of the rod helps teach our children how to live obediently under authority and avoid the folly of thinking they are the sole authority over their lives.
7. Proper use of the rod is not harmful to a child but results in their good.

Who are you going to listen to when deciding whether you are going to use the rod in your parenting? On the one hand, many voices in our culture today are against corporal punishment in any form. On the other hand, we have the One who formed your child in the womb, who gave them breath, who knew all their days before there was one of them, who has their hairs numbered, who loves them more perfectly than you possibly could, and who indicates in His Word, right here in the book of Proverbs, that corporal punishment does have a place at times. Who is a more knowledgeable and trustworthy source of what is best for our children? The answer is clear, but are you willing to trust Him?

To be clear, we are not saying that every way in which the rod is commonly used by parents today is right and proper and good. Many children are abused in various ways, including being physically beaten, and there is no excuse for this kind of treatment. There is a night and day difference between a parent lashing out and striking a child in anger or frustration and a parent calmly administering the rod in an appropriate manner out of love and concern for their child's well-being. People who have only experienced the former (striking in anger) cannot easily conceive that the latter (calmly administering the rod in love) is even possible. In the next chapter, we will address some of the more practical aspects of using the rod to help parents use it in a way that is a true blessing to their children, to do them good and not harm.

Discussion Questions

1. What was your childhood experience of "the rod," or corporal punishment? Were the ground rules clear as to when it would be used, or was it more based on the emotional state of your parents?
2. What things have you heard or read about use of the rod prior to now?
3. What was your mindset about use of the rod in child-training prior to reading this chapter? How have the things you've experienced or heard influenced your thoughts?
4. What are your fears, questions, and concerns as a parent about use of the rod? (Hopefully, at least some of these will be addressed in the next chapter.)

Chapter 18

The Rod: Practical Advice

> If we never have headaches through rebuking our children, we shall have plenty of heartaches when they grow up.
>
> – Charles Spurgeon

> Begin early to teach, for children begin early to sin.
>
> – Charles Spurgeon

We believe that the principles from Proverbs covered in the previous chapter are true and that the rod is a valid and essential tool for parenting. We also recognize that beyond these principles, the Bible does not give detailed instructions as to the specifics of how the rod should be used—when, how often, at what ages. These are all situations where wisdom is required. As we seek to be wise, we must consider other biblical principles and commands that apply, such as, "Fathers, do not exasperate your children, so that they will not lose heart" (Colossians 3:21 NASB). We can also benefit from the experiential wisdom of others: "Without counsel plans fail, but with many advisers they succeed" (Proverbs 15:22). Much of what follows below falls in the category of "advice," not absolute commands from Scripture. Parents may choose to implement the details differently than we did, and that is perfectly okay. We still want to describe what worked well for us, though, because we believe it could be helpful and encouraging to others who are starting on their parenting journey.

When to Use the Rod

Over time, we settled into using the rod only for three things: (1) willful disobedience, (2) lying, and (3) physically attacking another child.

Willful Disobedience

When a child has willfully disobeyed their parents, this is, by definition, rebellion, and it must be addressed in some manner. We found that the most straightforward approach was to use the rod anytime there was willful disobedience—intentionally, knowingly, thoughtfully disobeying clearly understood commands or instructions. We use the word *willful* here because we want to separate it from things like childish forgetfulness or other times when they may fail to follow through on our stated expectations for reasons other than sinful rebellion. Recall from chapter 13 that for a child's response to be considered obedience, it must be done right away, completely, and with a good attitude. If any one of those three elements was missing, we treated it as disobedience, even if it was something that seemed relatively minor.

Sometimes it was a challenge to determine the heart attitude or motivation of our child, but we could get a sense of their true attitude based on tone of voice used and their physical posture. If we detected some amount of "wanting" to obey, as though they were battling in their heart to try to obey with a good attitude, we would usually let it go. If, however, we could tell that they were completely grumbling in their heart to the point that it spilled out in a complaining response, we would treat that as disobedience. As discussed in chapter 13, requiring a verbal response from our child was incredibly helpful, because it took away the possibility for the child to say, "I didn't hear you say that," or "I didn't know you wanted me to do that." Requiring a verbal response also allowed us a better glimpse into their heart attitude in responding to us. A grumpy "Yes, Mom" followed by a sulking, stomping demeanor helped us to know they were not obeying in their heart.

As previously discussed, the clearer and more specific we can make our instructions to our children, the clearer it will be when they disobey. Saying something like, "I want you to do all the chores on your chore list every day for the rest of the time that you're in our family" is too overly broad, and it would be nearly impossible for a child to comply with this. But saying, "Please take out the garbage," is a clear, short-term command that the child can choose to obey or disobey, with a clear mutual understanding as to what the results would be in either case.

Lying

We purposed to use the rod every time we realized our child was lying.

I suspect that every child who has ever existed has learned to lie, and none of our eight children has proven this suspicion wrong.

Being a person who speaks the truth is of great value in all of life. Truth-telling is essential for trust in a marriage and in all other relationships, in a work environment, in a church fellowship, and so on. Sadly, honesty and trustworthiness have not been valued recently, and our culture assumes to some extent that "everyone is lying."

I (Cindy) distinctly remember a time that we had a plumber fixing our kitchen sink during a political scandal about an important public figure who had been accused of lying. I was horrified to hear this plumber continually wanting to talk about this scandal in front of my children and proclaiming repeatedly, "Everyone lies. Everyone cheats on their taxes. What is the big deal?" I think it never occurred to him how much this was undermining my trust in the nonitemized bill he handed me when he was done working. I add this example here because I want you, as a possible new parent of a young child, to take seriously the need to develop a love of truth-telling and an abhorrence to lying in your children by treating this as a serious issue. God treats this as a serious issue. Several proverbs deal with lying, but here are a few:

> Lying lips are an abomination to the LORD, but those who act faithfully are his delight.
>
> – Proverbs 12:22

> There are six things that the Lord hates,
> seven that are an abomination to him:
> haughty eyes, a lying tongue,
> and hands that shed innocent blood,
> a heart that devises wicked plans,
> feet that make haste to run to evil,
> a false witness who breathes out lies,
> and one who sows discord among brothers.
>
> – Proverbs 6:16–19

Because being a trustworthy truth-teller is so important, we must require this from our children from a very early age, before lying becomes a skilled habit. When a preschool-age child tells a lie to their parents, for example, saying that they didn't eat the cookie that's "missing," using the rod to discipline them will have much more of an impact than a lecture on the value of a "good name" (having a good reputation, including telling the truth—Proverbs 22:1). They absolutely need to know that telling a lie is wrong. In a sense, we want them to be afraid of telling a lie because of the possible ramifications. As they get older and can better appreciate the value of a good name or reputation, then their fear of lying can transition from a fear of physical pain from the rod to a fear of losing their reputation for telling a lie. If we fail to address lying with them, it can become established as a normal way of operating to get what they want or to hide sin, which is a very dangerous mindset as they mature.

If our child disobeyed and then lied about the disobedience, we sometimes had a policy of administering the rod twice—once for the disobedience and once for lying (the regular number of swats for each). If, however, they disobeyed but were honest about it, we had a policy of giving them only half of the number of swats for their disobedience. Our thought was that we still needed to address the disobedience, but we wanted to encourage them to be willing to confess what they did and be honest about it.

Attacking Another Child

The third and final category of activities in which we would use the rod is if our child attacked another child, including siblings or other children. Like lying, we wanted to establish from a very early age that this kind of activity was completely outside the bounds of what is allowable. Of the three infractions for which our children received the rod, this one was by far the least violated, because they learned quickly that attacking another child was a really bad idea.

We have heard some anti-spanking activists try to make the case that when we use the rod on our child, we are teaching them that hitting other people is a valid way to solve our problems. This is very mixed-up thinking and is kind of like saying that there is no way to distinguish between a person paying a speeding fine and a person being robbed at gunpoint. Both are examples of extracting money from someone with a threat of force, but in one case, the threat of force is from a legitimate authority (the government) properly exercising their God-given role to keep order, whereas the robber is simply stealing from another person and has no authority to do so. A child can clearly understand the difference between them striking out in anger at a sibling or playmate versus their parent punishing them in a calm and judicious manner for something they have done that they know was wrong. The parent has the God-given authority to do so, and the child does not.

It Should Be Judicial, Not Emotional

When a parent is administering the rod, it should be done in a calm manner and not based on emotions like anger or frustration. A parent should have the mindset of a good judge deciding what is best based on the facts and not based on how they feel at the moment. An upright judge hands down a sentence not because they are angry at the criminal but because the criminal has been convicted of breaking a law and therefore needs to be punished. This is the reason we have spent so much time pushing for parents to hold their children to an objective standard of obedience (expecting the children to obey at the first request) rather than a subjective standard of obedience (expecting the children to obey once we become upset enough to deal with it), as described in chapters 13 and 14.

Here is the reality: If you have committed to holding your child to a standard of obeying you at the first request and following up with the rod when they don't, then your use of the rod will normally be a duty you intellectually feel like you must do because you said you would rather than an emotional response. You may wish that you didn't have to do it, but you normally would not be angry or aggravated, because the child's rebellion has not been allowed to persist to the point that it has provoked you to aggravation or anger. This will allow you to calmly administer the rod without great emotion. By taking this approach, the parent is not put in the position of having to make a judgment call as to whether this instance of disobedience met some level of grievousness to warrant punishment. From a heart point of view, any form of disobedience is harmful if allowed to go unchecked.

In contrast, if you only use the rod as a last resort, after the child has crossed some kind of arbitrary "line" that is determined mostly by how annoyed or angry you feel, then you will almost always be angry at your child when you are administering the rod, which is counterproductive and potentially dangerous to them.

If you find yourself mostly angry when disciplining your child, then it is highly likely that you are waiting too long to discipline. You might think that if you were to follow up on the first sign of disobedience, you'll spend the entire day disciplining your child. We have generally found the opposite to be true. As discussed in an earlier chapter, a child will tend to live up to the true expectations of their parents. Once they realize that obeying the first time they are asked is the enforced standard, they will often adapt to that new reality, which results in much more peace and harmony in the home. When there is disobedience, it is dealt with quickly before emotions flare.

What If I'm Still Angry?

Even if we enforce a standard of obedience at the first command, most parents will still find themselves angry or irritated at times when their child has disobeyed. We need to be vigilant not to let our anger affect our interaction with our children, particularly when using the rod. If we are going to use the rod, we must do it in a self-controlled manner, not out of anger. As much as we want to be consistent in our parenting, it would be better to let an infraction go or postpone punishment than to use the rod in an angry manner. If you sense that you are too irate to administer the rod, one option may be to have the child wait somewhere while you have time to calm down. Another possibility would be to have your spouse administer the rod. We do not condone use of the rod in an angry manner.

To be clear, what we are talking about is being so angry that it affects how we act. It's possible for a parent to have some amount of anger but keep it in check as they administer the rod calmly and in a controlled and loving manner to their child. This is like a judge who is actually angry at what a criminal has done but tries to keep that from affecting his actual sentencing.

What Is the Right Age Range for Using the Rod?

We would be very hesitant to state a specific age range at which the rod should be used with children. However, most of what we've been talking about in terms of enforcing obedience at the first command is going to involve children on the younger side (preschool to early elementary). As children get older, the use of the rod tends to taper off, as parenting interactions with children transition from basic skills of obedience to things like responsibility and others-orientation, and deliberately talking with them about their heart issues. Older children are able to learn from consequences like the loss of privileges for their disobedience because they are old enough to mentally process the connection between their disobedience and the consequence, even if not corrected immediately. Every child is different, though, and parents will need to make judgment calls as to when to reduce or stop the use of the rod with their own children.

On the other end of the spectrum, children need to be old enough to understand why the rod is being administered. Generally, we observed that there is a time, typically at some point in the crawling stage, when children understand the concept of boundaries, that they will directly challenge the parents' authority. It may come out as something like this: they know there is a boundary they are not supposed to cross, look up to see if the parent is watching, and then cross the boundary to see what will happen. This is a critical time in child-training because this is when the parent has the opportunity to start to establish the pattern of obedience. Children are born as rebellers, and parents are given the task of teaching them how to obey. At the early stages, flicking your fingers on the hand of a crawling baby is an effective and appropriate way to communicate that they should not do something, like cross an established line or play with an outlet. There comes a point, however, when their rebellion is more overt and intentional, and use of the rod becomes appropriate at that point.

Talk with Your Child

When using the rod, it is also important to talk with your child. At a minimum, you should explain why it is that they are being disciplined. Often this would be something like, "I'm disciplining you because you didn't obey me right away when I told you to come inside." Depending on the situation and age of the child, you may also talk about:

- how difficult it is to obey
- how we need to ask Jesus to give us a heart that wants to obey
- how we struggle sometimes to obey
- how much we love them and how we would not be loving them if we just let them disobey

We would not recommend a checklist to cover every time—all these things should be covered occasionally but not each time, or it will be mechanistic. Furthermore, much of this "higher-level" discussion would be after administering the rod, as the child calms down and recovers.

We also found it helpful to communicate with our child about what was going to happen. For example, we'd say, "Because you disobeyed, I'm going to discipline you, and you're going to receive four swats." (We generally had a "standard" number of swats, which varied from child to child and at different ages. It seemed like some children were more responsive than others!)

The goal is to walk away from a situation where the rod has been applied with a sense of a restored relationship between the parent and the child. Ideally, the child will walk away with a better relationship with his parent than before the rod was administered. Beforehand, he had disobeyed his parents and was at some level in a state of rebellion with a sense of broken fellowship with his parent. Afterward, the rebellion and broken fellowship has been dealt with and is in the past, and the parent has an opportunity to express their love and support to the child. We always made a point to end a session with the rod with a hug and expression of love. Many times, the child would leave with a light heart, very much in contrast to the grumpy heart of rebellion that caused the situation in the first place.

It Needs to Be Painful to Be a Deterrent

The reason we use the rod is to cause momentary pain to produce regret in the child over what they did and to think twice before doing it again. It needs to be painful for it to have this effect. We have on more than one occasion seen a parent grab a child in diapers and just whack him on the behind (often with a hand), without removing the diaper. This is clearly not painful to the child, and usually just makes the child angrier. The point of using the rod is *not* to provide an opportunity for the parent to express his frustration or to let the child know that we are upset at them.

While it should be painful, we certainly do not want to cause any kind of injury to our child. We found that using something that is a little flexible that can cause a short-term sting was effective along these lines. This seemed to be better than something large or heavy, which could have a more jarring effect. We would always try out the rod on ourselves, on our thighs and palms, to feel how much it hurt, to help us determine how hard to swing the rod. Also, recognize that the approach will vary somewhat based on the age of the child.

We understand that the idea of intentionally inflicting pain on your child is hard to swallow. But recognize that a short-term sting that helps a child to gain self-control and learn to live under authority is well worth it. How much better to help your child gain a level of self-control and obedience than to grow up lacking those things, which can lead to much more serious consequences later in life than a short-term, stinging pain. We would rather our child learn self-control and obedience to legitimate authorities by our lovingly administered, temporary stings than be an adult lacking self-control and in rebellion to authorities and locked in a jail cell. For young children in particular, explaining rationale doesn't work—there needs to be an immediate and obvious deterrent or consequence.

One way to tell whether it is sufficiently painful is to observe the child's reaction to it. If administering the rod just makes the child angrier and more rebellious in their heart, then it may not have been painful enough. There ideally are times when using the rod, in the end, has a calming effect on the child—they have been disobedient, it has been dealt with, and there is a restored relationship between parent and child. This calming effect may be easy or hard to achieve depending on the personality of the child. However, if you find that using the rod with your child only has the effect of making them angrier, then it is good to evaluate whether it is truly painful to them.

It Should Be Done in Private

We do not want to embarrass our child in front of others, so we would recommend that the rod be administered in a private setting. Even within a home, we think it's a good idea that it be done privately rather than in front of siblings or other family members.

If you're out in public and your child disobeys, you can quietly tell them that you saw them disobey and that you are going to deal with it when you get home. If you do this, make sure that you do follow up when you get home. Of course, this approach will only work with a child who is old enough to remember the infraction long after the fact and connect it with the use of the rod.

No Fighting Back

Our goal in administering the rod is to address the rebellion in our children's hearts. As previously mentioned, before administering the rod, we normally would explain, in a calm and quiet tone of voice, what we were going to do: "In a minute, I'm going to have you lie down over my lap, and I'm going to give you four swats because you disobeyed me when I told you to pick up your toys. Do you understand?" If the child at this point kicks and fusses and resists, they are still essentially rebelling. When this happened, we would finish, and then calmly say something like, "OK, so I've already used the rod because you didn't pick up your toys like I asked. However, you didn't obey me when I told you to lie down over my lap, so I'm going to need to do it again." We think that it's crucial to attempt to address this heart attitude, which is the real issue at hand and not so much that they didn't clean up their room. Allowing a child to throw a fit when being disciplined without addressing it often fails to address the real issue of rebellion in their hearts.

Let's be honest, though. This didn't always work out perfectly. In many cases, after a round or two of this, the child would realize that they really did need to submit to their punishment, and then it would be over. However, sometimes they were worked up to a point that we didn't seem to be making any progress. Parents need to use their judgment about when to stop, and we can reach a point where we need to just finish up as best we can, change the situation, and move on, even if we didn't end up getting them to submit with a quiet spirit on that occasion. In such a case, it would be good to verbally follow up later, once things have settled down, to help the child respond better next time.

Also, there were rare occasions when I (John) made a trip home for the purpose of administering the rod when one of my children was not responding to Cindy well. This made a fairly strong point to the child that responding properly to Mom's correction was imperative and expected, and it was usually effective. Thankfully, this was only needed on an occasional basis since my work was about a twenty-five-minute drive from our house.

Use of the rod is one of the many areas in parenting where judgment calls will need to be made. As much as we would like to, we can't give you a set of rules to follow in a mechanistic fashion to have "success" as a parent with your children. We did find the suggestions given above to be helpful to us in our parenting, but we still had to use wisdom and balance the many Scriptural principles involved when dealing with any specific situation, and you will have to do the same. Many times we prayed that God would give us wisdom about how to handle a parenting issue with a particular child (as in James 1:5, "If any of you lacks wisdom, let him ask God, who gives generously to all without reproach, and it will be given him") or pleaded that God would give our children a submissive heart, recognizing that we had a limit as to how much we could just cause that to happen. Use of the rod is not a magic wand that automatically solves every problem, but it is an effective God-given parenting tool that can be beneficial for our children when used well.

What to Call It

Throughout this chapter we have talked about use of "the rod" just because we had to pick a term, and the biblical term seemed as good as anything for the purpose of writing chapters in a book. Within your own family, you are free to use any other term you would like. We have heard people call the rod by many names, such as the "instrument," the "wisdom worker," or the "board of education applied to the seat of learning." Likewise, the process of administering the rod has been called "disciplining," "chastising," or "correcting." Feel free to use whatever terminology works for your own family. One consideration when determining what to call the use of the rod in your own family is to perhaps use a word other than *spanking*, which generally has completely negative implications in our culture (often well deserved). Using a different term can help you and your family think about it in its appropriate, more positive, biblical manner.

Persevering

Sometimes in our parenting the use of the rod was effective, and other times it seemed like it wasn't. We have talked with numerous parents who have felt like administering the rod at times did not seem to be working. If you feel this way, our encouragement to you would be first to evaluate if you are using the rod in a way that keeps it from being effective. As described earlier, the two primary things to consider are:

1. Are you waiting until you are angered or frustrated over repeated infractions rather than applying the rod immediately when the disobedience occurred?
2. Is it sufficiently painful to the child?

If these things are not in place, then it's likely that the rod will not be effective.

The next thing to consider is how much time you are spending proactively training your child in times of non-conflict, as described in chapter 15. Proactive training should be the primary mode of training you are using with your child, and the rod should be secondary. If you are expecting the use of the rod to do all the work, you are going to be frustrated, and your child even more so. While we need to be faithful to use the rod when appropriate, if you see a problem occurring repeatedly, you should try to figure out how to address this problem with your child at a time when they are calm and receptive and the problem is not currently happening.

If you are proactively training your child and you are using the rod appropriately (early enough and painfully enough), and still feel like you lack success, then our encouragement to you is to press on in faith. Some children are more stubborn than others, and sometimes it just takes time and consistency. Many times, Cindy and I quoted Galatians 6:9 to each other when we were frustrated by not seeing immediate results in child-training: "And let us not grow weary of doing good, for in due season we will reap, if we do not give up."

From where we sit today, after going through the early years of child-training with our eight children, we can affirm that God was faithful to use our efforts, as imperfect and at times feeble as they were, and that every one of our children did eventually respond to some degree to our "staying the course" with both proactive child-training and the use of the rod. None of them are perfect, but we believe they are all better off than they would have been otherwise.

So, parent, recognize that it is good work you do when you seek faithfully to train your children, both with proactive training and with use of the rod. In due season you will reap if you do not give up!

Discussion Questions

1. This chapter is filled with suggestions about use of the rod in child-training. Which suggestions are similar to what you have been doing (or thinking about doing, if you're not yet a parent)? What suggestions are different?

2. What would you estimate is the percentage of time and energy you spend training your child proactively in times of non-conflict versus reactively, such as with the rod?

3. After reading the suggestions in this chapter, what, if any, are some things you would like to change about the way you use the rod? If there are changes you'd like to make, discuss how you might go about practically making these changes.

Chapter 19

Family Book Reading

> Life is too short to read a good book—read excellent ones!
>
> – Cindy Raquet

Reading books to young children is generally well understood to be beneficial in many ways. However, this chapter is about something a little different than curling up together on the couch with a good children's picture book from time to time.

I don't remember exactly how it started, but when our oldest child, Anna, was about three or four years old, we decided to read through the Chronicles of Narnia as part of the bedtime routine. (Honestly, I [John] think Cindy and I were just eager to have meatier bedtime reading and were getting impatient. It was mostly for us!) We had been reading picture books to the children at bedtime, but this was a new adventure—chapter books without many pictures. One had to just listen and picture the events in their own mind. At the point we started Narnia, I don't think that Anna understood much, but she didn't seem to mind sitting there for ten or fifteen minutes each night as we worked our way through each of the books.

By the time we made it through all seven of the Chronicles of Narnia series, bedtime reading as a family had become a well-entrenched family activity, so we continued on with another book, followed by another, and have done this fairly consistently to this day, approximately twenty-four years later. Since then, even our youngest of children have been along for the ride, sitting on someone's lap or playing on the floor, while listening to these "older" books. We think this has been a great benefit for them, and you would be surprised to discover how much a young child may be following the story line of a chapter book. We have also been recently told by a PhD brain scientist reading specialist that active, usable vocabulary can be picked up when listening to a book being read just as much as if reading the book yourself. What an easy and enjoyable way to add to your children's usable vocabulary and boost their own reading ability!

We have not kept a record of all the books we've read, but we estimate that we have read well over two hundred full-length chapter books. Some we have read more than once, as the children get older and the younger ones weren't old enough to remember the first reading. That sounds like a lot, but it was done just ten to fifteen minutes at a time. This is another example of how doing a little bit consistently over time yields tremendous benefits.

I think this is one of our favorite times of the day as a family. We do it right before the youngest go to bed, usually followed by prayer and singing a song together, jointly referred to in our family as "pray-and-sing." Sometimes the children will quietly work on a craft of some sort, but mostly they just sit and listen and snuggle with someone near them on the couch.

We love this shared history of having read so many excellent books as a family. These books have dealt with important topics of all different types—courage, suffering, history, foreign cultures, adventure, humor, worldviews. This builds up a common frame of reference that can be recalled in later conversations, such as "I know some of us are sick, but at least it's not as bad as the Spanish flu in *Hero Over Here*."

We have also valued developing a common appreciation of various cultures and time periods through the reading of historical novels. This has made us interested in things that we would not otherwise have noticed. One of my favorite examples of this was when our family had the incredible privilege of visiting the British Museum. A year or two prior to our visit we had read a book entitled *A Single Shard* by Linda Sue Park—an attention-grabbing book about a young boy in Korea in the twelfth century who was involved in the making of celadon pottery (a type of glazed pottery distinctive to Korea in that time). As a result of reading that book, one of our family highlights at the British Museum, believe it or not, was the nearly vacant display of ancient Korean pottery on one of the upper floors. If anyone else had been up there, they would have been humored to see a group of eight children, ages three to eighteen, and two adults so visibly excited to find the display of ancient twelfth-century Korean celadon pottery—in the same museum that houses the Rosetta Stone, Egyptian mummies, statues from the Parthenon, and many other well-known artifacts (which we also did enjoy, by the way, though those exhibits were packed full of eager visitors). We had a richer and more memorable—and unusual—museum experience simply because we read *A Single Shard* together as a family.

One other benefit of reading books together is that we can better deal with books that have objectionable elements in them. Some books are overall very good but may have some aspect in them inappropriate in various ways or which is not age-appropriate for all our children (e.g., they may be too scary or too graphic for very young children). But since we read them aloud, we can just skip over any objectionable elements, sometimes summarizing the important points. For example, we can merely say, “He was killed,” rather than read a description of a murder. Sometimes, we choose to read something but follow up with a discussion about it, such as asking the question, “Do you think it was right for the main character to lie in that situation?”

Recently, I have been taking the current nighttime reading book with me when I travel for work and, when able, make recordings in my hotel room for my family to enjoy at home at night in my absence. Cindy reports that hearing my voice reading the current story in the evening has had a calming and comforting impact on everyone, especially the younger children. In our family, I do almost all the readings, but there’s no reason that couldn’t be shared if there are two parents in the home. One of our daughters attending a nearby university has a lengthy commute each day and has asked to be included, so I now record our readings at home each evening, even when I am not traveling, just to send to her, as she also finds it soothing to hear a parent’s voice reading a good book while she drives, and the books are still that interesting. We’ve even had a college student who frequented our home enough to know of this tradition ask to be included in the audio file distribution as she headed overseas for her post-college job. She just wanted to enjoy that “family feel” and relish whatever the current book was along with us.

Finally, at a very practical level, we have found that having everyone together to read is a good way to settle everyone down before heading to bed. There’s a certain calmness to sitting together and just listening for ten or fifteen minutes that is hard to replicate at other times of the day.

You may be thinking, "How do I find a good chapter book?" This is a great question. Sadly, we find the library full of many books we choose not to read to our children because of the attitudes of the characters, the content of the story, and the lack of any significant redeeming value to the story. We have been greatly helped by the book recommendations of our homeschool curriculum (Sonlight) but many excellent curricula have similar book lists, and there are even whole books published with lists of good children's books. Cindy likes to say, "Life is too short to read a good book—read excellent ones!"[1] Don't settle for books that aren't redeeming or helpful. There are scores of excellent books available, many of which even warrant rereading.

What about the problem of books with scary or distressing themes or topics? That is another good question. We have read several books as a family that are emotionally challenging, especially for Cindy if she was currently pregnant (and therefore, more emotionally sensitive). However, reading through situations others are facing helps model for our children the character that will be needed when they face trials. (We will be covering how to help children face trials in more detail in chapter 22.) We have heard Andrew Peterson, a children's book author and songwriter, quote the author G. K. Chesterton when explaining why he has some scary and dangerous situations in his stories for children: "Fairy tales do not tell children the dragons exist. Children already know that dragons exist. Fairy tales tell children the dragons can be killed."

We will be talking about this more in a later chapter, but realize that even children's picture books can come laden with worldview influences you don't want your children to absorb. Be very discerning and careful as your children fill up your library bag with books you don't know anything about. If you find yourself reading a book and it has problems, feel free to stop and either talk about what the problems are with that book, or simply say that you have realized this book isn't good, and stop reading it. We frequently would be reading picture books to our children and find ourselves stopping and asking, "Do you think these children

1 It is possible this did not originate with Cindy, but we have not been able to locate another source. James Joyce is known to have said, "Life's too short to read a bad book." At some point in college, Cindy remembers being frustrated with so many books, most particularly on Christian topics, filling the shelves of Christian stores, that, while not untrue or completely frivolous, didn't seem worth the time spent reading them. With this phrase, she was giving herself permission to put down a book that didn't seem personally profitable and move on to something that was.

are treating each other the way they'd want to be treated?" or "Is it wise for these children to be hiding this information from their parents?" or "Are these children putting themselves in a dangerous situation by not obeying?" After discussing the book, we would put it away, and everyone recognized it was a book we weren't supposed to read anymore. Note that disobedience, foolishness, or bad attitudes are only a problem if they are without appropriate consequences or not addressed or resolved. The Bible contains lots of examples of disobedience or bad attitudes, but these are there for instruction.

Book Recommendations

Occasionally we have had friends ask us for book recommendations, which is why we have added an appendix which lists some of our favorite chapter books and children's picture books. Please recognize that as we write this, our youngest child is twelve, so it has been a while since we have been regularly getting picture books from the library. It's possible that some of the picture books we recommend are not readily available. If you can find them, that's great, but if not, there are certainly lots of other good books out there. You can probably get good recommendations from other parents you know who see things the same way you do.

Discussion Questions

1. While you were growing up, did your parents read to you? What kinds of books? What, if any, impact did those books have on you, and why were they memorable?
2. What do you see as potential benefits of reading good books together for your family? If you were to do it, what would be the best time of day for your situation?
3. Can you think of any books you've read in the past that would be good for family reading? What makes them good candidates?
4. Perhaps there are other activities or times when your family enjoys spending low-intensity, peaceful time together—can you think of other ways your family can be building a common culture while relaxing together? (Watching TV or a movie doesn't count).

Chapter 20

Family Culture

> Sometimes you will never know the value of a moment until it becomes a memory.
>
> –Theodor Geisel (Dr. Seuss)

Every family has a "culture"—that is, a certain way of doing things or way of thinking unique to that family (just as any business, church, or almost any other group has a distinct culture). As parents, you are establishing a family culture, whether you realize it or not. Family culture can include both serious things, such as having a culture where Christ is honored and where others are respected, and more lighthearted and fun things, like recreation. Many of these kinds of serious aspects of family culture are covered in other chapters of this book, so these are not the focus here. Instead, in this chapter we want to encourage you to think about ways you can proactively build a positive family culture through simple, fun, and memorable activities.

Why is it a good thing to work toward having a positive, unique, identifiable family culture? Here are several reasons:

- Having a strong family culture helps children realize they are part of something uniquely special as a member of your family. (All families are special and unique, but that's not always consciously understood.)
- Family culture can increase family unity, as people enjoy sharing in common activities.
- Family culture is a way to offset some of the negative aspects of

family interaction present in every family (due to the ongoing effects of sin).

- Building family culture can be lots of fun—and it's generally free as well.

Sometimes elements of family culture can happen spontaneously, with no prior planning, such as having impromptu snowball fights. Other things require intentionality on our part, at least a little bit. Some might involve ways you celebrate holidays. Others may be more regular, everyday occurrences.

One thing to emphasize is that, by definition, your unique family culture should be just that—unique. That means that you can relax and just establish a culture that fits your family personality—and the personalities of its members. You are not trying to make your family like someone else's but trying to allow your family to thrive in the special ways God has put you together.

Also, keep in mind that just about anything your family does regularly that you really enjoy doing together becomes a part of your family culture. It doesn't have to be something odd like "We really get a kick out of playing charades while scuba diving!" Even relatively normal things, if generally enjoyed by all, or most, of your family members, become a part of your positive family culture, such as taking a walk around the neighborhood after dinner.

Just to get your juices flowing, here are some things we would consider to be part of our family culture. While you are obviously free to adopt these if you'd like, our goal in giving them is to show you examples of simple, free, easy-to-pull-off activities that can build a family culture, not to imply that every family should do these. In fact, please don't, because then our family culture will become less unique!

Jammie Rides: We don't remember exactly how this started, but one night we needed to run an errand fairly late in the evening, shortly after the children would normally go to bed. At this point we had four or five small children. We decided that we would put the children to bed but then yell out, "Jammie ride!" from the bottom of the stairs and have them all run downstairs in their pajamas. I carried each of them into the car, and they had the unexpected adventure of riding in their pajamas to wherever we were going. Once they got over the initial shock of their dad yelling, "Jammie ride!" while they were supposed to be going to sleep, they thought it was a blast. We have done this on occasion, and even now, with older children, they still enjoy a good jammie ride. I've seen high schoolers, after getting the secret word of a jammie ride for the younger kids, go get their pajamas on early so they can fully participate, sometimes even asking me to carry them to the van.

Mary and Joseph's Journey: Most families have unique family traditions around various holidays. One of our favorite traditions involves a manger scene we've had our entire married life. When we put it out, we actually tend to have the stable empty, because before Christmas the shepherds would have been in the fields, Mary and Joseph would have been in Nazareth, and the wise men were somewhere far away in the East. Then, starting from the opposite side of the house, each night Mary and Joseph "move" a little closer to the stable as they journey to Bethlehem. We time it such that they arrive in the stable on Christmas Eve, and then baby Jesus appears, with the shepherds, on Christmas morning. Once Jesus is born, the wise men start their journey. We have observed the children through the years "plan" the trip for Mary and Joseph (including "camping" in the forest as they pass under the Christmas tree). Our particular manger scene has a removable baby Jesus, so the youngest children of the family have always enjoyed hurrying downstairs on Christmas morning to see the baby finally in the manger and then excitedly telling every family member, "Baby Jesus is born! He's in the manger!"

Driving around the Christmas Tree: Perhaps one of our favorite family culture activities is one of our most odd. This happened spontaneously one year, then became an unbreakable tradition. Each year during the Christmas season, we all pile into our fifteen-passenger van and drive to a nearby town that has a large, decorated Christmas tree in the center of town, right in the middle of a fairly large traffic circle. We then drive again and again around the traffic circle while loudly playing "March of the Kings" by Bizet over the car speakers, which builds up to an exciting climax at the end (and we speed up at the end as well). Depending on when the song starts, we might go fifteen times around the circle before it's all over. To many of you this might sound odd, but to the Raquets, it's practically a sacred (and very well-loved) ritual.

Made-Up Songs and Cheers: When our children were all in the ten-and-under age group, we frequently made up silly songs or cheers about everyday activities. Sometimes these were recycled tunes from other songs, and sometimes they were original melodies. "The Silly Goose Bedtime Parade," or the diaper-changing version "The Silly Goose Diaper Parade," were songs made up to make the journey up the stairs with a toddler more enjoyable.

It's the silly goose bedtime parade!

We're marching all around; we're having a good day.

It's the silly goose bedtime parade!

We're coming to your town; we're having a parade.

Simple, silly stuff, sure, but it made going up the stairs a fun parade rather than a chore.

We made up songs about lunch foods; songs about tired, cranky babies; songs and a cheer for driving home from grocery shopping[1]; and even a family lullaby, which always seemed effective in calming sad babies. Music can calm and cheer and add a spring to your step, and it did a lot to encourage my (Cindy's) heart when I was wearying in well doing. So, feel free to sing—it may become a family tradition!

Ice Cream: I (John) grew up in a family where there were specific "rules" for ice cream:

Rule 1: If you are scooping ice cream and someone else hears you, they yell from wherever they are, "I'll have one small scoop for man!" (as in Neil Armstrong's, "One small step for man"). When the person scooping hears this, they must scoop for whoever else requests it.

Rule 2: If you successfully get a bowl of ice cream scooped and no one heard you, then you loudly slam the freezer door shut, to let everyone know that you got away with it. At that point, they have to scoop their own.

When we were getting married, at the rehearsal dinner Cindy was ceremoniously given a "silent ice cream scoop" so that she could survive in our family. While we haven't kept up the same tradition, ice cream is still an important part of our family culture. Our main tradition concerning

---

1 The "Grocery Brigade Cheer" was something John and the children would deliver over the phone as they drove home from the grocery store: "Vegetables, diapers, and shampoo/Eggs and milk and ice cream too!/If you need food, we'll come to your aid/ Because we are the Grocery Brigade!" Family songs and cheers obviously don't need to be serious or profound to become a strong family tradition!

ice cream is that at the end of some dinners the children will try to come up with reasons why we should have ice cream, and sometimes I say yes and sometimes I say no (depending on how good the reason is). However, if Cindy bats her eyelashes at me (literally), then I always give in (and the children know this).

A few things to note about the activities listed above:

1. They are essentially free.
2. They take little to no preparation.
3. They involve everyday objects and common family activities.
4. They are easy and fun to do.

What things would you like to build into your family culture? Look for opportunities to develop these kinds of activities or "ways of doing things" that can help you build a strong and enduring family culture.

Discussion Questions

1. Which of the bulleted "reasons to have a strong family identity" given at the beginning of this chapter are most important to you and why?
2. Is it a common experience for you to do something as a family that everyone really enjoys—where people say something like, "That was really fun"? How many activities like this can you think of from the past month?
3. List activities or characteristics specific to your family—what makes your family unique? If your children are old enough, ask them, "What do you think makes our family special?" and "What things would you miss if you had to leave our family?" (Feel free to adjust these questions based on the age and maturity of your children—it may not be the wisest thing to ask some four-year-olds an abstract question about leaving your family.)
4. If you would like to build a stronger family culture, brainstorm two or three things you can do to improve this. Be creative. Think in terms of things that are inexpensive or free, are easy to do, and don't take

a lot of planning or time. If it's too hard or too complicated, you're unlikely to actually do it! If possible, plan when you are going to do these things over the next few weeks, and give it a shot.

Chapter 21

Whining

Whiners usually play alone.

– Cynthia Lewis

We don't think there is an existing parent who has not periodically struggled with their child whining. That being said, parents can have a significant impact in terms of how much their child whines. As in many aspects of parenting, however, reducing whining requires more of a change in us and how we parent than a change in our children.

Why do children whine? Our opinion is that children whine primarily because it is effective. They have learned over time that when they whine, they get their way more than when they don't whine. It really is as simple as that.

Some of you who are reading this may not believe this and attribute whining to being tired, to their personality, or to other things. We would challenge you to pay attention the next time your child whines, and observe whether they get what they want or not. You may be surprised how often whining does work, even though that's not your intent as a parent.

How is whining effective? One way is that it gets the parent's attention. If a child starts whining, their parent's attention is often drawn from whatever they were doing to the child. This may be because the child doesn't have any other effective way to get the parent's attention. Parents frequently try to do two or three things at once, and the calm voice of a non-whiny child may not ever get noticed; whining has a way of diverting the parent's attention to the child. This is particularly true in public environments, such as at a store, in a restaurant, or on an airplane, where parents are highly motivated to stop their children from whining to avoid embarrassment.

Another way whining is effective is when parents capitulate and give the children what they want. For example, consider a child in a grocery cart who sees some candy and asks if they can have some. When the parent says no, the child cranks things up a notch and starts whining about it, perhaps even getting to the point of screaming—which is basically whining at full volume. How the parent responds in this circumstance will show whether they have a short-term or a long-term view. If they have a short-term view, meaning that they are mostly worried about fixing things in the present, they will relent and go ahead and get the candy for the child. This will almost certainly cause the whining to cease, and the problem seems to be solved—that is, until the next time the child is in the store and is even more emboldened to whine again, since it worked last time. But if the parent has the long-term view, they will put up with the short-term annoyance of a whiny child and not give in to the request.

How to Prevent Whining

So then, how can a parent keep their child from whining? We and many other parents have found that this can best be done by following one simple rule: *Never, ever give in to whining.*

We need to do everything we can to ensure that whining is simply not effective from the child's viewpoint. This includes not giving them what they are whining about but also not allowing their whining to draw our attention to the issue they are whining about (even if we don't give them what they are requesting). Of course, this is much easier said than done, because it requires lots of intentionality and consistency, especially at times when our focus is directed elsewhere from our child.

If whining is not effective, then the child will generally stop whining, or at least it will become a rare occurrence. The hard part here is consistency. If whining is effective only 10 percent of the time, the child will still whine, because it is *sometimes* effective. It's only when it is really made 100 percent (or at least 99.9 percent) ineffective that significant progress can be made.

How to Respond to Whining

So you have decided you want to nip whining in the bud and no longer want to allow it to be effective. Your child begins to whine about something. What do you do at that point? There is no one-size-fits-all response, but here are some potentially good responses, depending on the situation.

Verbally correct the child. If a child begins to whine, rather than respond directly to the issue at hand, it is often much better to verbally tell the child that they should not whine. By doing this, you are in effect changing the subject from whatever they were whining about to the fact that they are whining. The important thing here is to verbally correct their whining but do nothing that addresses what they are whining about. If a child starts whining that they want to go outside, it does no good to tell them that they need to stop whining, but when they do, we let them outside. Children are very savvy about these kinds of things, and they will quickly realize that there is now a new intermediate step in the process, where they stop whining and then the parent gives them what they were originally whining about. When you verbally correct them, treat their whining as a serious matter to be addressed.

Ignore the child who is whining. Sometimes, rather than addressing the child and verbally correcting them, it may be best to simply ignore their whining altogether. This can work well if several children are vying for your attention. Ignoring the one who is whining may be the best course of action and may help correct the problem, reinforcing that whining is ineffective.

"Mommy doesn't hear you when you whine." A child may have a valid request, such as being thirsty, in which case verbally correcting them or ignoring them may not be the best course of action. We discovered a modified form of ignoring them in which we make it well known that we cannot listen to whining, and that Mommy (or Daddy) "won't hear you when you are whining." We simply can't respond in any way until they stop whining and ask a question in a normal tone of voice. Normally, this requires some encouragement along these lines, and it can be helpful if an older sibling or the other parent can come along and coach them about "how to talk so Mommy can hear you." When we have done this, it was not meant to be deceptive, and we usually say it with a smile—more like it's a game we're playing, not that Mommy really can't physically hear them when they're whining.

Enforce a "You can't get whatever you're whining for" rule. This is one of our favorites, and it works better with slightly older children (perhaps age four and up). The idea is to talk ahead of time and have a well-known family rule that says that if you are whining about something, then you are prohibited from getting whatever it is that you are whining for. It's like the law of the Medes and Persians, which cannot be revoked, even by the king who made the law. We treat it as though our hands are tied—when they whine, we have no choice but to make sure that they don't get what they were whining about. Then, when whining happens about some particular issue, everything stops, and the parent says, "I just heard some whining. I need to know what you were whining about because I can't give it to you." This actually makes whining counterproductive, not just ineffective. Occasionally I (Cindy) have heard a whiny voice in another room and have run into the room to ask what the whining was about—since I needed to know what it was they couldn't get because they were whining about it. It's amazing how quickly whining tends to stop when this is the result. This can be said with a smile on your face and cheerfulness in your voice but with steely resolve nonetheless.

Good for the Parents *and* the Children

Having non-whiny children is more enjoyable than having children who whine, so in that sense reducing our child's whininess is beneficial to the parents. However, we believe that the benefits are, in fact, even greater for the child.

At a fundamental level, whining is an outward expression of a heart attitude that says, "I am unhappy because I am not getting what I want." It is reflective of a self-absorbed mindset, which is very natural for children, especially young children. As we work with our children to reduce their whining, we can affect not just their behavior but also the way they think. Allowing our children to whine essentially reinforces their selfish thinking because it shows them that if they are selfish and express that in a certain way (by whining), they can get what they want. If we attempt to stop the whining before it begins, they are not reinforced in this way of thinking. Attempting to reduce our child's whining does not automatically make them unselfish. We believe teaching them not to whine at least encourages them in that direction, especially if we are addressing a heart attitude of selfishness in other ways (e.g., by teaching them to consistently think about how what they are doing impacts others, as described in chapter 11). Put another way, we can work all day teaching them to have a generous and unselfish heart, but if we allow them to whine, we can end up undoing much of this instruction. There is a connection between what we are thinking in our hearts and what we say. Jesus Himself said, "Out of the abundance of the heart the mouth speaks" (Matthew 12:34).

One of our older children mentioned that training children not to whine has benefits even into adulthood for the child. Every adult is faced with numerous situations where their current circumstances aren't what they would most enjoy or appreciate. Being taught not to whine as a child helps them prepare for adulthood as they practice good habits of heart training and accurate thinking. Rather than complaining (an adult form of whining), they learn to recognize that a sovereign, benevolent God is orchestrating the steps of their life, for their good and His glory, and to whine is to complain against Him. They can respectfully call out to God for help to understand their circumstances and for grace to bear up under them, but they are less tempted to rebelliously whine about them in their heart. Of course, none of us does this perfectly, even if we were trained not to whine as a child, but our battle against having a complaining attitude can be made less difficult with good habits of heart maintenance.

Compassion, Not Judgment

Let's say that you read this chapter, realize you have actually been encouraging whining in the way you interact with your children, and over time, you make changes that help to significantly reduce whining in your children and are delighted in the results. However, you head to the store one day and notice other people's children who are really whiny. In such a case, remember what we mentioned in chapter 16. If we are not careful, we can end up with a judgmental attitude that looks down on other parents, forgetting that we were in the same spot at one point in time. As parents, we should make a concerted effort to guard our own hearts and to think in terms of compassion rather than judgment for a fellow parent who is struggling with his or her children. It's important for us to realize that, especially with strangers, we don't know the full story and shouldn't take pleasure in comparing our children with other people's children in the area of whining (or any other area, for that matter). They may be having a bad day, they may have an unsupportive spouse, they may have never seen good examples of parenting, or they may simply have never thought through the issue. In areas where we have seen progress in training our children (especially externally visible things like whining), let us not think we are so wise, but let us consider instead our gratefulness to God for His help and progress in this area of our parenting.

Discussion Questions

1. How well do you notice whining when it is happening in your children? As a first step, spend a few days simply attempting to notice when whining is occurring. You may be surprised how common it is and that you normally don't consciously notice it.

2. How have you attempted to correct whining in the past? Has it been effective?

3. In what situations do you struggle most with your children whining? How can you proactively attempt to reduce the whining in those situations?

4. Whining is one outworking of a self-oriented heart. What are other outworkings of a selfish heart? To what extent are the approaches to reduce whining described in this chapter extendable to address other outworkings of selfish hearts in your children?

Chapter 22

Protecting Our Children

> It would be better for him if a millstone were hung around his neck and he were cast into the sea than that he should cause one of these little ones to sin.
>
> – Luke 17:2

How much should we protect our children? This question continually comes to mind from the day our child is born onward, and the answer constantly changes as our children grow and mature. It is often challenging to figure out how much we should protect our children in any specific situation. This chapter will provide some principles you can use to guide your thinking in a variety of circumstances.

Parents Are the Primary Protectors

Parents have the primary responsibility for protecting their children. Think about it—no one else in the world has your child's interests in mind more than you, the parent. Parents should be providing a protected environment in which a child can grow and mature in a healthy manner. This includes not just physical protections, such as buckling children in car seats and storing medicine in a safe place, but also protection from inappropriate emotional burdens, bad influences, and false or dangerous ideas.

When parental protection breaks down, a child is left in a vulnerable situation. This is why orphans are particularly emphasized in Scripture as those who need protection; they lack the normal, primary mode of protection—parents. Others in society also have a role in the protection of children, such as other adult family members, teachers, police, or social workers, but a child's parents are most responsible for protecting their child.

But stating that you are the primary protector of your children does not mean that you must always protect them from everything. There is a need to teach children how to deal with the things they will face as they mature into adults, which leads us to the second principle.

Have an "Arrows Sent Out" Mindset

Consider the following verse: "Like arrows in the hand of a warrior are the children of one's youth" (Psalm 127:4). A warrior's arrows are made for sending out, not for simply staying put in the quiver. In a similar way, our children were not placed in our family for the purpose of staying there forever but to be sent out as adults to make their own mark on the world. In the big picture, a parent's job is to prepare their "arrows" to be eventually launched into the world, not to remain forever in our household "quiver."

Maintaining an "arrows sent out" mindset is very helpful when figuring out how much and when we should protect our children. It also can help us in other aspects of parenting. As we teach and train our children, what are we teaching and training them for? To be sent out! Our ultimate goal is not to protect them but to send them out. Keeping this goal in mind is an important way to have the right attitude toward our children throughout the entire parenting process. This brings us to the third principle to consider.

It's a Matter of *When*, Not *If*

At the point that a child is no longer living in their parents' home, the parents' role of directly protecting their child is more or less finished. For better or worse, the child is now living on their own, no longer under the direct protection of their parents.

As we think about whether we should protect our children from something, the question is really not *if* we should protect them but *when* we should stop protecting them and what we need to do to help them get to that point. As an example, consider the use of sharp knives. A two-year-old simply does not have the maturity to use sharp kitchen knives. However, at some point, probably somewhere between the ages of five and ten, with proper training and supervision a child can learn to use a kitchen knife well for some purposes. It would be strange and dangerous to give a sharp kitchen knife to a two-year-old. It would also be strange to be "protecting" a sixteen-year-old by not letting them use sharp kitchen knives. At some point they will need to learn to use them, and simply keeping knives out of their hands for their entire time in our home isn't appropriate.

Now, let's consider something perhaps even more dangerous but less visibly evident—ungodly worldviews. As an illustration, consider the viewpoint taught in Scripture that God exists and is the Creator of all things. In contrast, many in our society believe that there is no God and that everything that exists came to be through unguided natural processes. If we are wise parents, we will want to make sure that by the time they leave our home, our children have not only been taught the truth of God as Creator but we've also exposed them to things other people believe and worked through why we believe what we do. However, just like with the knife, the timing of when we do this is crucial. It would not be wise to put our very young children, before they are mature enough to know how to handle that kind of information, in an environment where the predominant attitude and teaching is that there is no God and that everything happened by natural processes. It's a matter of *when*, not *if*.

Young children do not think like adults—they tend to take everything they hear at face value, and they lack mature critical thinking skills. We do need to help them develop those, but the best way to do this is to work with them and give them time to mature, not to expose them to lots of false ideas before they have the ability to critically evaluate what is being said.

Overprotection

Recognize that, whether we are talking about physical dangers or worldview dangers, we can be overprotective as well. In terms of physical danger, when children play outside or participate in any kind of sport, there are always elements of risk. Sometimes they may do something somewhat risky, and it may go well or poorly. We don't want to protect our children to the point that they never suffer a skinned knee or a bruised elbow. Growing in resilience and courage does require learning to take reasonable risks.

An example of worldview overprotection, obviously dealing with older children, would be not exposing them to other points of view at an age -appropriate time, before they leave our nest. We have met some Christian college students who were shaken to the core when they realized for the first time there were competing ideas to what they had been taught and that they had never been taught how to evaluate these competing world-views. We think this kind of exposure is something that should be done more in the teen years rather than at younger ages.

Dealing with Trials and Grief

Sometimes parents think they need to insulate their children from any negative emotions or sadness. While we certainly would not want to burden young children with situations or information they are not mature enough to handle, we have found that it has been beneficial for our children to be brought into some of the griefs and sadness we were experiencing.

Take, for example, a miscarriage. Some parents who have gone through an early miscarriage make the decision to hide all of that from their children, and there is nothing overtly wrong or sinful about doing that. However, we have found that children handle that kind of sadness in a very different way than parents do. We went through a number of early miscarriages and, of course, were very sad and emotional when each happened. We decided to tell our children about them in an age-appropriate way, saying that a baby had started to grow in Mommy's tummy, but the baby died, and Mommy and Daddy were sad about that. Our children's reaction to that was often to look a little bit sad but then go off and play, not bearing the full weight of it all the time, like we were.

We believe there were several benefits of taking this approach. First of all, children tend to have a sense of the emotional state of their parents, and they saw us sad but knew the reason why, so they didn't have to wonder and come up with their own ideas about why we might be sad. Also, they were able to practice showing compassion for those who are sad, as they would do what they could to encourage us. For example, we had one daughter give Cindy one of her teddy bears after a miscarriage because she knew Mommy was sad and needed it more than she did. This was a precious interaction and meant quite a bit to both our daughter and to Cindy. We would not have wanted to prevent that opportunity for our child to selflessly sacrifice something precious to her to try to encourage her mother. Another benefit of being open with our children about grief is that we were able to demonstrate to them that sometimes people are sad but God is faithful and loves and cares for His people, even when they are sad. We had a sense that directly and openly dealing with grief with our children was a healthy way to teach them how to navigate times of sadness or grief.

Times of grief will come that you will be unable to avoid exposing your children to anyway, like the death of a grandparent, sibling, or other family member. We experienced a midterm loss of a baby, which was very unexpected and difficult for us. Looking back, we would not have wanted to "protect" our children from that season of grieving and sadness because God clearly used so many things from that time to work in the hearts of our children. Some of them mention today how they considered the realities of life and death and their own sin problem more seriously because of that loss. They also valued their next baby brother as more precious, recognizing the gift they had been given, no matter how much extra work he might have added to the family. The example of our church family coming around us and ministering to our needs during those first few weeks was also a powerful testimony to them of God's tangible care through His obedient people.

Of course, you should use your judgment about how much of your emotional struggles or griefs you want to share with your children. If you do decide to talk with them about these things, try to be straightforward and speak in a way that is appropriate for their age.

By the way, because children tend to be direct and straightforward, they sometimes respond to other people's grief in a more helpful way than adults do. We remember that after our first miscarriage, before we had had any children, we were understandably sad. Many of the adults we knew weren't really sure what to say, so they just tended to avoid the subject. However, one little girl came up and simply said, "I'm sad that your baby died." That was one of the most comfortable and encouraging responses we received from anyone during that whole process.

I (Cindy) had seasons of struggling with postpartum depression and sadness related to some health issues I was struggling with. It was challenging as a mother feeling like I was a negative influence in the lives of my children and husband, as if I were a dark cloud in their world. I would have loved to hide these emotions from the children, but I just couldn't. John often encouraged me that it was actually good for our children to see me go through times of sadness and depression and not be a "supermom" in their eyes, who never had trials or discouragement. He would encourage me that they would certainly have sickness and challenges themselves in their adult years and as potential parents ("These things I have spoken to you, so that in Me you may have peace. In the world you have tribulation, but take courage; I have overcome the world" [John 16:33 NASB]), but that it would be helpful for them to remember that we did, too, and looked to Christ, did not give up, and continued to take baby steps of faithfulness in our roles as their parents, even during struggles with sadness and health.

Worldview Influences

When it comes to protecting our children from bad influences in books and movies, many parents are concerned about things like avoiding bad words and activities that they disapprove of, like smoking. While it is probably good to think about these kinds of things, more insidious matters are often present in movies and books, including attitudes and worldviews. We would encourage you to consider the underlying attitudes when evaluating whether a movie or book is okay for your children to watch or read and not just focus on avoiding a list of words or activities.

For instance, many books and movies may not contain swear words or overtly bad activities like violence or bullying but instead portray a situation in which the children in the story are the ones who have the most accurate picture of reality and save the day, in contrast to the adults who are all basically bumbling idiots. We would suggest there is potentially greater harm done to the heart of a child by watching such a movie than one in which there may be a few objectionable elements but in which the underlying attitudes are wholesome and true.

Another example would be avoiding a movie or book because there are bad people in it. The most important question is probably not, "Are there bad people?" but rather, "How are the bad people portrayed?" The Bible is full of bad people, but being sinful or wicked is never portrayed as being a good thing.

Learn to be a student of the attitudes and worldviews that are often behind the scenes in books and movies. You are missing an important aspect of protecting your children if you allow these kinds of things to influence them. Don't focus just on the external—also consider the effect on their hearts. When children are older (probably over age ten), you might be able to have them watch some of these kinds of attitudes or worldviews, but then "shred" the movie afterward and point out the wrong ways of thinking, thereby teaching your children how to critically watch entertainment. For younger children, however, it's probably best just to avoid exposing them to these sorts of things, since younger children don't have the mental ability to think about the abstract concepts involved.

Protecting from Abuse

Sadly, this chapter would not be complete if we didn't cover the need to protect our children from all forms of abuse, especially sexual abuse. Sex is a wonderful, God-designed gift, but sin has grievously distorted it in a diversity of ways. In particular, the prevalence of pornography in our society has changed how men and women think about each other and has probably been a factor in most instances of sexual abuse. We implore you not to be naïve about potential harm that can come to your child if you put them in dangerous or compromising situations. Here are some things that we encourage you to consider.

We recommend carefully considering the risks of leaving your child alone in the presence of any other adult, particularly men. Many abuse situations have occurred involving a friend or relative known and trusted by the parents. Even if you fully trust someone, we still recommend that you avoid placing your children in a position where they could be vulnerable. When we first began employing babysitters, we used a few young men we knew and trusted from our church. While we don't know of any dangers our children were exposed to during those times with our friends, after several years and having heard too many horror stories of others, we decided that, as a policy, we were not going to do that anymore. From then on, we stuck with female babysitters only. While using only female babysitters may reduce the risk, it does not eliminate it, and wisdom is still required.

We also recommend teaching your children what is and isn't appropriate in terms of how other people relate to them. We found a book that was helpful along these lines called *The Swimsuit Lesson* by Holston and Freeman. This book suggests having your children go change into their swimsuits before coming to listen to you read this story, and then explains to them that areas that are covered up by swimsuits are special areas that shouldn't be touched by other people. We also made a point to tell our children that if someone were to touch them there or do anything that made them at all uncomfortable, they definitely should tell us about it and that they weren't going to be in trouble in any way. We recommend that you discuss this with your children and make sure that they have an age-appropriate understanding of when people are treating them improperly and what to do about it.

Sadly, many people we know who had pornography exposure had it early in their lives. Even for young children, be very wary about access to computers, phones, tablets, and other internet-connected technology. Recognize that they could also get exposure to pornography when visiting other homes. Be vigilant, recognize the dangers out there, and take appropriate precautions plenty early. We would recommend that you use filtering and monitoring software on all your devices. It's hard for us to give specific recommendations because technology changes frequently, so ask other parents or church staff for their current suggestions.

Wisdom Is Needed

Clearly, protecting our children is a task that requires parenting wisdom with many judgment calls to be made. Our children are continually growing, and the decisions about what to protect them from need to change as our children mature. You are the only parents of your children, so stand firm and make the decisions you think are best for them.

Finally, it's good to recognize that we ultimately cannot and should not protect our children from every potential danger. We do what we can, but in the end, we must recognize that we do not have the ability to prevent absolutely every bad thing that could happen to our children. All of life involves some element of risk, and we should seek to live life wisely, ultimately trusting in our Lord to protect us and our children from harm and to be with us and our children when we go through providentially ordained trials.

Discussion Questions

1. Describe the level of protectiveness in your home growing up. Do you feel like one or the other of your parents was overprotective or underprotective?

2. Looking back on your childhood, are there specific things you wish you had been more protected from? Are there things you wish you were less protected from?

3. Considering your own children, are there areas where you aren't sure how protective you should be? What factors in this chapter would apply for that situation?

4. How did your parents handle times of sadness or grief when you grew up?

5. How have you handled times of sadness or grief with your children? Were you happy with how that went?

6. What criteria do you use when evaluating whether your children can watch a particular movie? Have you ever shown something to your children and wished later that you didn't? Describe that situation and what you would have done differently.

7. Give examples of movies or books that had good attitude or worldview aspects to them. Discuss what was good about them.

Chapter 23

Using a Schedule

> The rich fruit of spontaneity grows in the garden that is well tended by the discipline of schedule.
>
> – John Piper

This chapter has particular relevance for families with more than one child in which one parent stays at home and the family manages numerous priorities (e.g., homeschooling multiple subjects or many outside daytime activities). If this doesn't sound like it applies to you, feel free to skip this chapter.

At several points in our parenting, Cindy was having a hard time managing all the children's activities. There were just too many things going on and too many considerations to be made to be able to "wing it" and keep everyone moving in a positive direction. She was attempting to balance things like nursing a baby, managing the impact of piano practice times, figuring out when to do school with each of our school-age children, having administrative time (scheduling, emails, grocery and menu planning, etc.), and daily chores and cleaning.

It was very frustrating to try to keep all these activities going in an even slightly organized, coherent fashion, and it took an incredible amount of effort just to keep everyone coordinated.

Thankfully, we ran across a helpful book that discussed family scheduling entitled *Managers of Their Homes* by Steven and Teri Maxwell.[1]

---

1 Steven and Teri Maxwell, *Managers of Their Homes: A Practical Guide to Daily Scheduling for Christian Homeschool Families* (Leavenworth, KS: Titus2, 2016). This book has many helpful tips on how to adapt a schedule to suit your family, with several example schedules. If you are intrigued by this topic, the book is worth your reading. The chapter on occupying younger children is particularly valuable.

In it, they discussed an approach to scheduling that we more or less followed to great benefit.

Our process of establishing a schedule was as follows:

1. **Make a list of all the things that need to happen, including who is involved and the amount of time we'd like to spend on it.** Examples: Mom does phonics with Eric (30 min.), Anna practices piano (30 min.), Ellen does math drill (15 min.), everyone eats lunch (30 min.). We found that allocating time in fifteen-minute increments worked about right for our family. I normally did this on a spreadsheet, with the time required recorded in one column per person so that I could easily total the time for each person (see next step). Make sure to include everything that you would need time for, not forgetting things like phone calls, devotions, getting dressed, exercise, and the like.
2. **Add up the time required for each person.** If you have more things to do than time to do it, then this is the point where you know that you must make some prioritization decisions. Are there things you just won't do or perhaps will do for less time than you originally desired? Prayerfully consider how the time for each member of the family would best be used, and adjust the time requirements accordingly. Once everyone has enough hours in the day to do the things that are listed, then you know that, in theory, you should be able to fit everything in.
3. **Make a draft schedule.** This is the fun part (seriously). It's kind of like a gigantic puzzle, where you need to fit a bunch of things together in a way that makes sense. The book we read recommended cutting out pieces of paper and moving them around, but I found that simply creating a table in a word processor worked best for me. We broke the day into fifteen-minute increments and had one column per person. As an alternative, Titus2 (publishers of *Managers of Their Homes*) now offers an online schedule-making program called ScheduleBreeze. It color codes everyone and follows each of the steps explained in the book and is a relatively easy way to make and maintain a family schedule.
4. **Try out the schedule for a couple of days.** No matter how hard you try, there likely will be parts of the schedule that are not workable for one reason or another (e.g., someone is scheduled to

practice the piano at the same time the toddler is supposed to nap in an adjoining room).

5. **Adjust the schedule as needed to work out the kinks.** Shift things around until it seems to be working.

We found that the most important period of the day for us to have a schedule was from getting up in the morning through dinnertime. Evening activities in our family tend to vary quite a bit, so defining a fixed schedule for the evening didn't make as much sense for us. An example schedule is given in appendix 2.

One important point is that the schedule is meant to be a help and not a hindrance. It is a framework for how the day is planned to be spent, not something that must be adhered to at all costs. We all have various interruptions or changes that occur from time to time (e.g., someone calls with a crisis, a child gets sick, Mom is tired and needs to take a rest), and when that happens, schedule adjustments can be made. But we found that having a schedule in place enabled us to adapt to these kinds of interruptions more cheerfully. In reality, what we consider "interruptions" are actually more accurately thought of as "God's plans for this day," as described in Proverbs 16:9, "The mind of man plans his way, but the LORD directs his steps." Rare was the day when we were able to follow the schedule exactly as written. Nevertheless, if there was a providential interruption to our plan for the day, we could just pick the schedule up again at whatever point made sense.

Recognize, too, that a family schedule is not permanent. It can be changed or rescinded as you see fit. For our family, we find that it typically needs to be updated on an annual basis (or a month or so after the birth of a new baby).

We have been making family schedules for about twenty years now, and while the details have changed over time as our family has grown and our children have gotten older, we still have seen many tangible benefits of this approach:

- **It enables a conscious prioritization of our time.** The act of writing down the ways we would like to spend our day and consciously making tradeoffs ensures that we are doing this intentionally and with some careful thought. If we go through each moment of each day just doing what seems best at the time, we may not make the best decisions.

- **It significantly reduces the amount of thinking required to keep the household running well.** By developing the schedule ahead of time, everyone knows what they should be doing at any given time, and it is not up to Mom or Dad to constantly be directing them or having to make real-time decisions for each member of the family, while simultaneously tracking what the rest of the family is doing, which can be overwhelming.
- **For young children especially, a schedule can enable much greater contentedness.** Without a schedule, what normally happens (at least in our home) with young children is that they will do something for a while until they get bored, at which point they will be clamoring for something else to do. We found that if we used the schedule to proactively have them switch activities every thirty to forty-five minutes, they were much more content, rarely complaining about what they were doing or asking to do something different. The schedule provided a pacing and level of predictability in which they thrived that would not be there otherwise.

Should You Make a Family Schedule?

While there are many potential benefits of a schedule like we have described, this approach may not be for everyone. By personality, some people like to follow a schedule better than others. Also, the need for a detailed family schedule varies depending on the number and ages of your children. The more people living and interacting together, the higher the potential benefit of a schedule.

Nowhere in Scripture is the command, "Thou shalt have a detailed family schedule." Like many ideas in this book, this is something that you can consider and adapt to your family situation in whatever way seems most appropriate.

Discussion Questions

1. Has there ever been a time in your life where your time was scheduled out to a high level of detail (e.g., summer camp, a retreat, military training)? Was the schedule in these instances a comfort or an annoyance to you? Why?

2. Do you feel like you generally are able to spend your time wisely? Are your children under your care spending their time wisely? Would going through the process of consciously prioritizing your time be helpful to you at this stage of your life?

3. How much time and effort do you spend trying to coordinate the activities of your family? What is the most frustrating part of this?

4. If you were to make a schedule, what kind would be the most helpful? A full fifteen-minute, person-by-person schedule like that described in this chapter? Or a more limited schedule dealing with just one or two of the more challenging-to-schedule parts of your day?

Chapter 24

Sitting Still

> A man without self-control is like a city broken into and left without walls.
>
> – Proverbs 25:28

One of the most frustrating situations for a parent is when your young child is making disruptive noise or commotion in a church service, musical concert, recital, wedding, or funeral. The time to work on teaching this, though, is generally not during the event itself. We found that training our children ahead of time to sit quietly was essential to reducing the stress and tension of being at a public event with young children.

How Can You Train for This?

From a young child's perspective, these kinds of events are essentially boring situations where they must sit still with nothing to do. To replicate a similarly dull situation in which to practice, we decided to train our children to sit on our laps in a boring location—in our living room with nothing at all happening in the room (or perhaps listening to a sermon recording or podcast). We would do this at times when the children were well rested and not cranky, to make it as easy as possible for them to respond well to the training. For very young (pre-talking) children, we would simply place them on our lap, put our arms around them, and sit there. If they started squirming or whining or even screaming, we would calmly but firmly hold them and tell them they needed to sit still and be quiet. If the child rebelliously resisted this, we would sometimes have to discipline them, but most of the time, simply talking to them and physically restraining them would do the trick. At first we would start with just a few minutes, but over time they learned how to sit still and remain quiet, and we could practice for longer and longer periods. Once they had the concept, nighttime reading (see chapter 19) became a good time to regularly practice this. When we then found ourselves in a situation like a church service, we could hold the young child on our lap in the same way, and the child would understand that this was a time to be quiet and still. We don't think our young children would have learned to sit still if we only gave negative correction in the heat of the moment.

What about Older Children?

Older children—maybe three- to seven-year-olds—would practice sitting quietly during the nighttime reading by sitting on chairs with their hands in their laps. We called this "self-control practice" and found this practice necessary at times to stay current with this vital skill. If we had recently practiced, both they and we knew they were perfectly capable of sitting in a non-distracting way out of respect for those around them. Once they had the basic concept instilled within them, we would talk with them on the way to the event about the need to sit still and why this was important.

When Can You Do This?

This kind of training is only effective when the child has reached a certain stage of development. A newborn clearly cannot understand what it means to be still and quiet in this way. For each of our children, there was a challenging time, usually before the age of one (we don't recall their exact ages, and each child was different) when they still didn't seem to understand this concept and were quite capable of making significant disruptive noise. It seems there was always a phase for each baby when a quiet room was an unavoidable temptation to try out their voice with cute little squeals and sounds, and no amount of training at home worked because of the incredible attraction to test the echo in a large church sanctuary or concert hall. During this short period, we usually had to simply remove them from the public setting so as not to be disruptive to others around us. However, somewhere between ages one and two, they developed the ability to learn to sit quietly on our laps through training at home.

Distract or Train?

Many parents attempt to deal with the challenge of having children be quiet in a public event by providing some kind of distraction for the child (toys, coloring books, etc.). While occasionally providing distractions is necessary and appropriate, we feel that this is not a good long-term strategy, especially as children get older. It is one thing to provide a chew toy to a teething baby but quite another for an older child to routinely require some distraction in order to be entertained during an event. We have experienced this challenge ourselves. When we tried bringing quiet toys and coloring books to an event like a church service, the toys provided something to be fought over or dropped and lost, causing an outburst of sadness—exactly the opposite outcome of our purpose for bringing the toys! Additionally, we want the children to learn to participate in the event, and simply providing distractions does not move them in that direction. If the child's expectation is that they need something to distract them to "make it through" such an event, we are setting them up for a struggle to pay attention in the long run.

What about Nursery?

While we believe there are many benefits to teaching your young child to sit quietly, having a nursery available can be a great benefit to parents (especially mothers), as it enables them to be able to focus completely on the church service or event and have a break from training young children. This is an area where parents should feel free to decide what is best for their family. Even if a child regularly stays in a nursery at a young age, this does not prohibit you from working with your child on the skill of sitting still at home, and this training can be of great benefit for the time when the child transitions out of a nursery.

Benefits to the Parent and the Child

We recognize that doing this kind of training takes significant time and effort. However, working hard to proactively train our children to sit quietly at an event has been a great blessing to our family. It has significantly reduced the stress of attending these kinds of events and removed a major point of frustration in parenting. For the child, developing this form of self-control is a necessary and valuable part of growing up. Additionally, we were able to take them to events such as symphony concerts and other special occasions without concern that they would be a distraction to others. Had we not taken the time to train them along these lines, we probably would have simply avoided going to these events, and they would have lost out on such opportunities. Just the reduction in stress for the mom or dad alone makes this a worthwhile expenditure of time and effort. It is extremely stressful to attend something important, like a wedding or funeral, and spend your time focused on distracting your child rather than observing the occasion.

We Are All Works in Progress

Some of you may be thinking, "Yes, this sounds great, but there is *no way* my child could learn this kind of self-control right now." Among our eight children, some developed this skill much more quickly than others. A few were downright tricky and persistent and took significantly more training to be able to sit and not distract others. However, we maintain that this is a necessary life skill and particularly important to learn for those who struggle with it. We have not regretted persevering in this area with our more challenging sitters or determined rebels. While the training period can seem long and endless, in retrospect, it wasn't excessively long and yielded years of pleasant public event attendance with our young child.

Finally, remember to be gracious to other parents in this area, as we have mentioned before. God has appointed you as parents to have primary responsibility for *your own* children. Other parents who struggle with unruly children in a public environment should be viewed with compassion and not judgment.

Discussion Questions

1. When you consider bringing your child or children into a public event, what thoughts or feelings do you have?
2. What things have you tried so far to help your children be able to sit quietly at public events? Have these been effective?
3. If you had confidence that your child would behave appropriately at a public event, what, if anything, would change in the way you operate as a family?
4. Is the idea of proactively training your child to sit in a long public event something that makes sense for your family right now?

Chapter 25

Mealtimes

> You know you're a mom when...you understand why momma bear's porridge was cold.
>
> – Unknown

For many, the logistics of preparing and eating a meal together can be challenging. Even when families do eat at the same time, distractions like TV or texting keep people from having a normal, face-to-face conversation. But we believe that the discussion around the dinner table (or lunch or breakfast table) can be valuable for the whole family. It's an opportunity for (1) parents to catch up with each other and discuss the events of the day or to plan the next day, (2) to find out how everyone's day went and to process together anything noteworthy that happened, good or bad, and (3) to talk together about what is going on in the world outside of the home.

These kinds of conversations have great value for children as they observe and learn how to think about these topics. Even for babies and toddlers who aren't talking yet and can't participate in the conversation, mealtimes provide an opportunity for them to observe the natural give-and-take of conversation. Much of what children learn is what they absorb rather than what is directly taught to them, and this is particularly true around the dinner table, as children observe how their older siblings and parents handle real-life situations, how they think about things outside the home, and how they talk about other people. None of this happens if the meal consists of everyone sitting in the same room jointly watching whatever is on television or interacting with other electronic devices.

We have found that having regular meals together gets more challenging as the children get older and our schedule involves more out-of-the-house activities. Nonetheless, the times when we *can* eat together are precious. It is important to have realistic expectations here. Not every meal ends up with a deep theological, political, scientific, or philosophical discussion. Many conversations are about everyday topics, which are important too. However, now and again, weighty topics suddenly pop out during a meal discussion. For example, one evening a spontaneous comment about an older member of our church led to an in-depth discussion about the challenges people face as they age. This opened the eyes of several of the children to an issue they'd not thought about in that way and gave them the others-oriented, "what it's like to walk in their shoes" perspective in a helpful and comfortable context.

So, take advantage of mealtimes. Don't be afraid to talk together about things that don't directly involve the children. They benefit by hearing these kinds of discussions, and you benefit by having them.

Guess Who's Coming to Dinner?

Having visitors share a meal with you can be a particularly enriching time, especially for the children. Whether it's a visitor from a foreign culture or the neighbor next door, everyone has a story to tell about their life experiences, and we have found that this depth of communication seems to happen most naturally toward the end of a shared dinner. We have heard the most amazing stories and learned so much as we have invited acquaintances to dinner and simply asked about their lives. Our children have many fond memories of guests John has brought home who were work associates from out of town and, frequently, from out of our country or culture. Having "eyewitnesses" from all over the world makes the places and events we read about in books come alive.

It's Not Always Easy

Mealtimes can be one of the most challenging times for parenting, especially with young children. Many things are happening all at once during a meal, and competing factors work against some of your expectations for a quiet, enjoyable mealtime:

- **Desire for communication.** Meals, especially supper, are times when everyone is together and there is a desire for conversation between various members of the family. However, this requires an understanding by all concerned about how to participate in a group conversation (as opposed to one-on-one). A significant portion of the communication that happens at meals may not involve younger children.

- **Lots of direction given.** During meals, various instructions or commands will be given, especially when teaching a young child how to eat their food and how not to throw their food on the ground.
- **Lots of potential for disobedience.** More expectations of behavior occur during meals than in other contexts (e.g., how to eat, how much to eat of what, not playing with food or throwing it on the ground). As a result, there is greater potential for disobedience or rebellion during a meal than at other times.
- **Tiredness.** Depending on nap schedules and the time of the meal, mealtime can often be at a time when a child is feeling tired and, of course, hungry. This doesn't always lend itself to the most pleasant of interactions.
- **Desire to feed your family well.** Among all the other things going on during a meal, parents also have a desire to provide healthy food for family members. So, what children eat and how much they eat is of interest.
- **Fighting against picky eating.** The mealtime is when we deal with the pesky issue of trying to have children eat what is put in front of them rather than become picky eaters.
- **Presence of visitors.** Even though having visitors at meals can be a rewarding experience, it can increase the intensity and stress of almost all the other factors described above.

So, as you can see, mealtimes have the potential to be some of the most stressful times of the day. But we can reduce mealtime stress and take full advantage of the valuable time we spend eating together by doing just a few things.

The Battle over Food

At family meals, we attempt to have our children eat the good food put before them, but they often realize that it's pretty easy for them to refuse to eat something. If we are not careful, meals can start to feel like a battle of wills.

No parent really wants mealtimes to become a battle over food. But how do we prevent this? One option would be simply not to fight the battle and just give in to what the child would prefer to eat. However, this generally results in creating picky eaters and can prevent children from eating a variety of healthy foods. Besides this, it makes a lot more work for the person preparing the meals, who now must become a short-order cook and prepare custom meals for individual members of the family.

Over time, we developed a few simple rules that seemed to work well for us in terms of balancing the desire to have the children eat what is put before them with the desire to keep mealtimes from being a battle:

1. You must try everything that is on your plate. ("Try" simply means to take one bite.)
2. You may have seconds only after you have finished everything on your plate.
3. If there is dessert, you may have it only if you've finished everything on your plate.

We found that this simple approach took away a lot of the conflict over food. Rather than the parent and the child developing lawyer-like negotiation skills regarding how much they need to eat of this or that, it's now up to the child how much they want to eat. Generally, it's not too hard to get them to take the single bite to meet rule #1. Once that is done, it's completely up to the child as to how much they want to eat of each item on their plate. For example, if you are having peas and French fries and the child doesn't finish the peas but wants more French fries, you simply say, "Yes, you may have more French fries once you have finished your peas. If you don't want to finish your peas, that's okay, but you won't be able to have more French fries. It's completely up to you." At this point, there is no longer a battle going on between the parent and the child. There is, however, a clash going on within the child between the part of him that wants fries and the part that doesn't want to eat peas, but that's potentially a *good* battle!

It has been quite humorous at times to watch the child make the internal calculation about whether it's worth it to choke down whatever it is that they don't like to get what they do. Sometimes they simply decide not to eat the rest of the peas (which is completely fine with us, so that's not a conflict). Other times, though, they decide that more fries *are* worth it, so they go ahead and eat the peas. What has been interesting to us is to observe how they eat the peas (or whatever it is that they don't want). Occasionally, they really do have to struggle to eat the rest because they truly do not like it. But quite often, once they have made the decision, they gobble down the peas without much difficulty. This shows that the desire not to eat the peas was more a desire to exert their will than a true hatred of peas.

Another benefit of this approach that we've observed is the children over time actually start to like the foods they initially didn't care for. Many foods are an acquired taste, and by truly tasting them every meal that they're served (rule #1), they can eventually acquire a liking for them—or at least they no longer hate them.

It is important for parents to be wise about the quantity of servings we give our children when using this approach. If we are serving something to the child that we know they don't like, we won't give them a huge, heaping serving of that item. Rather, we'll give them a relatively small serving (more than one bite, though). This way, we make it easy for them to finish the serving and be able to have more of other things that they do like.

Practical Suggestions for Little Ones

When a child is not yet talking, meals can be particularly challenging. We learned from others two helpful ideas to make this time more pleasant for everyone. First, we taught some simple meal-oriented sign language to our children to enable better communication—things like *please*, *thank you*, *more*, *water*, and *all done*. Some of the fussing that normally happens is simply the child trying to communicate, and giving them some signs to use before they are able to talk can reduce the amount of general fussiness during meals.

Secondly, we taught our children in the spoon-feeding stage to hold on to the sides of the highchair tray when we were feeding them. This kept them from trying to grab the spoon or put their hands in the food and contributed to more sanity during this challenging stage. It also began the process of teaching them overall self-control.

This is even easier if you start off feeding your spoon-fed child by seating them on your lap with you holding their free hand. For example, if you are right-handed, sit with your already-bibbed child on your left leg, with their right arm tucked under your left arm and wrapped around your back. Hold their free hand gently in your left hand. Now you can use your right hand to scoop soft foods onto a baby spoon and offer it to your child, and they don't have a free hand with which to explore the food on the spoon, which would be a natural response. This keeps them from learning that habit of battling the spoon full of food heading toward their mouth.

A Good Ending

Another goal we've had is to have everyone stay at the table until we're all done. Small children generally would prefer to leave as soon as they have finished or lost interest in eating, but if they do that, they will miss out on the conversational benefits previously described. Additionally, remaining at the table is a good way to practice self-control and to show a respect for others. We required our children to ask to be excused, which gave us the opportunity to say no (and possibly to explain why) if everyone was not finished and we wanted them to remain. This is a situation where parents can use their judgment, since there may be contexts in which it makes sense to dismiss younger children earlier than the rest— for example, if they're overly tired, if there are visiting children who want to leave the table or have already left the table, or if the discussion is getting rather long and adult-oriented.

In the spirit of being responsible and seeking to be a blessing to others, we have, at times, encouraged our children to say, "Thank you for the nice meal," to whoever prepared the meal and to take their dishes to the sink. These are the kinds of others-oriented habits we want to encourage in our children (and ourselves).

May God enable your mealtimes to be times of refreshment, conversation, learning, and encouragement!

Discussion Questions

1. In a typical week, how many meals do you eat together as a family? Are you happy with this number?

2. If you would like to eat together more often, list the primary reasons you don't eat together. What could you change in order to address one or more of these reasons? Do these changes fit with your overall priorities?

3. On a scale of 1 to 10, rate the quality of interaction when you do have meals together. Which of the following are hindrances to good communication during your mealtimes?

   a. The meal is so rushed there's not much time to talk.

   b. We're not sure of what to talk about.

   c. We often are watching television or a video while eating.

   d. There are often battles over who eats what and how much.

   e. Everyone is so tired and cranky that communication is difficult.

   Can you think of other hindrances that pop up at your family mealtimes?

4. Identify one or two things you intend to do to improve your mealtime communication over the next few days or weeks.

Chapter 26

Raising Interested Children

> I am proud to have been born in Iowa. Through the eyes of a ten-year-old boy, it was a place of adventure and daily discoveries—the wonder of the growing crops, the excitements of the harvest, the journeys to the woods for nuts and hunting, the joys of snowy winters, the comfort of the family fireside, of good food and tender care.
>
> – Herbert Hoover

The title of this chapter is not a typo—we would like to describe the idea of raising "interested" children, as opposed to interesting children. Here's the difference: An *interesting* child is a child that other people want to listen to or know more about, but an *interested* child is a child who wants to listen to or know more about other people or other things. We wanted to encourage our children to

- be interested in the world around them and, in particular, the people around them.
- be excited about learning new things and meeting new people.
- develop habits of learning new things on their own and to enjoy the process along the way.
- see the connection between the created universe and the Creator and to be interested in the things the Creator has made, because all created things reflect the Creator.
- wonder why things work the way they do and to have a sense of wonder at what God, the ultimate designer, has made.
- enjoy learning things together as a family.

Not everyone values these kinds of things, and that's okay. But if you share some of these desires, this chapter provides some thoughts about how to help our children be interested in the world and people around them.

Be Interested Yourself

Having interested children is almost certainly something that is caught, not taught. If you are consistently interested in the world and the people around you, then your children will likely pick up this perspective as they increasingly interact with the world and people around them. Cindy and I both had parents who themselves were interested in many things as we grew up, and we naturally absorbed this way of thinking. Our desire is that our children would keep this mindset going forward.

What if you are not personally drawn to being interested in learning but you would like your children to be interested? We would encourage you to attempt to grow in this area, perhaps starting with something you do find interesting. Do you like sports? Do you have a hobby? Do you know someone who is fascinating to talk with? Being interested does not mean you need to be interested in anything and everything; what is probably most important is that your children see you being interested in something and see you seeking to learn more about it.

Express Wonder

Psalm 19 starts out with a description about how the created universe points toward the Creator:

> The heavens declare the glory of God,
>   and the sky above proclaims his handiwork.
> Day to day pours out speech,
>   and night to night reveals knowledge.
> There is no speech, nor are there words,
>   whose voice is not heard.
> Their voice goes out through all the earth,
>   and their words to the end of the world.
>
> – Psalm 19:1–4

There is much around us that can inspire wonder, especially when we look at it closely and get a glimpse of the marvelous design of the

Creator. We can also see God's handiwork when we see what people can do, whether it be sports, leadership, art, music, writing, acrobatics, feats of endurance, or any number of activities people can do at a very high level.

When we verbally express wonder or amazement at things like this, our children pick up the cue that there is something interesting here. And if in our expression of wonder we point to the Creator, they start to make that connection as well.

Learn Things Together

Learning something together as a family can be an enjoyable and beneficial experience. This can come in many forms, from taking a course on a new topic to learning a new hobby together.

But learning together doesn't need to be as formal as taking a course. If you are talking with someone, you can learn a lot by just asking good questions about their life or experiences. Even rather common questions like "Where did you grow up?" can be followed up by questions like "What was it like growing up there?" or "What has changed since the time you grew up?"

Having people join you for a meal is a great opportunity to have your children get to ask questions like this of people with unique experiences. As we mentioned in a previous chapter, just by having some out-of-town work associates over for dinner, our children have learned about diverse countries and cultural backgrounds. It is so much more memorable to actually talk to someone from India or Argentina or who farms for a living or who is a medical doctor than to just read about their country or vocation in a textbook.

Avoid an "I Must Be Entertained" Mentality

Learning and being interested is something we do, not something that happens to us. In contrast, entertainment is a more passive activity, usually involving us sitting and watching something.

Though it is sometimes helpful and appropriate to use entertainment of various forms to keep children occupied, it can be tempting to let this become the norm. Entertainment by its very nature is entertaining and is designed to hold people's attention. If someone (adult or child) indulges in lots of entertainment, they can get used to things that easily hold their attention and become bored with things that are potentially interesting but less entertaining (such as reading a book).

We think it is helpful to keep the amount of time children are engaged in entertainment relatively low and, instead, encourage them to go outside, play with toys or games, build something with blocks or Legos, or take part in any number of other engaging activities. Sometimes they just need a little suggestion, such as "Can you draw a picture?" or "Why don't you play with the dress-up clothes?" If children go through life expecting to be continually entertained, it tends to be miserable both for them and for the parents who feel like they need to keep them entertained.

If one of our children came up to us and said, "I'm bored," we would smile and come up with a chore that needed to be done. (Not that chores are bad things—see chapter 9.) The children quickly learned that claiming boredom was interpreted as volunteering to do anything that needed to be done, and not surprisingly, we almost never heard that phrase.

Computers vs. Play

Today's children have access to various electronic devices, including video monitors, computers, and smartphones. We have felt free to severely limit our children's use of these kinds of devices, especially at younger ages. While there is nothing objectively wrong with interacting with the world through electronics, it seems that, in some sense, interacting with the real world is fuller and richer and more "real" than interacting through electronics. The person who is physically with you should have priority over the person at the other end of the smartphone chat. Running around and playing outside and interacting with nature can be a much richer experience than looking at a screen of some kind. There is also increasing evidence that excessive screen time has a negative impact on children.

We would encourage you to decide how much and what kind of electronic entertainment (including social media, for older children) your child should use, based on your parental judgment. Then, manage their use of electronics to match what you have decided. If you don't actively manage this area of your child's life, they may very well become much more hooked on electronics than you want them to be and potentially less interested in the world and people physically around them.

Discussion Questions

1. Are you an interested person (as defined above)? Rate yourself on a scale of 1 to 10, where 1 means you are interested in almost nothing, and 10 means you're interested in everything and everyone. Has that changed over time?
2. If you have children, how would you rate them on the same scale?
3. How important is it to you that your children grow up to be interested people? Are you content with how that is going, or are there things you'd like to change?
4. How much do your children seek out entertainment versus other forms of occupying their time (such as playing, reading, building things)? Are you okay with this balance, or would you like it to change?
5. Now, ask the same question of yourself: How much do *you* seek out entertainment versus other forms of occupying your time? Are you okay with this balance, or would you like it to change?
6. If you have children, how much do you feel pressure that you must keep them entertained?
7. How much and what kind of electronic interaction or entertainment do your children use? Is that acceptable to you, or would you like to make some changes? If you'd like to make changes, discuss how you'd like to go about doing that. Consider whether making changes in your own use of electronic interaction and entertainment should be part of the picture.

Chapter 27

Babies

Babies are such a nice way to start people.

– Don Herold

For most people, the parenting journey begins with a baby, usually with a combination of excitement and apprehension. This chapter is not a comprehensive overview of how to care for a baby but describes a few perspectives we've found helpful to keep in mind in those first several months of parenting babies.

Relax and Enjoy the Ride

When a new baby is born, especially if it is the first child, the whole world changes. There seems to be so much to learn, even in terms of some of the most basic aspects of caring for a baby. It can seem like leaving the house, with just the three of you, can be a major undertaking and require more planning and packing than you could have imagined before the baby was born. Parents who are intentional or intense by nature can often find themselves being extremely concerned about whether they are "doing it right."

A newborn's life consists mostly of eating and sleeping, and after a couple of weeks, some periods of wakefulness are thrown into the mix. During this early stage, the goal is to make sure that the baby is fed and given some good cuddling time with parents, their diaper is changed when needed, and he or she has a safe, comfortable place to sleep and a safe way to ride in the car. That's about it. This is not the time to be worried about whether we should be playing language-learning recordings (should it be Latin or Greek?) or making sure the baby has the ideal stimulation or educational environment.

The first few months in a baby's life are a good time for the whole family to simplify things and just focus on getting through the basics of each day: "But if we have food and clothing, with these we will be content" (1 Timothy 6:8). Even this can be a challenge, particularly if a baby struggles with colic or acid reflux or other conditions that can cause lots of crying or unhappiness.

Parents have around eighteen years to parent their children, and they don't need to figure everything out in the first few months. We would recommend that you, as best you can, try to relax and enjoy the ride with a new baby. In the moment, it can seem like time is really dragging, especially if there is a lack of sleep for parents or child. But this is a relatively short phase in the big picture of life, and it is truly a precious time. Focus on the basics, and leave the rest for later.

A sense of humor can be helpful, however. We can remember some stressful times when one of our babies was being particularly fussy and crying as Cindy was trying to comfort him, and I (John) started taking a video of this "special bonding time" between Cindy and the baby. That thought was such a ludicrous description of the situation that we both burst out laughing, and it took the edge off and helped us relax and have some perspective.

Try to remember how amazing a baby is. God fashioned this little one, right under your noses, as a unique individual with an amazing blend of your distinct traits and several more unique to them. They have all these astoundingly functional tiny parts and are on an almost nonstop mission to learn how to use them by exploring the world around them. They can melt huge macho adults with their tiny little smiles and express joy in such a unique "whole body wiggle" way—they are usually quite delightful little people to have around. Our whole family has truly mourned these last ten years or so when we've no longer had a baby or toddler in our home. If you have one, gather up the family, set a rested and fed baby on a blanket on the floor in the middle of the living room and—voilà! You have free entertainment for the next short while.

The Three-Month Rule

Through the process of having eight babies in our family over about fifteen years, John began to encourage me with the "three-month rule." He would tell me that I should allow myself at least three months, from the birth of a new child, before dwelling on things like, "This new routine is never going to work!" or "How will I ever ______ now?" or "When will we ever ______ ?" He was right. It always seemed overwhelming and impossible to think about or make plans about big picture things during those first three months of change, but after that season things had settled out into the new normal, at least for most of our children, and we were able to tackle those bigger questions and plans.

Many changes occur in a household when a newborn comes into the picture, including schedule changes, sleep-pattern (or non-sleep-pattern) changes, and postpartum hormonal changes for moms who have given birth. Everything takes longer and can seem more complicated than you might expect before the birth. I distinctly remember the first time we left our house to visit a store after our first child was born—it seemed like we needed to take so many things (car seat, stocked diaper bag, cushions of various kinds, nursing pillow, extra supplies, etc.) that I felt like we were preparing more for a camping trip than a trip to the store. It seemed to take forever to collect everything, have the baby finish feeding, get the car loaded, and leave. In contrast, just a few weeks earlier, prior to the birth, leaving to go to the store was a one-minute process—we would just get in the car and go.

We found that it helped not to expect anything to feel normal for those first three months after a baby was born as we were adjusting to life as a family of three (then four, then five, etc.). However, after about three months, things did start to feel normal, to the point that it was a little hard to remember what things were like before the baby arrived.

Postpartum Hormones

I (John) would like to address the dads in particular in regard to the sensitive time after a woman gives birth. You need to realize that huge hormonal changes are taking place in your wife in the days and weeks after the birth. This can cause greatly varying effects from pregnancy to pregnancy. I distinctly remember an incident shortly after our first child was born. We were loading our newborn daughter into the car to take her home from the hospital, and a man was walking through the parking lot near us with an oxygen tank over his shoulder. Cindy, normally a very sane person, was panicking because she was absolutely convinced this man was going to hit me over the head with the tank and steal the baby. Shortly after that, on the way home, a little bit of water spilled out of a vase in the back of the car, and my beloved but very hormonal wife was distraught about it at a level I would expect at a death of a close family member. At that point, I wasn't sure who needed my help more—my child or my wife. Husbands, this is a time when you need to be very understanding and supportive of your wife, even if she is not very rational. Her body has gone through huge hormonal fluctuations between growing a baby to giving birth to transitioning to milk production—that's a lot of hormonal changes. If you went through the same thing, you wouldn't do any better!

Also, recognize that some women will struggle with symptoms of depression, sometimes referred to as the "baby blues." This is somewhat normal and often dissipates after a week or two. However, sometimes it can linger much longer than that, and if this is the case, we recommend that you discuss it with your doctor. Again, husbands, this is a time to be patient and supportive of your wife. Don't expect her to just "snap out of it" because it's irrational. These kinds of feelings in this situation are usually hormonally induced, and she can't just think her way out of the situation.

Breastfeeding

This section applies to those who choose to breastfeed their baby. Breastfeeding is a relatively easy and inexpensive way to feed a baby *in the long run*. However, the first few days or weeks can be challenging, as everyone is adjusting to the process in various ways. It takes some time before nursing becomes a nearly effortless, enjoyable time for both mother and baby.

If you plan to breastfeed, we highly recommend you begin to educate yourself on this process before the baby is born. A helpful book on this subject is *The Nursing Mother's Companion* by Kathleen Huggins. An experienced mom gave me (Cindy) a copy at our first birth, and we have found it an extremely useful reference through nursing each of our eight children, even the challenging ones. It has been updated seven times (and we've had several of the updates, all worthwhile). It includes such things as an appendix written by a doctor of pharmacy that describes which over-the-counter and prescription drugs are best choices when needed based on what gets concentrated in breast milk. Sadly, not all doctors are up to date on this kind of info. There are also quick-start guides and sections for nagging middle-of-the-night troubles that can spring up when nursing, when it is hard to find an awake person for help. It is extremely helpful to have a "hit the ground running" perspective about what you do and don't want to do during those first few days after the birth if you want to get your best possible start at breastfeeding, so I highly recommend getting information like this *before* heading into a birth.

We suggest that you seek help and advice from experienced lactation consultants and midwives (possibly including experienced moms) when you are having challenges breastfeeding. Though hospital nurses on maternity care floors have had training in helping new moms begin to nurse their babies, we've had several who have never actually nursed a baby themselves, so keep this in mind if you need some expert help. Most hospitals have a lactation consultant who can visit you in your hospital room and with whom you can make appointments after you've left the hospital.

Other kinds of specialty doctors can help in this area as well. One of our children was greatly helped by the expertise of a doctor of osteopathy who had special training in cranial osteopathy. We had been to several lactation consultants, and none of them could figure out why our baby had a very ineffective sucking ability and was losing weight. This doctor understood the nerve and muscle arrangement in the baby's head and mouth and finally figured out how to teach him to make suction.

Most children don't need help with learning to breastfeed, but I write all this to encourage you that support is out there if you need it. Don't delay to get help if things aren't working well in those crucial first few weeks. It is worth an initial short-term struggle to have the ideal infant food that is free and nearly effortless, for as long as your child needs it. Bottles, pumping, and formula are sometimes necessary and can be a huge blessing, but they all require more effort and expense in the end.

It is a bit of a challenge for moms, when exhausted and uncomfortable from birth, to prioritize setting good nursing habits, but I almost always looked back and wished I had been a bit more attentive to little things, like sore nipples or clogged ducts, before they became bigger problems. John would often serve as my coach and essential second set of hands when getting things started off the first several feedings, and I would encourage you husbands out there to offer as much helpful assistance as you are able.

Another thing to consider, when beginning breastfeeding, is the need to get your milk supply well established and to avoid, as much as possible, the discomfort of engorgement when your body is trying to figure out what the supply and demand needs will be. Though everyone is very tired after a birth, we have found that things tend to go better if we wake up a sleepy baby and encourage them to eat on a somewhat regular schedule in those first few days. Some babies are very, very tired after birth, and it is tempting to just let them sleep undisturbed until they wake up. However, this is not always the best concerning breastfeeding. Regular breastfeeding will help mom not be as uncomfortable and engorged as her milk is coming in and will help keep the baby from some of the effects of jaundice, which can make them even sleepier.

So, as crazy as it sounds, in those first few days or weeks, we actually tended to set an alarm to wake up and feed the baby in the middle of the night, perhaps three to four hours after the last feeding. This helped us avoid having a ravenously hungry baby, who at this point was vigorously crying and gasping air that would need to be burped later, trying to nurse on an overly full breast. It was much pleasanter to gently wake the baby, nurse, then get everyone settled back in to sleep with a bit less drama and tears, for both baby and mom. This also tended to provide another good chunk of sleep for everyone that night. Obviously, do what seems best in your circumstances. Perhaps your baby is very tiny and wakes frequently, and this suggestion sounds ludicrous. But we want to encourage those with sleepy newborns who need to eat more than their bodies yet realize that there are many good reasons to wake a peacefully sleeping baby in those early days.

Eat, Play, Sleep

Looking back, we are convinced that some of our first few babies were cranky more often than they might have been because they had not learned to sleep well and had not had enough rest. It didn't occur to us that a baby might need to learn the skill of getting to sleep and being able to stay asleep long enough to get much-needed rest. When we had an infant who struggled to sleep, it was tempting to get into a feeding and sleeping habit that might not have been ideal for the baby or for the mom. It sounds too simple to make that much of a difference, but switching around the order of how we structured these three things—eating, playing, and sleeping—seemed to make all the difference. (By *playing*, we mean the time that a baby is awake, not that you have to play with the baby every moment they are awake. Babies learn by exploring their world and observing, and it is good to let them do some of this without your involvement.)

The routines we established for feeding and napping our earlier babies cultivated some difficulties that could have been avoided by this sequence. When we started, the baby would usually wake up, observe their world, and then, because they were getting tired and cranky, and probably pretty hungry, I would feed them. When we did this, they would tend to nod off after just a little snack, not sleep as long, and be on a fairly unpredictable cycle of sleeping and eating, with snacking and dozing little bits throughout the day. As the richer milk comes later in a feeding, "quick snacks" aren't as filling, and I don't think our earlier babies gained weight as well as they could have—one of a baby's most important tasks.

In contrast, we found that when we fed the baby shortly after they woke from a nap, they were awake and energized enough to get a good, full meal. They were also awake enough to be sufficiently burped to get out those uncomfortable bubbles. Then they could observe their world and smile at their fans until they showed signs of tiredness. Preferably at those first signs of sleepiness, or even perhaps a bit before, we would cheerfully, lovingly, swaddle the baby and lay them in their cradle or crib and work toward their learning how to fall asleep without needing us as a sleep prop. Ideally, they would get a decent nap, untroubled by gas bubbles or a not-full-enough tummy, and wake ready for a good feeding.

This was the ideal, the goal toward which we were working those first few months. Did we ever rock our baby to sleep or let them just nap in our arms? Of course we did. Is it okay to comfort a crying, exasperated baby? Yes. The eat-play-sleep cycle wasn't a rule or law, just a more helpful way to sequence and bring a bit of gentle, predictable order to their disorganized newborn life. We found baby seasons much more pleasant for all involved when we made this little tweak to our normal baby-care mode.

We are offering this just as a bit of encouragement for family and parental sanity—context is essential. Babies (and mommas) get sick, houseguests pay visits, schedules are thrown off, and babies teethe, so use your head and make adjustments as needed in your situation.

Sometimes babies have colic or reflux or other issues they are dealing with and cry more than usual. These can be trying times. Babies—and parents—do need sleep. If you have a baby who seems to cry quite a bit of the day and night and appears to be in pain, we strongly encourage you to see your doctor. Many situations, like food intolerances, reflux, or other health issues, like ear infections, can make a baby miserable. Try to get help so you can both get needed sleep. This would be a great time to recruit grandmothers, or honorary grandmothers, to walk with the baby or take the baby for a car ride, which often helps fussy babies get a much-needed nap. Reach out to your church family or neighbors and see if you can get even just a short "walk around the block" date with your spouse, away from the crying baby, just to keep perspective. Colicky babies do grow out of it—ten-year-olds aren't usually keeping us awake because of hours of crying. You will make it through, and if you can get help, that may make the difference in your sanity.

Cherish the Blessing

As I (Cindy) write this, I have so many fond memories of my husband, melted in the presence of baby cuteness, saying precious little things in an adorable voice to the infant who had captivated his heart. I never could have imagined what my husband would have been like with a baby in his arms. Raising our children has been the most enjoyable and rewarding joint project we have ever shared as a couple.

It can be overwhelming when we focus on the awesome responsibility and stewardship we have been given by God in this little image-bearer with whom we have been temporarily entrusted. It is good to take this stewardship seriously, but also remember that it was God who formed this child, who knit them together in their mother's womb (Psalm 139:13), and knew all the plans for their days before one of them began (Psalm 139:16). It's not completely on your shoulders. Take one day and one baby step of faithfulness at a time—and you'll be able to accomplish God's purposes for you in the life of this child.

There are times you just need to hug this precious little one, thank God for them, and go to sleep, resting in the knowledge that ultimately this child is God's creation and He will give the wisdom and resources needed for the task. Ask Him for wisdom, and rest. You've been given an incredible gift—one that will likely go out as an arrow from your quiver and make a mark on the world you could not make yourself.

This little person has gifts and talents different than yours, reflecting their Creator's awesome creativity. Their presence in your life will be like installing little mirrors all over your house, showing you more about yourself than perhaps you wanted to know. If you have eyes to see and a heart to learn, raising children can be one of the most sanctifying and maturing things you can undertake. We are so excited for what God has planned in your life through the presence of a little one in your womb, arms, or home.

Discussion Questions

1. What was the attitude toward babies in your family when you were growing up? Did your parents have similar or different attitudes?
2. What thoughts come to mind when you think about a baby coming into your home?

The rest of the questions are based on your situation.

Questions for those who have had a baby come into your family by birth or adoption:

3. What were some of your fears or concerns prior to the baby's arrival?
4. What things about having a new baby surprised you? What were difficulties you didn't expect? What were positive aspects you didn't expect?
5. About how long did it take you to feel like living with the baby was normal and routine?
6. Do you find it hard to step back and enjoy the wonder of having a young baby in the home? To what extent were you overwhelmed and stressed vs. content and joyful? Did that change in one way or another over time?
7. How much was the father involved in the care and support of both mother and baby during the first three months? Discuss whether there are changes in dad's involvement that could be helpful if another baby came along in the future.
8. Did you have an "eat-play-sleep" routine, an "eat-sleep-play" routine, or no routine at all? How did that go? What, if anything, might you want to change for the next baby?

Questions for those who have not yet had a baby in the home but might at a later point in time:

9. How much exposure to young babies have you had?

10. Do you think you will like the young baby stage? What things do you anticipate enjoying, and what things do you think will be difficult?

11. Potential fathers, how much involvement do you anticipate having in caring for mom and baby the first few months? Discuss as a couple how you would like this interaction to go.

Chapter 28

Toy-Time Tapes: Teaching and Training Your Children When You're Not Present

Children are like wet cement. Whatever falls on them makes an impression.

– Haim Ginott

Sometimes you hear of something that sounds like a great idea, you try it out, and you find that it is, indeed, incredibly valuable. One such priceless idea that affected our parenting is what we call "toy-time tapes."[1]

We read about this concept in a book entitled *Creative Family Times*[2] and a similar concept in *Practical Homeschooling* magazine back in the early 1990s. The basic idea is that there are many things we would like to teach our children and have them learn by repetition, and that making a recording of these things, made by us in our voices, is a valuable tool.

When we made up our family schedule (see chapter 23, "Using a Schedule"), we generally set aside a forty-five-minute period each day for each of the younger children that we called "toy time." This was a time when a child was expected to stay in a particular room by

1 We named these "toy-time tapes" early in our parenting years because we used cassette tapes. Later we burned CDs. Today, a toy-time tape would most likely be a playlist of custom prerecorded tracks, as described later in the chapter.

2 Allen and Connie Hadidian and Will and Lindy Wilson, *Creative Family Times: Practical Activities for Building Character* (Chicago: Moody, 1989).

themselves and listen to a recording we had made especially for them. It was usually their bedroom, a playpen or crib, or some other room in which there were toys that they could also play with while they were listening, since forty-five minutes would be a long time to sit and listen to a recording. Our children generally enjoyed and looked forward to this time of individual play and listening to the recordings.

We will talk a little later about why we found this so valuable. However, so that you have a better idea of what we are discussing, we want to describe the typical content of the recordings.

What Can I Put on the Recording?

There is almost no limit to the kinds of things you might want to put on a recording for your children to listen to repeatedly. Some ideas are listed below. Note that what you put on your recording may be somewhat dependent on your child's age, although keep in mind that it's fine for them to start memorizing things that they may not yet fully understand. The ideas below are listed by category, but you can put them on your own recording in just about any order that makes sense to you, probably mixing things up a bit for variety. You can include more than one of some of the ideas. For example, you could choose to sing two or three hymns, not just one.

Introduction and Conclusion

- Initial, personalized greeting—something along the lines of "Hi, Henry! This is Daddy! We have made this toy-time tape for you. Right now, it's time for you to listen to this and play with your toys, and you can follow along and learn all the things that we say on this recording."
- A conclusion at the end, stating that you hope they enjoyed the recording, you love them very much, and you hope they enjoy the rest of their day.

Songs

- Sing the verses of a hymn.
- Sing other songs you'd like to teach them (including any family favorites).

Scripture and Theological Training

- Read a short psalm.
- Read a well-known passage of Scripture.
- List Old Testament books of the Bible in order.
- List New Testament books of the Bible in order.
- Go through catechism questions and answers (pick your favorite children's catechism). You can just state the question and answer or, optionally, comment on the answer. A catechism is ideal for a toy-time tape because it is designed to teach important spiritual concepts in a simple question-and-answer format.

Important Facts to Know

For teaching important facts to your child, it's sometimes good to state the fact and then ask them to repeat it back, leaving a pause in the recording for them to do so. (Example: Mom says, "Nathan's birthday is April 17, 2010." Dad says, "Okay, Anna, now it's your turn. Nathan's birthday is _________. Did you say April 17? You're right!")

- Your street address
- Your phone number (or Mommy's and Daddy's phone numbers, if there's not a house phone)
- Birthdays of the members of your family
- The child's birthday
- Months of the year
- Days of the week
- Names of relatives and where they live

Math Concepts

- Verbally go through relevant addition, subtraction, multiplication, or division facts or tables. (Example: Multiplying by 3s: 3x0=0, 3x1=3, 3x2=6, etc.). It can be helpful to add a pause and have the child guess first for some of these. For example: "Okay, now, what is 3x6? [Pause] Did you say 18? If you did, you're right!—3x6=18."
- Skip counting: This is counting by 2s, 3s, 4s, etc. For example, skip counting by 7 would sound like "7, 14, 21, 28, 35. . ."

Being able to skip count is very helpful when it comes to knowing multiplication or division well and for commonly used math concepts like factoring.

How Our Actions Affect Others

One parent can "interview" the other parent and ask situational behavior questions, and the other parent can give the answer. It's also good not to just say what they should *do* but to also work in *why* they should do that.

- Sitting in church. Here's an example of what we mean:
  Mom: "How should we act when we're in church?"

  Dad: "We should sit still and pay attention to what is happening in the service."

  Mom: "Why should we sit still?"

  Dad: "It's important for us to sit still so that we are not distracting the people around us. When we move around and wiggle, it makes it hard for people next to us or behind us to pay attention to what is happening."

  Mom: "Why is it important to pay attention in the worship service? "

  Dad: "Because we learn about God in the worship service, and there is nothing more important for us to learn about!"

  This is just an example—use your own words and thoughts.
- Going to a store. (How do we act? Do we touch things? Why not? What do we do if someone says hello?)
- Going to a relative's home. (Go over what the expectations are, what they can and cannot do, etc.)
- How to respond when an adult greets you.
- When I want more of something, what do I say?
- What do I say when someone says thank you?

Other

- Recite short poems.
- Answer science questions (e.g., Why is the grass green? The grass is green because...).

- Read something you want them to memorize.
- Add just about anything you want your child to hear!

Why Toy-Time Tapes?

There are several reasons we found toy-time tapes to be so helpful:

- **Hearing parents' voices.** In our family, Dad was at work during the day and Mom was at home, so the toy-time tape was an opportunity for the children to get input directly from Dad in the middle of the day (or when he was traveling). As a result, for our recordings, we tended to favor Dad's voice over Mom's (although both were heavily involved). It also was a recording of Dad and Mom working together, with both of their voices involved, to emphasize that they function as a team under God's authority, even when only one of them is there during the day.
- **Easy, painless way to memorize.** After a child has heard the toy-time tape dozens of times, they will know just about everything on that recording thoroughly, with a minimum of time and effort on the parents' part. This frees up time for the parents to do other things when they are with the children in person. Some of our family's favorite hymns are those that were on the toy-time tape, and our children know all the verses by memory. They often smile at us and each other when those hymns come up in a worship service.
- **Well-defined time to learn to play alone.** The toy-time tapes were an automatic way for the child to know when their time alone was done. Having the recording play in the background helped them to quickly understand what was expected of them during this time, and knowing that they were productively occupied and engaged provided a break for Mom. Sometimes we even had them simultaneously play their recordings in separate rooms. We think that it is a valuable skill to be able to entertain yourself at times, and toy time with the recording was a good time to practice this skill. This may take some initial training to teach your children to stay in their room for the duration of the recording, but we found the effort exerted to do this was well worth it.

Practical Suggestions for Making the Recordings

Technical Suggestions

Back when we first did this, we pretty much had to use cassette tapes, so the production of the material was a bit tricky. Today, digital recording is fast and easy for most people (using smartphones or computer microphones), so it makes sense to separately record individual tracks and then combine them all at the end as a playlist. We found it helpful for slightly older children to be able to start and stop the recording on their own, which might be a good reason even today to burn the sequence of audio files to a CD and make use of an inexpensive CD player. We recommend that you avoid using a device the children interact with when you are not around, especially if it is connected to the internet. It is beyond the scope of this chapter to give detailed technical instructions on how to best make a set of audio files and then play them back in a particular order. If you do not already know how to do this, then our best advice is to track down someone who does and have them help you.

Change Things Up

Try to have as much variety within the recording as you can so that it holds the child's interest. Some things are more engaging than others. Varying the overall topic, who is talking, and how long the segments are will help the child to stay more engaged.

Also, if you are using digital audio files, it is generally very easy to make changes to the recordings. After your child has listened to the same recording for several months, they will be excited to get a new recording with new things in a new order, even if some of the individual tracks are the same. A new recording can even be a much-appreciated (and free) Christmas present or birthday present.

Be Creative and Fun

Our biggest advice in terms of producing the recordings is to try to be as enthusiastic, creative, and fun as possible. Change the inflection in your voice, joke around, and talk to them as though they are right there in the room with you. You can even repeat short things at different volumes, tones of voice, or accents. This chapter is just a starting point—if you decide to make a toy-time tape, customize it to match your personality, and have fun with it!

Discussion Questions

1. Growing up in your family, how did you learn things like your address, sibling birthdays, months of the year, or the other things that are listed as ideas in this chapter?

2. In what ways do you think toy-time tapes could be helpful to your family?

3. What do you think are the benefits and the drawbacks of using a toy-time tape to teach your children vs. teaching them directly (in person)?

4. Are there challenges you foresee in producing a toy-time tape? Practically speaking, how might you overcome these challenges?

Chapter 29

Bible Memory

> I have stored up your word in my heart, that I might not sin against you.
>
> – Psalm 119:11

Many Christian adults value the Scripture they have memorized but wish they had even more of God's Word stored up in their hearts. We parents have a fantastic opportunity to help our children memorize Scripture at an early age when it is quite easy for them to do so. We have been amazed at how quickly and easily the children are able to commit to memory large passages of Scripture while working together on it for only a few minutes a day. This is yet another example of how a small amount of effort, consistently applied over a long period of time, can yield tremendous results.

We are about to speak passionately on a topic we feel strongly about, however, as we have said before, just because we are passionate about this doesn't mean it is something God has placed on your plate right now. Please carefully and prayerfully consider any new ventures before feeling any burden to incorporate them into your routine. We do not want this to be overwhelming to already overwhelmed parents.

For the past twenty-plus years, we have started off most school days having a ten to fifteen minute time of Bible memory. This has enabled our children to learn dozens of full chapters of the Bible. This may sound like a lot, but it was simply the result of working at it consistently over time, not an innate, unusual ability to memorize. It is clear to us that our children can memorize things much more quickly than we adults can. But the ability to memorize is also a learned skill that improves with practice.

While our desire for our children to memorize Scripture was primarily to have God's Word hidden in their hearts to be recalled later, we also believe there is an academic benefit in developing the skill of memorization. We hesitate to talk about how much Scripture our children have memorized because we fear this would sound like bragging or make us out to be some elite, uniquely capable Bible-memorizing family. I can assure you we are not—we even struggle to remember the passages we've memorized. However, we firmly believe this type of Bible memory is achievable by anyone with just a little consistent time each school day. And even if we don't remember the passages perfectly over time, we still have created a much greater familiarity with large passages of Scripture, which the Holy Spirit can bring to mind later. If we haven't reviewed a passage in a while, it might be rough the first few times through it, but it comes back much more quickly than starting from scratch. Our older children tell us they continue to appreciate having large passages of Scripture tucked away in their minds as they have grown older.

Practical Suggestions

How to Start

Gather the children and read aloud the first verse of your chosen chapter of the Bible. (More in a minute about what types of chapters would be good to start with.) The goal is to have recited together the words of this first verse with the children more than seven times before the end of the session.[1] This is our approach:

1. I (Cindy)read the entire verse and comment on what it means, especially if there are complicated concepts that might need explaining to the ten-and-under crowd.
2. I break it up into phrases and have them say it back to me.

   Mom: "Bless the Lord, O my soul…"
   Children: "Bless the Lord, O my soul..."
   Mom: "And all that is within me, bless his holy name…"
   Children: "And all that is within me, bless his holy name..."

1 I (Cindy) heard at a Child Evangelism Fellowship training course that hearing and speaking something seven times puts it in a different part of your memory.

3. I do this again, making the phrases longer.

   Mom: "Bless the Lord, O my soul, and all that is within me…"
   Children: "Bless the Lord, O my soul, and all that is within me…"

4. Then I read it out loud but leave words out that they try to fill in. This works very well for reviewing the previously learned verses too. I do this several times, leaving out different words each time through.

   Mom: "Bless the ________"

   Children: "Lord"

   Mom: "O my ________"

   Children: "Soul"

5. When I think they can say the entire verse, we say it together several times. To keep this interesting, you can say it loudly one time, whisper the second time, say it very slowly or quickly, or do "popcorn" where we say the verse, one word per person, around the room in a circle until we have said the entire verse.

Each day after that, I review the previous verse or verses and then introduce a new verse.

When I (Cindy) started this, our children were ages six, four, two and a half, and almost one. Our goal was to memorize Psalm 103 and surprise Daddy with it. It was truly priceless to see his shocked face as the young children went on and on through all twenty-two verses of this chapter. Since they were young, we also had some motions we put to the verses for emphasis. I had also spent some time working on their public speaking skills as we got closer to the presentation, which is challenging at this age: standing still, looking Dad in the eye, and trying not to fidget (though it was far from perfect). The joy in the children's faces during their presentation to Dad was a precious confirmation that it was worth all the effort to pull off this surprise.

I wanted them to have God's Word stored up in their hearts for the Holy Spirit to use later in their lives, but I also wanted to acknowledge their efforts, beyond the joy of surprising their dad. Thankfully, at that time a company called Keepers of the Faith[2] had Bible memory pins that

2 While the folks who ran Keepers of the Faith retired, the award pins are still available at keepsakeawards.com, or you can search for "Keepsake Awards" on Amazon.

were perfect for this. I eventually made banners for each of the children (nothing tricky or involved: I glued felt over a gold painted dowel rod and added gold rick-rack to hang the banners) so they could display their Bible memory medals in one place. While there were several chapter-specific medals available, for most of the chapters we have learned we've just ordered a generic "Bible memory" medal and wrote on the back with a small permanent marker which chapter was memorized and on what date. We continue to "surprise" Dad with Bible memory presentations, but he is not so surprised to know we are working on it.

That first time through Psalm 103, only the six-year-old and four-year-old could do it on their own, out loud, without help. Thankfully, the Keepsake Awards provides the option of both gold and silver Bible memory medals, and we were able to award silver medals for good effort to the toddler crowd since they had worked hard but didn't really know the passage word for word. Don't be surprised at how well younger children can do, however. We have had times when a preschooler seemed to know a chapter better than their older siblings.

Where to Start

While this method would work for any portion of Scripture, certain aspects make some chapters easier to work on than others. For example, we did memorize Proverbs 3 one time, but it was one of the most difficult passages we have worked on since the flow from one verse to the next is not always logically connected. I think Psalm 103 is a great place to start, as well as Psalm 1, Psalm 19, Psalm 139, Psalm 145, or Psalm 146. Though longer, the Sermon on the Mount (Matthew 5–7) flows very nicely and contains so much of Jesus's teaching. Luke 2 is nice to work on around Christmas. First Corinthians 13, Romans 12, Ephesians 6, John 15, and Isaiah 53 work well for memorization. We were working on having all of 1 and 2 Peter memorized, but never got as far as the last chapters of these books. If your children are young, you may think, "I have all the time in the world; this will not go quickly," but it does. As the years have gone by, we have felt some time pressure, wanting to get through certain chapters before the next child graduates and eventually leaves the nest, not wanting them to miss out on some key chapters that their older siblings knew well. We have tended to cycle back through some of our favorites so the next set of children can benefit from them.

Why Entire Chapters and What about Verse Numbers?

While there is much benefit in knowing specific verses and their locations in the Bible, we wanted to work on long chapters to get more doctrine in context into the children's hearts and minds. It is fairly distracting to this goal to add in each verse number as you are working on a chapter. Besides, verse numbers weren't a part of the original texts. Our children can certainly go to the Bible and quickly scan through that chapter to find the verse number of a specific passage since they know in which chapter it is located. They have, in different situations and contexts, learned specific shorter verses and their verse references, and we strongly encourage this as well; we just didn't work on this much after starting in with the larger chapters.

We have also enjoyed some playful competition in recent years with our college-age children with the excellent Scripture memory app The Bible Memory App (formerly Scripture Typer). I highly recommend it, but only if you have already dealt with all the distractions and dangers that computer, tablet, and phone use can introduce.

Discussion Questions

1. What role, if any, has Bible memory had within your own life? If you have memorized Bible passages before, how has this helped you in your Christian walk?
2. What are your thoughts on memorizing whole chapters versus memorizing smaller passages (perhaps with chapter and verse numbers)?
3. What would you like to see, in terms of Bible memory, in your children when they leave your home? What steps can you take now to work toward these objectives?

Chapter 30

Be Bold

> The wicked flee when no one pursues, but the righteous are bold as a lion.
>
> – Proverbs 28:1

Parenting well is not a task for the fainthearted, especially within a culture that is increasingly non-biblical in its worldview. If we strive to be excellent parents and give our children a God-centered world view, there will be times when we stick out like a sore thumb. The goal of this chapter is to encourage you to parent with boldness, considering what is best for your children and not considering what others think about you.

Maintaining High Expectations Can Be Awkward

Sometimes you may find yourself in a situation where you are holding your children to a different set of expectations than everyone else around you, and you may feel significant social pressure to cave in. For example, suppose you are at a pool, and there are clear signs, which your children can read, that say "NO RUNNING." However, as you look around, virtually every child seems to feel free to run because they are almost all doing so. What are you going to do? If you make sure your own children don't run, you risk offending other parents who may feel like you're judging them. If you do allow them to run, you're essentially teaching them that rules by those in authority (the people who run the pool) can be ignored.

Don't be afraid to be the awkward parent who is holding their children to a different set of expectations than the other children around them. Of course, this should be done in a way as to minimize offense, but sometimes there is no way to remove all possibility of offense. ("If possible, so far as it depends on you, live peaceably with all" [Romans 12:18].) You are responsible for your own children, and being primarily concerned about what other parents think about you is not a worthwhile parenting strategy.

Don't Fall for the "Expert" Model of Parenting

Our society puts extreme value on the "expert," whether it comes to science or politics or cooking or parenting methodologies. If someone is declared to be an expert, we feel like we must follow what they say.

There are many so-called experts who will proclaim all kinds of things about what parents should and shouldn't do. Some of this advice might be good, but some of it can be based on faulty worldview assumptions (e.g., a child is inherently innocent and only corrupted by society) or questionable social science methodologies. Obtaining a high level of education in a parenting-related area does not automatically make one a good parent. For example, we have been aware of child psychologists who have completely unruly and rebellious children.

Parents today have lots of parenting advice thrown at them. Our recommendation is to consider everything you hear, but give the highest weight to people who have children that are the kind of children you admire and would like your own children to grow up to be. If someone is a so-called expert, either because of educational training or simply because they have written an article about parenting, I would take whatever they say with a grain of salt and compare it with many other pieces of advice before fully absorbing it (see Proverbs 11:14). Rather than look to the self-declared "experts" out there, find a few families you know with older children whom you admire, and ask those parents for advice—they are the *real* experts.

Don't Fall Prey to Modern Parenting Fads

In a closely related topic, we would recommend that you be highly skeptical of any parenting advice that is "new" and "better." We are not in any way meaning to imply that everything that previous generations did, parenting-wise, is automatically the best way to go. Every generation of parents tends to have their own strengths and weaknesses and their own blind spots. But the "latest and greatest" parenting advice should generally be considered suspect.

Many modern parenting magazines are a good example of this. They exist to sell things to you through their advertising, and the articles are present primarily because no one would buy a magazine that is only advertisements. Worldview matters when it comes to things like parenting, and most of what you see in a parenting magazine is not coming from a biblical worldview. It certainly is not wrong to read these magazines, and some of what they say may be helpful, but you will likely struggle if parenting magazines are your primary source of parenting input.

The Standard Is Not "What Are Other People Doing?"

People, by nature, compare themselves with others without thinking about it. We tend to follow the lead of what others are doing, and whatever is common within our community is what seems "normal" and "appropriate" to us.

In the Christian life, and with parenting in particular, we are often called not to follow the society around us but to seek something better. In a nutshell, we are called to raise our children in the discipline and instruction of the Lord (Ephesians 6:4), that they would love God with all their heart, soul, mind, and strength and love others as themselves (Matthew 22:37–39). One goal of our efforts should be that our children would become people of solid biblical character.

Suppose these things are your objective, but you happen to live within a community where great value is placed on getting children into an elite university so they can have a high-paying career and financial success. To that end, you notice that virtually everyone around you is working vigorously to get their children into the "right" kindergarten, the "right" sports team, the "right" ballet school, the chess team, the robotics team, and all of the other high-level activities that will give them the "right" credentials to set them on the "right" career path. Without thinking about it, you might start to feel significant pressure to make sure that your children fully participate in all these "right" activities, not so much because you've thought it through, considered your ultimate parenting goals, and decided that these were the best ways to raise your child in the fear and admonition of the Lord. Rather, the desire to pursue these activities is something you've absorbed from the culture around you because everyone else is doing them, so you think you probably should too. This is just one example of where you, as a parent, are called to be bold and aim for what is best, which may be something different than what everyone else around you is doing. Social pressure is powerful, and boldness may be needed to go against the flow.

Don't get us wrong—nothing is overtly problematic with any of these "right" things in and of themselves. In fact, many of them can be good for building character, among other things. However, if they become our primary goals as parents, we have likely allowed society to set the standard for us.

Other examples of allowing what others do to set the standards for us could involve how we allow our children to dress (sexually suggestive vs. modest), what they read or listen to, usage of electronic gadgets, how they are allowed to speak to family members (tearing down vs. building up), what movies they watch, or where they are allowed to go without a parent.

Don't be afraid to stick out from the crowd. Recognize that you are the only parents for your own children, and as a result, you have a higher level of responsibility for your children than anyone else in the world. Do what, in your judgment, is right and good, and don't bow to peer pressure from the world around you.

Don't Be Shamed by a "Large" Number of Children

This book is written to cover parenting issues, not address the question of how many children you should have. That being said, we wanted to devote a small section to encouraging those of you who do happen to have large families (with *large* being defined as having more children than is typical within your community).

In our experience, we were tempted to feel a certain amount of embarrassment when we had many small children, in part because strangers felt very free to make rude and highly personal comments to us as we were just walking around in public. When we were expecting our fourth child, people would say things like "Was this intentional?" "Don't you know that there's a population problem?" "How do you feed them all?" "Don't you know what causes that?" (Sometimes, to that last question, we would reply, "Well, we think we've figured it out, but if it's what we think it is, we're sure not going to stop!")

Interestingly, as the children got older, the rude questions stopped, and we think it's because it became self-evident that our group of now older children were a "mighty force" for good rather than just a drain on our resources. It's amazing what a group of eight older children can accomplish. They can do things, go places, and encourage and serve others in ways that we, as just two parents, simply cannot go and do.

Honestly, it took a certain level of boldness for us to continue to have children when many in society were looking down on and ridiculing us. In hindsight, we have absolutely no regrets, and are extremely glad we were willing to stand against society's opinion in this area.

So our advice to you is to work out this issue between you, your spouse, and God, and then be bold enough to ignore whatever others around you think, whether you end up with one child or many.

Be an Example of Bold Leadership to Your Children

So far, everything in this chapter has addressed the need for boldness in the task of parenting. In addition, we can have a significant and positive impact on our children when we live boldly in other areas of our life. Our children will see us standing up for what we believe, which will invariably encourage them to be bold in their own lives.

Perhaps you are in a situation where you should speak up about something when no one else is. Maybe you find a need to point out a legitimate safety concern when it might be awkward to do so. Or possibly you need to make a stand and leave an event before it's over for some good but unpopular reason. For example, we had a friend who would take the time when she went grocery shopping with her young children to collect a copy of all the sexually suggestive magazine covers in the checkout lane and go stand in line and ask to speak to the manager. She would ask the manager if he or she would like their own children having to look at these photos while they were getting their family groceries. This took extra time and was awkward and inconvenient, but her children sure learned by example, and I think the store eventually had a lane available without these types of magazines. This is very much like the example of the persistent widow (Luke 18:1–8). As you walk through the various situations in your own life, stand up, do what's right, and do it boldly!

Discussion Questions

1. Think of a time when you were tempted to lower family expectations for your child to avoid an awkward situation. What did you do? Looking back, would you have done anything differently? Note: There is often a judgment call required—sometimes it may be appropriate to relax expectations in some contexts. Discuss the factors to consider when deciding whether to awkwardly hold your child to higher expectations than others versus temporarily lowering expectations.
2. Can you think of examples of parenting advice given by so-called experts? Was the advice helpful or not? Where do you get specific parenting advice? Think of as many sources as you can.
3. If practical, obtain a modern parenting magazine and leaf through the articles. Discuss the worldviews behind them if they can be discerned. Evaluate the advice given, and determine which advice would be helpful and which could be detrimental to your ultimate goals as parents.
4. Think of ways you have felt "peer pressure" as a parent. For each of these examples, identify whether this parenting peer pressure was a good influence or a bad influence. (Realize that there can be good peer pressure.)
5. Try to identify one or two specific areas where you feel convicted to change the way you operate and become bolder in your parenting.

Chapter 31

Faithfulness, Not Results

> Well done, good and faithful servant. You have been faithful over a little; I will set you over much. Enter into the joy of your master.
>
> – Matthew 25:23

The passage given above is in the middle of a parable Jesus told about three servants (Matthew 25:14–30). One was given five talents (a "talent" is a sum of money), another two, and another one. The servants who were given five talents and two talents were faithful to use those talents as the master intended (by investing them). They were both commended equally, even though the one with two talents only made two additional talents, whereas the one with five talents made five. In contrast, the third servant, who only had one talent, hid that talent in the ground and didn't invest it as the master wished and was strongly rebuked by the master. The master appears to be much more concerned about his servants being faithful than the actual results (which is why the servant who only earned two talents but was faithful was commended just as strongly as the one who earned five talents).

Our family has developed a saying, "Faithfulness, not results," to encourage each other along these lines. In fact, one of our older children had this phrase carved out of wood and hung on our wall before she moved into her own apartment. This phrase applies to many aspects of life, but it most certainly applies in the realm of parenting.

"Faithfulness, Not Results" as Applied to Parenting

Parents can often fall prey to some wrong ways of thinking. On the one hand, we may think that "children will be children," and that what we do as parents has little effect or impact on their lives. On the other hand, we may think that how our children turn out is completely determined by us and by the decisions we make. Both viewpoints are misguided and unbiblical and can lead to damaging approaches to parenting and much unnecessary stress.

If you are a parent, then God has entrusted your child to you—your child is like the "talent" in the parable described above. God has called you to be a faithful parent, and to do everything you can to raise up your child in the discipline and instruction of the Lord (Ephesians 6:4). You are called to be faithful. Your focus should be on being faithful as a parent and trusting that God will use your efforts as His vehicle of blessing for your children. However, the results are ultimately up to Him, not you.

This concept is incredibly freeing because we can focus on things that are to a great extent under our control (our faithfulness) rather than things we cannot ultimately control (our children's response). To be sure, God has set things up such that there is a strong connection between what we as parents do and how our children respond, but it is a wrong or even arrogant attitude to think that we completely determine how our children think and behave by our parenting.

Practically speaking, how does a "faithfulness, not results" attitude change the way we parent?

- **A "faithfulness, not results" attitude keeps us from getting discouraged.** All parents face times of discouragement when it seems like what we are working on is never going to "catch" in our children. If our focus is entirely on the results (the children finally "getting it"), then we cannot help but be discouraged. But if our primary focus is on attempting to be faithful to God in this undertaking, then it reduces frustration and discouragement. Clearly, it will still be discouraging if our children are not responding as we wish, but at least we don't have the added unnecessary pressure that comes with measuring success by something we cannot fully control.
- **A "faithfulness, not results" attitude helps us to be patient with our children.** If the primary question in our minds is "Am I being a faithful parent?" and we can by and large say

that we are, then we can take comfort that we are doing what we are supposed to be doing. This will certainly reduce our impatience with our children when they are not responding well. It reminds us that the results are God's work, in His time, and not ultimately our responsibility.

- **A "faithfulness, not results" attitude can reduce sinful pride.** If we believe that our children's behavior is completely a result of our parenting, then in times when they do behave well, we are tempted to take undue credit in the form of sinful pride. If our primary focus is on being faithful and if we recognize that good results are really a blessing from God, then our response will be gratitude to God for using our efforts in the lives of our children rather than pride.
- **A "faithfulness, not results" attitude acknowledges the need for God's grace in our lives.** When we think along these lines, our need for God's grace can be seen in two ways. First, none of us are 100 percent faithful to parent the way we should. Sometimes we do things we shouldn't, or we fail to parent as we should. We are dependent on God's grace in our lives to help us grow in faithfulness as we parent, and we are dependent on God's grace to overcome the effects of our parenting weaknesses and failures in the lives of our children. Second, because we recognize that we do not fully determine how our children turn out, we see the need for God's work of grace in our children's lives to learn and grow in the ways He has for them.
- **A "faithfulness, not results" attitude avoids unhealthy pressure on the parent-child relationship.** When a child fails to live up to our expectations (as they often do), we can feel significant pressure to immediately "fix" them because their actions reflect directly on us. This can lead to an unhealthy level of "performance pressure" in which the parent-child relationship becomes primarily about the child's performance. Having a "faithfulness, not results" attitude helps break down this kind of pressure because we are more focused on being the parents we should be than on how a child is responding. This attitude also helps us to resist feeling parental peer pressure in which we compare ourselves with other parents. If our primary goal is to be faithful to God in our parenting, then we are much less concerned about what other people think about us in this area.

- **A "faithfulness, not results" attitude changes the way we pray.** Fervent prayer about our parenting and for our children is more likely to occur when we recognize our helplessness and complete dependence on God in any situation. A soldier under fire in a foxhole doesn't need to convince himself of the need for prayer—he will likely spontaneously cry out to God. The same principle applies to us as parents. When we recognize we are completely dependent on God to use our parenting efforts to create fruit in the lives of our children, we will pray more naturally and earnestly for God to work in their lives.
- **A "faithfulness, not results" attitude is helpful to model for our children.** When our children see this concept modeled by their parents, it can be a strong encouragement to them as they grow in faithful obedience to God based on a relationship with Him, not based on a legalistic mindset of earning God's favor or their parent's favor by their performance or success.

A "faithfulness, not results" mindset is an abstract concept, so younger children may not really understand what the words mean. However, it is good for us to talk about the concept at a level the child can understand. For example, suppose that a seven-year-old is starting to play a team sport like soccer but they struggle with some of the skills required to play well. We should primarily encourage our child along the lines of their character and effort rather than focusing primarily on the results of how they played. We might ask things like "Are you working as hard as you can?" and "Are you listening to your coach?" Working hard and listening to the coach should be the goal, not some standard of performance. Of course, there is nothing wrong with also praising your child when he or she plays well, but that is not the primary focus.

It's Sometimes Challenging to Discern

One word of caution, especially for those of you who already have a more laissez-faire approach to parenting—you need to think carefully and be honest with yourself when determining whether you have been a faithful parent. There are times where our child's behavior is significantly affected by our sinful or unwise actions (or lack of actions). Using the "faithfulness, not results" mindset to excuse us from what is actually unfaithful parenting is not helpful.

Sometimes, it is difficult for us to discern to what extent we are failing as parents or to what extent we are doing what we should (i.e., being faithful). It can be helpful to have open and frank discussions with our spouse or close friends to give us better insight into this question than we can discern on our own. No parent is perfect and 100 percent faithful, but it is an area in which we can grow by God's grace.

"Faithfulness, Not Results" as Applied to Life

The concept of "faithfulness, not results" applies to many areas besides parenting. We can teach this principle to our children by showing them, through our words and actions, how we seek to be faithful in all aspects of our lives and leave the results up to God. Here are just a few non-parenting examples of this principle in action:

- **Too much to do.** We have more to do than we can possibly get done (at work, at home, over a weekend, etc.). In this circumstance, we need to ask ourselves whether God expects us to do more than can possibly be done (and the answer would be no). Since this is the case, then we should seek to use our time as best we can, focusing on the things we think God would most want us to do, and then be content with whatever the results may bring. This is an incredible stress-reducer for those of us who live hurried, hectic lives.
- **Evangelism.** As Christians, we are called to be faithful witnesses of the gospel to those around us. We are not called to save the people around us—that's God's job. We can be faithful witnesses but have little or no observable response. If this is the case, we can rest in the fact that God is concerned about our faithfulness, but the results are His responsibility. Even Jesus had times and places where He was faithful to do everything the Father gave Him to do but had little or no results to show for it in terms of the response of the people (see Mark 6:1–6). Once again, we need to be honest with ourselves about whether we are truly being faithful. Living with a "faithfulness, not results" mentality does not mean we are off the hook. It just means that we should be focusing on being faithful rather than focusing on the results.
- **Interpersonal encouragement.** When we live in community with others, there are times when we may need to challenge

someone we love and call them to live to a higher standard. For example, we may notice a prideful attitude in a friend that is really affecting their relationships with others, and we feel convicted that we should bring this up with our friend. Such encouragement is not always well received. If our friend does not respond well to our attempts at encouragement, we can feel defeated if we do not remember that we are primarily responsible for our actions (faithfulness) and not responsible for our friend's reaction (results). If we are mostly worried about how someone will respond, we are much less likely to confront someone when they need to be confronted.

- **Performance at work.** In any kind of a work environment, we should be focusing on being faithful to do what we are responsible to do to the best of our ability rather than focusing on the results (e.g., promotions, being appreciated by others, getting the sale). Good results tend to follow when we are faithful, but that is not always the case for a variety of reasons, many of which are outside our control. A "faithfulness, not results" approach in the work environment very much fits with Paul's encouragement to the Colossians: "Whatever you do, work heartily, as for the Lord and not for men, knowing that from the Lord you will receive the inheritance as your reward. You are serving the Lord Christ" (Colossians 3:23–24).

Cultivating a "faithfulness, not results" mindset in ourselves and in our families keeps the focus on the right things and keeps us from becoming too performance oriented.

As we come to the close of this book, our desire and prayer for you is that God will enable you to see your children as the true gift and blessing they are. May God give you the determination, energy, and wisdom to train your children diligently, both proactively in times of non-conflict and when they have disobeyed. May He give you the ability to be consistent in your parenting. May God grant both you and your children an others-oriented mindset in which you look not only to your own interests but also to those of others. May you have the courage to stand against the dominant culture that doesn't recognize God and will not agree with your convictions. In the middle of your busy life, may God grant you the eyes to see what a short time you have to invest in your children. May He eventually send your children out into the world as arrows, ready to accomplish whatever it is that He has molded them to do. Finally, and perhaps most importantly, may your parenting be filled with grace, recognizing that your children are fellow sinners along with you in need of a Savior.

Discussion Questions

1. Can you think of an instance from your past where you think you were too focused on results? How would a "faithfulness, not results" mindset have helped you in that situation?

2. Do you struggle with focusing too much on how well your child performs, as opposed to focusing more on your child's character? What factors do you think cause you to have too much focus on performance? What thoughts run through your mind when your child doesn't perform up to your expectations?

3. Do you struggle with being too lax as a parent, with a "kids will be kids" mentality, when there are issues in a child's life that you, as a parent, have a responsibility to address? Can you think of some issues (character or otherwise) where your children could benefit from godly parenting?

4. Can you think of a time when you shied away from talking with someone because you were afraid of how they were going to respond? How would a "faithfulness, not results" approach have helped you in that situation?

5. When we say "faithfulness, not results," to what or to whom exactly are we being faithful? (There are many answers.) Give specific examples.

6. List some good examples of the "faithfulness, not results" mindset in the Bible or in literature. What are some examples of where this attitude was lacking (with the focus on external results outside of one's control)?

Epilogue

While our book manuscript was being edited, we had an eventful day that made me (John) consider some bookend thoughts related to this book. Two things happened that day that caused me to step back and think about the bigger picture.

The first big event was the marriage of a young couple whom Cindy and I had the privilege of leading through premarital counseling. Seeing this couple get married urged us to emphasize to you the priority of the marriage relationship. Marriage is the beginning of a family, and that primary relationship continues, according to God's plan, "until death do us part." Children are usually an important, but typically temporary, stewardship for that couple. Parents need to prioritize their marriage relationship for the good of their children. Parents who love each other, are committed to one another, and invest time and effort in growing their relationship, even while parenting young children, are, as a residual effect, simultaneously investing in the lives of their children because children thrive when they are in a home with a stable parental relationship.

So, parents, love your children by investing in your spouse! Invest time and energy communicating and spending intentional time with one another, even when children are young and finding a babysitter is challenging. Your children's well-being and sense of stability are directly related to the strength and health of your marriage. We are thankful that we prioritized date nights even when our children were young (though it wasn't easy, and we often thought the Herculean effort required might not be worth it). When life was particularly busy and stressful, and maybe we weren't communicating as well as we both knew was needed, we would remind each other "This relationship is key! Too much rests on this to let it melt into a merely tolerable marriage or business partnership!" It is good for your children to see you prioritizing your relationship. We both recognize that we have been particularly blessed by seeing loving, dedicated marriages modeled by our parents. Thanks to them, it has been our "default setting" in times of trial.

The second big event that day was the death of my father. As I found myself helping my children mentally process their grandfather's death while we were all gathered at the hospital, it occurred to me that most of what I had to say to them were things my father had said to me when other people had died—things like "This dead body is just the earthly shell" and "The person we loved is no longer here but is in the presence of the Lord" (if they were known to be a believer in Christ). When I look back on my childhood, it struck me how consistently my father had taught me how to deal with the happenings of life by applying principles from Scripture, and how many of the things I have taught my children were simply my repeating what he had taught me. I am so grateful for my father's (and mother's) teaching, and my children have indirectly benefited from that same teaching.

So, parent, recognize that the time goes by more quickly than you can imagine, and know that how you teach and train your children will directly impact their children (your grandchildren). What will be said about you at your funeral by your children and grandchildren? The time and energy you invest in your children will almost certainly have a greater impact on future generations than anything else you can do in this life.

I'll close with a slightly modified version of Galatians 6:9:

And let us not grow weary of doing good, for in due season we [and our children, and our grandchildren, and our great-grandchildren...] will reap, if we do not give up.

Acknowledgments

This book project has been much more manageable and enjoyable than we could have ever imagined thanks to the support of several friends and the professionals they contacted on our behalf. Our heartfelt thanks for all the help and encouragement we've received goes especially to these many dear saints.

Thanks to all of you who said, "You should write a book on parenting!" I (Cindy) would never have imagined it was possible, but with your persistence, my dear husband's visionary and "possibility thinking" gifts, and much grace from our heavenly Father, look what God has done!

The book would not have come into being without two dear friends, a former babysitter of ours and her husband, who have encouraged us, cheered us on, offered to do initial editing, read every word, and gave much helpful feedback over the length of this five-year-plus project. They have "field tested" much of this content on their six children and have truly propelled us on, pressing for when it would be published, that they might share it with others. We are so thankful for having such a like-minded brother and sister in Christ who have sacrificed so much for the glory of Christ and the growth of His kingdom around the world. You know who you are.

Truly this book would not have come about without the lessons we learned the hard way, sometimes at the expense of our original guinea pigs—our own children. We are so thankful for the gift of each one of them and for God's gracious working in their lives. The oldest six were the initial readers of each chapter, and they added anecdotes they remembered and even a few hearty amens in a few places, as they have had opportunities to babysit or nanny and saw many of these principles in action or saw the need for them to be applied. Their enthusiasm for this project has been an extra blessing we didn't expect. We had hoped when we started this project many years ago (long before any of our children were married or even dating) to have this finished before our first grandchild made their grand debut, and by God's gracious providence, that may be the case (by just a few weeks).

We are indebted to several brave couples who agreed to be "test readers": Kent and Dawn Lietzau, Dan and Amber Gallagher, and Ben and Carrie Leach. We were so blessed by your feedback and encouragement—thank you, friends.

We are grateful to Dr. Sam Waldron who, without being asked, offered to read our manuscript and then recommended it to our publisher. Without your help, we would probably still be flailing around trying to figure out how to get the manuscript turned into a book!

We are particularly humbled and grateful to have such capable and like-minded professionals agree to work with us on this project.

Thank you to our publisher, Jeff Johnson, at Free Grace Press, for taking on this manuscript with such enthusiasm and kindness. We never imagined working with a publisher could be such a pleasant arrangement. Each phone call or email put our hearts at ease, and we are so honored to have our book published in the company of so many men whose work we admire. Thanks for adding this project to your already full plate.

Special thanks to our editor, Liz Smith, for taking on our project. From the beginning we wanted this to be a smooth, easy read and craved a talented, Christ-exalting editor. We despaired of finding an experienced individual who would have the time, or heart, to work on our manuscript (which is what led us to ask Dr. Sam Waldron about how to find an editor in the first place). We are so thankful that our providential question led to you via Jeff at Free Grace Press. He assured us he knew just the person for this project. He mentioned she was in great demand, but he would ask her to set aside time for our manuscript. We are so glad he did and that you were willing to pencil us in. We are confident this work would not accomplish the purpose for which we have labored and prayed without your finishing touches. Thanks for giving all these words careful scrutiny and for the many helpful suggestions. We greatly value your labors.

Appendix 1

Book Recommendations

Chapter Book Suggestions for Reading Aloud or for Older Children

The Wingfeather Saga by Andrew Peterson

1. *On the Edge of the Dark Sea of Darkness*
2. *North! Or Be Eaten*
3. *The Monster in the Hollows*
4. *The Warden and the Wolf King*

We enjoyed these four books immensely as a family. In fact, John would record the chapters he read aloud at night and send them digitally to our children spread around the globe at the time because they were such good books. They are delightful portrayals of strong family relationships and the very real challenges that sin and pride bring to keeping those relationships functional. They contain quite a bit of suspense, action, and danger, but under all is a confidence that "The Maker" is at work through it all. Probably our favorite nighttime reading books ever, up there with The Chronicles of Narnia. The first book starts a bit on the silly side, but if that is not your cup of tea, stick with it; it all becomes relevant in the end, and much less silly and more heartwarming as it goes along.

The Chronicles of Narnia by C. S. Lewis. These seven fabulous short chapter books are filled with allegory covering many different Christian themes. Simple, impactful, and yet so rich, you can reference the allegorical examples in many areas of life as you teach your children.

The Mysterious Benedict Society by Trenton Lee Stewart. A most creative story about four uniquely gifted children who must work together to thwart an impending evil. One of the many delightful aspects of this story is that there are adults always trying to help and working for their welfare (as opposed to the common theme of children always saving the day and all the adults being irresponsible or inept).

The Candymakers by Wendy Mass. It may not seem so special at first until you realize it is a children's version of the movies *Vantage Point* or *Hoodwinked* with the same events seen from many different perspectives. This book demonstrates that all is not always what it seems on the outside.

The Sign of the Beaver by Elizabeth George Speare. A survival story of a settler boy in Maine who is befriended by local Native Americans.

A Murder for Her Majesty by Beth Hilgartner. A compelling story set in a cathedral during the reign of Elizabeth I in England. There is some bad language, so read aloud so you can edit. Many characters in the book demonstrate selfless kindness.

The Wilderking Trilogy by Jonathan Rogers.

1. *The Bark of the Bog Owl*
2. *Secret of the Swamp King*
3. *The Way of the WilderKing*

This trilogy is very loosely based on the story of David and Saul. It has gripping adventure, strong family and friendship examples, and a lot of grins and good humor along the way.

Caddie Woodlawn by Carol Ryrie Brink. The adventures of a girl in Wisconsin in the late 1800s, based on the true life of the author's grandmother.

The Good Master by Kate Seredy. This book chronicles the antics of a family, with a fabulous father figure, in Hungary in the countryside before war in Europe. The book demonstrates the effects that loving parenting can have in the lives of children.

The Singing Tree by Kate Seredy. A sequel to *The Good Master* with the same great father figure and interesting characters. However, this book is a bit darker because of the war, so read aloud to process or edit as needed.

Beyond the Desert Gate by Mary Ray. An engaging historical fiction story about first-century Palestine. This book follows three brothers from a loving family who grow up in a brutal world and sometimes find themselves on opposite sides of the battles going on around them. Some of the themes include the dynamics of the Roman Empire versus the Jews and even some of the effects Christians had on this dynamic. This book contains some realistic and challenging themes, so best read aloud.

The Master Puppeteer by Katherine Paterson. A young hero unravels a mystery in eighteenth-century Japan. This book gets the reader inside Japanese culture, and the story takes place in the setting of Japanese puppet theatre.

A Single Shard by Linda Sue Park. This is the book that inspired our family to race up the stairs to the lesser frequented parts of the British History Museum to see real examples of ancient Korean celadon pottery. This a well-crafted story and includes details about ancient Korean culture and pottery production, which is a joy to read.

Red Sails to Capri by Ann Weil. A short book with lively characters that serves as a memorable introduction to many distinctives about the small island of Capri. Appropriate for younger children.

The Wolves of Willoughby Chase by Joan Aiken. Misadventures of two cousins in a large house in England. While the distantly related adults left in charge have evil intent, the parents return from their travels in the end and set all to rights.

Young Fu of the Upper Yangtze by Elizabeth Foreman Lewis. A thirteen-year-old boy moves from the Chinese countryside to the city of Chunking in the 1920s. In the city he learns many life lessons amid adventures in the city, guided by a kind and wise mentor along the way.

The Wednesday Wars by Gary D. Schmidt. Very well written and thoughtful book about a sixth grader's experience discovering Shakespeare amid what was going on culturally in America surrounding the Vietnam War. This book thoughtfully looks at the cultural tensions and aspects of family relationships during this time in history.

The Westing Game by Ellen Raskin. A riveting adventure game ensues when the potential beneficiaries of a huge estate must win the Westing Game to inherit.

The Ivan Books by Myrna Grant. Challenging and exciting short stories about life as a Christian family in the Soviet Union, meeting underground, being interrogated, hiding Bibles, and so on. Ivan's family demonstrates courageous sharing of Christ, wise living in a closed society, and joyful, trusting hearts in God through all hardships, though sometimes it is a process. There are six books in the series.

The Rani Adventures by Ron Snell.

1. *It's a Jungle Out There!*
2. *Life Is a Jungle*
3. *Jungle Calls*

Fun stories from a kid's perspective about growing up as a missionary kid in the jungle. Filled with real-life adventures and very funny. Our adult children still read these.

The Green Ember Series by S. D. Smith.

1. *The Green Ember*
2. *Ember Falls*
3. *Ember Rising*
4. *Ember's End*

This is an action series featuring rabbits with strong sibling relationships, courage, determination, and, as the author says, "rabbits with swords."

The Black Star of Kingston by S. D. Smith. This is an early prequel to the above series.

The Last Archer by S. D. Smith. An "in-between-quel," part of the previous books told by the perspective of a different character.

The Golden Goblet by Eloise Jarvis McGraw. An Egyptian boy who just wants to be a goldsmith becomes stuck under the care of his evil stepbrother who uses the boy to his own ends. As the story continues, the boy discovers his stepbrother's plot and learns the value of friendship and a simple life.

God King: *A Story in the Days of King Hezekiah* by Joanne Williamson. A great historical fiction book about Israel, the Assyrians, and the Egyptians during Hezekiah's reign. This book has memorable characters and gives an interesting and accurate take on this biblical story.

The Endless Steppe by Esther Hautzig. This interesting book is about a girl who grows up in Siberia and learns to live with very little.

The Wheel on the School by Meindert DeJong. A heartwarming story about a class of determined children who work through many obstacles to bring storks back to their village, sweetly affecting all the villagers with their project. This story is a wonderful example of determination and working together.

Charlotte's Web by E. B. White. This is a heartwarming classic children's book about an unlikely friendship between a pig and a spider. A memorable read for all ages.

Master Cornhill by Eloise Jarvis McGraw. In London, a young boy finds his life turned upside down because of the bubonic plague. As he seeks to discover what he is supposed to do with his new life, he meets new friends and others who help him put his life in a new direction. This captures the culture and setting of London during the plague and the great fire.

Johnny Tremain by Esther Forbes. A story set during the Revolutionary War in America, with appearances by well-known real-life characters such as Paul Revere and Ben Franklin.

Little Britches by Ralph Moody. A true story about a young boy and his family settling in the foothills of the Rocky Mountains. It exemplifies a young boy learning to shoulder responsibility through the example of his father and through difficult situations he encounters. We read this aloud as there were a few edits needed, but well worth it for the exemplary story.

Carry On, Mr. Bowditch by Jean Lee Latham. Inspiring true story about a man who changed the way navigation was done in his time, all while being completely self-taught. This story shows the value of initiating your own learning, enduring when life is tough, and the value of hard work over the long haul. This is a particular favorite of our family, and we reference it frequently.

Bound for Oregon by Jean Van Leeuwen. The story of a Christian family going to Oregon, with all the hardships that go along with the trail. Strong father figure and realistic family interaction. This book is based off a true story.

Banner in the Sky by James Ramsey Ullman. An incredibly gripping story about the first ascent of a fictional mountain in the Swiss Alps. This was definitely a family favorite, though it may need some discussion about following authority as the main character is not always the best at that.

Shadow Spinner by Susan Fletcher. This is a retelling of the story of Scheherazade. This book has great characters and shows the power of stories to shape the people who hear them.

God's Smuggler by Brother Andrew. This is a wonderful and entertaining book about the adventures of Brother Andrew as he smuggles Bibles into the Soviet Union to encourage the church there. God's power to do amazing things is demonstrated again and again in Brother Andrew's escapades.

The Kite Fighters by Linda Sue Park. This beautiful story is about two brothers and kite fighting in ancient Korea. This book gives a good sense of some of the elements of Korean culture through real and compelling characters.

The Great and Terrible Quest by Margaret Lovett. A medieval tale with excellent characters, an element of mystery, and a quest to find the lost king who will end the corruption prevalent in the kingdom. Some characters learn courage and others persevere through great difficulty in this tale.

The Bronze Bow by Elizabeth George Speare. A story about a broken boy with a broken family who hates the Romans and joins the zealots but finds redemption and transformation through a new teacher called Jesus, whose way is different than any the boy has heard before.

The Land I Lost by Quang Nhuong Huynh. This is an entertaining book about growing up in Vietnam before the war. The stories in the book seem from a very different world and are often shocking but gripping. Our children were amazed by the variety of animals this culture encountered and trained for a variety of useful purposes.

Owls in the Family by Farley Mowat. A hilarious and sweet story about a family who loves animals and the unique challenges that follow adopting two owls into their home. Our family really enjoyed this book when we read it out loud and even sent it overseas to some friends of ours.

The Great Wheel by Robert Lawson. A young Irishman goes to America to work for his uncle and becomes part of the project to erect the first Ferris wheel in Chicago at the turn of the century.

The Alcatraz Books by Brandon Sanderson

1. *Alcatraz Versus the Evil Librarians*
2. *The Scrivener's Bones: Alcatraz vs. the Evil Librarians*
3. *The Knights of Crystallia: Alcatraz vs. the Evil Librarians*
4. *The Shattered Lens: Alcatraz vs. the Evil Librarians*
5. *The Dark Talent: Alcatraz vs. the Evil Librarians*

These books, written by an extremely sarcastic author, are the most creative and some of the most enjoyable stories we've read. Imagine a world where librarians control all knowledge and are part of an evil cult, to the extent that they have hidden whole continents and name prisons after famous "Free-Kingdomers" in an effort to defame them. The titles may seem dark, but it's really all in good fun.

Ashtown Burials Series by N. D. Wilson

1. *The Dragon's Tooth*
2. *The Drowned Vault*
3. *Empire of Bones*

These books are better for older children. The title "burials" made me (Cindy) think this series wasn't for me, but they are very imaginative books about humans dealing with trans mortals—powerful beings who can't die and have been the stuff of legends throughout human history. When these transmortals transgress a written covenant with mankind, they are "buried"—incarcerated to prevent harm. The series follows three ordinary children, with ordinary and uniquely challenging problems, adapting and growing under the tutelage of some exemplary, and less exemplary, characters. At times funny and at other times inspiring. We've read them many times, they are that good.

Picture Books for Younger Children:

If your children are too young for chapter books, here are many of our favorite picture books:

Going to Sleep on the Farm by Wendy Cheyette Lewison and Juan Wijngaard. Beautiful illustrations from many different vantage points as all the farm residents fall asleep. Watch for the toy animals and the animals on the quilt as well!

Our Animal Friends at Maple Hill Farm by Alice Provensen. This large picture book features endearing animal personalities and daily events on a farm.

Good Morning Sweetie Pie and Other Poems for Little Children by Cynthia Rylant.

A New Coat for Anna by Harriet Ziefert. Anna and her mother make friends in post-war Europe as they trade goods and services to make Anna a much-needed larger coat.

Storm is Coming! by Heather Tekavec. Farm animals, after being warned that a storm is coming by the farmer, huddle in the barn and wonder what sort of fierce, feared creature is a storm.

What's That Awful Smell? by Heather Tekavec. The farm animals all try various solutions to solve the smell they think originated with a new baby piglet.

Happy Mother's Day by Steven Kroll. This story demonstrates how each child participates in honoring their mother on Mother's Day in their own age-appropriate way.

Happy Father's Day by Steven Kroll. Same theme as above, as children honor their father on Father's Day.

Blueberries for Sal by Robert McCloskey. A toddler "helps" her mom pick blueberries, while a bear cub similarly learns to gather berries with its mom.

Make Way for Ducklings by Robert McCloskey. A policeman gets involved as a duck family promenades around Boston in earlier times.

One Morning in Maine by Robert McCloskey. Vivid descriptions of two children's mornings in the natural surroundings of Maine.

Time of Wonder by Robert McCloskey. A detailed description of a family's experiences around a Maine island as they experience a severe weather event pass through. It sounds scary but is a good example of artistic descriptions of nature and weather.

Little Whistle by Cynthia Rylant. These beautifully illustrated books are about a guinea pig and the toys in a toy store that interact together when the store is closed. The personalities of the toys, including the need for the baby dolls to have the care babies need, are precious.

Little Whistle's Dinner Party by Cynthia Rylant.

Little Whistle's Medicine by Cynthia Rylant.

The Crinkleroot Book Series by Jim Arnosky. These have beautifully detailed illustrations aimed at teaching children the differences between moths and butterflies, how to identify trees, etc. Short and accessible for elementary children.

All About Series by Jim Arnosky. These are similar to the books above, telling about a specific animal, like sharks, lizards, turkeys, or owls, with engaging illustrations and information.

All Those Secrets of the World by Jane Yolen. A precious story about a four-year-old trying to process her father being away at a war while living at her grandmother's house.

Owl Moon by Jane Yolen. I think this may have been our favorite book when our oldest was a toddler. The illustrations are amazing. And it's fun to get to make the sound of a great horned owl repeatedly! A father and young daughter stay up late on a frosty night to see a great horned owl and are not disappointed. Toddlers have fun looking for small animals in the edges of the woods on each page.

Honkers by Jane Yolen. This one always started the tears flowing when I was pregnant! A young girl is sent to live with her grandparents while her mother is on bed rest for a pregnancy. While at the farm, the girl hatches and befriends a Canadian goose. The teary part is when the goose flies away and the girl goes back home to her family. Minimal watercolor illustrations are very effective.

Tacky the Penguin by Helen Lester. Our children were tickled by the sense of humor in these books. Tacky is an odd penguin, very different from his penguin buddies, which leads to some very humorous situations. In the end, they always conclude that Tacky is "an odd bird, but a good bird to have around."

Tackylocks and the Three Bears by Helen Lester.

Tacky in Trouble by Helen Lester.

Tacky and the Winter Games by Helen Lester.

Three Cheers for Tacky by Helen Lester.

Tacky and the Emperor by Helen Lester.

The Library by Sarah Stewart. Humorously detailed illustrations and a creatively told story, in poetic form, of a bookworm as she grew up and eventually donated her book collection to form the town library.

The Gardener by Sarah Stewart. A farm girl, who is a gardener at heart, is sent to the city to live with an uncle who runs a bakery. This determined gardener manages to transform the world around her through resourcefulness, hard work, and a few seeds from her grandmother.

Ruby Mae Has Something to Say by David Small. We found this a hilarious book about a normal woman from Nada, Texas, who was given courage to speak by a contraption from her nephew. Her newfound courage leads her all the way to the United Nations!

Mailing May by Michael O. Tunnell. A small girl is enabled to visit her grandmother across the Idaho mountains by the ingenious work-a-rounds of her parents and the U.S. Postal Service.

Bubba and Beau, Best Friends by Kathi Appelt. Another family favorite, these are short books with big pages and few words, perfect for reading aloud before bed or to a group of small children, especially if you put on a Texas drawl. Very Texas in culture (and we aren't even Texans), Bubba is a baby and Beau a puppy, and they and their parents, Mamma Pearl and Big Bubba, share simple adventures.

Bubba and Beau Go Night-Night by Kathi Appelt.

Bubba and Beau Meet the Relatives by Kathi Appelt.

The Book of Jonah by Peter Spier. A well-illustrated book that honors the biblical narrative of the story of Jonah. May be a bit too intricate for preschoolers.

Father, May I Come? by Peter Spier. One of my all-time favorite picture books. You may have to look hard for this one, as it is out of print. A young boy in 1687 wants to come along as his father responds to rescue a boat that has run aground on the Dutch coast. What is so special about this book is the comparison, across time, of a boy in an identical situation in more modern-day Holland and the changes in way of life and technology that influence the way this problem, a foundering boat, is handled. Modern-day equivalents to ancient trades are pictured in the excellent illustrations. The book includes sons admiring fathers, heroism, courage, and care for those in need. What could be better?

Something from Nothing by Phoebe Gilman. A Jewish folktale of how the blanket of a baby gets transformed, as the child grows, into a jacket and other smaller things, until all that is left is the story. The parallel story going on in illustrations of the mouse family below the house is worth the book, even if the story wasn't already delightful.

Mike Mulligan and His Steam Shovel by Virginia Lee Burton. This story of determination and hard work has endured from when I was a child. My children enjoy it just as much as I did.

Katy and the Big Snow by Virginia Lee Burton. Katy is a personified snowplow who helps rescue a town after a big snowstorm. Part of the fun is seeing the town emerge on the map as each street is plowed, in priority order, to get necessary services out to the needy townspeople.

Berlioz the Bear by Jan Brett. This author is known for her captivating illustrations, often with hints at what will happen on the next page in the margin illustrations. There are many books by this author; these are just a few of our favorites.

The Mitten by Jan Brett.

The Gingerbread Baby by Jan Brett.

A Street Through Time by Anne Millard. Follow a piece of land through history with beautifully detailed illustrations.

Children Just Like Me: A Unique Celebration of Children Around the World by Anabel and Barnabas Kindersley. Charming photographs of children in their daily lives from all over the world. It helps our children see how children all around the world participate in similarly "normal" things like they do, but it also shows them how different some of those normal things are, like what they eat or wear.

Click, Clack, Moo: Cows that Type by Doreen Cronin. Farmyard silliness that had our children giggling and grinning.

Dogs Don't Wear Sneakers by Laura Numerof.

Anno's Journey (and many other Anno books) by Mitsumasa Anno. A bird's-eye view of the travels of Anno through northern Europe. His travels bring him through events from stories your children may be familiar with, and there are many rewards for the visually observant.

Babies in the Bayou by Jim Arnosky. These are simple stories by naturalist author and illustrator Jim Arnosky.

Rabbits and Raindrops by Jim Arnosky.

Raccoon on His Own by Jim Arnosky.

Otters Under Water by Jim Arnosky.

Raccoons and Ripe Corn by Jim Arnosky.

Billy and Blaze by C. W. Anderson. These are classic stories of adventure and responsibility with a boy and a horse. Our children loved these.

Blaze and the Gray Spotted Pony by C. W. Anderson.

Blaze Shows the Way by C. W. Anderson.

(And all the other Billy and Blaze stories)

The Big Alphie and Annie Rose Storybook by Shirley Hughes. Sweet stories of a young brother and sister and their British mum and dad by author and illustrator Shirley Hughes. Her other books listed are full of poetry about young family life.

Out and About: A First Book of Poems by Shirley Hughes.

Chatting by Shirley Hughes.

Hiding by Shirley Hughes.

The Nursery Collection by Shirley Hughes.

Rhymes for Annie Rose by Shirley Hughes.

Bernice Gets Carried Away by Hannah E. Harrison. A selfish cat learns a great lesson. Delightful artwork.

Water Is Water by Miranda Paul. Excellent picture book about the water cycle. It is in rhyme, with lovely, engaging pictures of a family throughout a year.

Mr. Putter and Tabby Collection by Cynthia Rylant. There are many books in this excellent series. They are terrific readers, so you may want to save them for your children learning to read, but they are also terrific read aloud stories. The main characters are a single older man and his single elderly female neighbor, and the adventures they have with their cat and dog. We love how this shows some of the joys and challenges of one's later years in engaging literature for young children.

Good King Wenceslas by John M. Neale. This book has *amazing* illustrations. The text is the familiar song, but the illustrations start with a child in a square staring at the statue of this king and imagining what the story would have been like. The drawings are from many perspectives, and I feel cold just looking at them!

Spot the Differences: Art Masterpiece Mysteries by Alan Weller (Dover). Side-by-side famous art paintings with subtle differences to sharpen observational skills and learn about art and artists along the way.

Come Look with Me Series by Various Authors. This is a series of books, created by Gladys S. Blizzard, of famous paintings for young children. The book includes questions to ask your children as they look at the paintings, to help them engage with the art, so it is a perfect series for those who want to expose their children to art history but have had little exposure themselves.

Appendix 2

Sample Family Schedules

Example Family Schedule: Morning

Time	Mom	Anna	Nathan	Ellen	Carol	Rose	Henry	Eric	Dad
5:30 AM	Sleep	Sleep	Sleep	Sleep	Sleep	Sleep	Sleep	Sleep	Devotions
5:45 AM									
6:00 AM									
6:15 AM									Shower
6:30 AM	Feed Eric							Fed by Mom	Make Breakfast
6:45 AM		Get Up / Get Dressed				Get Up / Unload Dishwasher	Get Up / Get Dressed		
7:00 AM	Bible Story / Feed Eric	Bible Story						Bible Story / Eat	Bible Story
7:15 AM	Breakfast							In High Chair	Breakfast
7:30 AM	Dress / Devotions	Time w/ Eric	Morning Chores	Morning Chores	Finish Breakfast			Time w/ Anna	To Work
7:45 AM				Devotions (Guest Rm)	Morning Chores	Morning Chores	Morning Chores		Work
8:00 AM	Dress / Devotions	Morning Chores	Time w/ Eric	Devotions (Guest Rm)				Time w/ Nathan	
8:15 AM	Time w/ Henry			School Prep			Time w/ Mom		
8:30 AM	Bible Memory / Fix Girls' Hair								
8:45 AM									
9:00 AM	Time w/ Eric	Morning Chores						Time w/ Mom	
9:15 AM	Put Eric Down							Nap Prep	
9:30 AM	Free	Recess						Sleep	
9:45 AM									
10:00 AM		Harp	Schoolwork	Schoolwork	Schoolwork	Get Ready for Tape Time	Get Ready for Tape Time		
10:15 AM		Schoolwork				Tape Time	Tape Time		
10:30 AM	Feed Eric	Science	Science	Science	Science			Fed by Mom	
10:45 AM									
11:00 AM	Free	Craft w/ Henry, Rose	Lunch Prep / Schoolwork	Lunch Prep / Schoolwork	School	Craft w/ Anna		Tape Time	
11:15 AM								Tape Time	
11:30 AM		School or Baking			Time w/ Eric	Read in Front Room	Read in Front Room	Tape Time	
11:45 AM					Read to R, H, E	Read w/ Carol			

Example Family Schedule: Afternoon

<table>
<tr><th>Time</th><th>Mom</th><th>Anna</th><th>Nathan</th><th>Ellen</th><th>Carol</th><th>Rose</th><th>Henry</th><th>Eric</th><th>Dad</th></tr>
<tr><td>12:00 PM</td><td colspan="7" rowspan="2">Lunch</td><td rowspan="2">Lunch--Fed by Child (rotating)</td><td rowspan="22">Work</td></tr>
<tr><td>12:15 PM</td></tr>
<tr><td>12:30 PM</td><td colspan="8" rowspan="2">History Read-Aloud</td></tr>
<tr><td>12:45 PM</td></tr>
<tr><td>1:00 PM</td><td rowspan="2">Time w/ Ellen</td><td>Devotions</td><td rowspan="2">Piano</td><td rowspan="2">Time w/ Mom</td><td rowspan="2">Devotions</td><td colspan="3">Play in Front Room</td></tr>
<tr><td>1:15 PM</td><td>Eric to Nap</td><td>Prep for Mom Time</td><td>Finish Chores</td><td>Eric to Nap</td></tr>
<tr><td>1:30 PM</td><td>Phonics</td><td rowspan="2">Math</td><td rowspan="2">Devotions</td><td rowspan="2">Violin (Living Room)</td><td>Schoolwork</td><td colspan="2">Phonics</td><td rowspan="4">Sleep</td></tr>
<tr><td>1:45 PM</td><td>Time w/ Rose</td><td>Read to Henry</td><td>Time w/ Mom</td><td>Read w/ Carol</td></tr>
<tr><td>2:00 PM</td><td rowspan="2">Time w/ Nathan</td><td rowspan="2">Harp</td><td rowspan="2">Time w/ Mom</td><td rowspan="2">Math</td><td>Birthday Cards</td><td>Get Ready for Nap</td><td>Get Ready for Nap</td></tr>
<tr><td>2:15 PM</td><td>Read to R, H</td><td>Read Before Nap</td><td>Read Before Nap</td></tr>
<tr><td>2:30 PM</td><td rowspan="2">Feed Eric</td><td>Polished Cornerstones</td><td rowspan="2">Math</td><td rowspan="2">Piano</td><td rowspan="2">Math</td><td rowspan="10">Nap</td><td rowspan="10">Nap</td><td rowspan="2">Fed by Mom</td></tr>
<tr><td>2:45 PM</td><td>Laundry</td></tr>
<tr><td>3:00 PM</td><td rowspan="2">Time w/ Carol</td><td rowspan="2">Piano</td><td>Plants Grown Up</td><td>Polished Cornerstones</td><td rowspan="2">Time w/ Mom</td><td rowspan="2">Toy Time in Basement</td></tr>
<tr><td>3:15 PM</td><td rowspan="3">Schoolwork</td><td rowspan="2">Schoolwork</td></tr>
<tr><td>3:30 PM</td><td rowspan="2">Time w/ Anna</td><td rowspan="2">Time w/ Mom</td><td>Time w/ Eric</td><td>Time w/ Carol</td></tr>
<tr><td>3:45 PM</td><td>Time w/ Eric</td><td rowspan="2">Piano</td><td>Time w/ Ellen</td></tr>
<tr><td>4:00 PM</td><td>Free</td><td>Schoolwork</td><td>Time w/ Eric</td><td rowspan="2">Art</td><td>Time w/ Nathan</td></tr>
<tr><td>4:15 PM</td><td>Free</td><td>Time w/ Eric</td><td rowspan="2">Art</td><td>School or Dinner Prep</td><td>Time w/ Anna</td></tr>
<tr><td>4:30 PM</td><td rowspan="4">Dinner Prep</td><td rowspan="6">School, Baking, or Dinner Prep</td><td rowspan="2">Voice Practice</td><td rowspan="2">Art</td><td rowspan="4">Sleep</td></tr>
<tr><td>4:45 PM</td><td rowspan="5">School, Baking, or Dinner Prep</td></tr>
<tr><td>5:00 PM</td><td rowspan="4">School, Baking, or Dinner Prep</td><td rowspan="4">School, Baking, or Dinner Prep</td><td rowspan="2">Set Table</td><td rowspan="4">Free</td></tr>
<tr><td>5:15 PM</td></tr>
<tr><td>5:30 PM</td><td rowspan="2">Feed Eric</td><td rowspan="2">Free</td><td>Fed by Mom</td><td rowspan="2">Home</td></tr>
<tr><td>5:45 PM</td><td>Fed by Mom</td></tr>
<tr><td>6:00 PM</td><td colspan="9" rowspan="2">Dinner</td></tr>
<tr><td>6:15 PM</td></tr>
</table>